*To Ed Jackson, life-long friend,
comrade-in-arms, and fellow traveller,
who did more than anyone else to ensure
the publication of this book.*

Preface

I AM, AT LEAST by reputation, a sex radical: gay activist dating back to the Cretaceous period, defender of pedophiles, defender of (and participant in) sex work, sometime porn actor and maker, shameless voyeur (no window is safe if my binoculars are at hand), perpetual sourpuss on the subject of gay marriage. I came of age in the 1960s and 1970s, an era when most of those character traits and activities were illegal at worst and shameless at best. Some still are. Others — gay marriage, for example — have switched sides, transitioning from what many people thought of as an unthinkable and illegal travesty to a ritual celebrated in a growing number of jurisdictions, Canada included.

I am not by nature an activist or a theoretician, but I happened to be in the right place at the right time: Toronto, in the early 1970s. A small-town boy, I found the city exciting and challenging, but manageable. And, since family was far away in northern Ontario, I could risk coming out of the closet, which sounds strangely old-fashioned now but was so very important then. You had to find others. You had to find your tribe. If you were a twenty-something, as I was, it seemed as if the gay world you discovered was exactly the same age, though I'd soon learn that it had a history going back decades; like me, it was eager, horny, curious, not careful, open.

The people I met often had similar backgrounds to mine: small-town boys, frequently the first in their families to go to university, not committed to a career path, looking for sex, looking for love. It was a world of possibilities, at least for white, cisgender young men — an imbalance it would take decades to rectify. You might decide to join an organization, attend two meetings, and by the third find yourself heading a committee or carrying a banner at a demonstration. Like so many others, I got hooked on empowerment, the transformation of the Helpless Queer with no history and an unlikely future into Someone, into a group of Someones who uncovered a history, who found heroes, who grabbed today and shook it until tomorrow fell out of its pocket and there was a place for us.

Though not charismatic enough to be a leader or analytic enough to be an ideologue, I eased my way into the militant tribe of early gay liberation by being willing to write and willing to practise it until stories rang personal and true. My eventual career as a mainstream journalist grew from the sense that every official story has a hidden, truer tale buried in it.

That's true of my story too.

But this book isn't my whole story. It's not an autobiography; it's an account of my sexual and political awakening and subsequent activism. My goal here is to bring to vivid life some critical moments in the early years of the struggle, sometimes moments that I helped make happen and sometimes moments that happened to me. It's not a full history of the times, either. AIDS activism, the distinguishing feature of the 1980s and 1990s, makes the smallest of appearances here, though the disease claimed several friends and colleagues. I mourned and marched but played no organizing role in the fight for treatment options or the politicization of the doctor/patient relationship. Instead, I personalized the politics by joining a care team for Michael Lynch, activist, poet, father, and friend, and by recording day by day in my journal the ways a community can organize palliative care. Though the struggle to legalize gay marriage eventually sucked up all the oxygen in the room, I paid it no mind, persuaded that the proper strategy to achieve equal marriage was to take it away from straight people. That wasn't a popular approach.

Even less popular was "Men Loving Boys Loving Men," my attempt in *The Body Politic* (*TBP*) to humanize and demystify intergenerational relationships. The resulting police raid and criminal charges, which led to a week-long trial, tested the support of the wider gay community for the frank discussion of an unpopular subject. It was almost a testing ground for the role *The Body Politic* would play after the 1981 police raids on Toronto's gay bathhouses, though in that case its role was to inspire resistance and create support for equal rights — what some thought of as the "radical gay agenda."

Is there a theme here? Perhaps it's the importance of serendipity. As a young man, I had no goals, dreams, or schemes (if you don't count studying to be a scientist, and I was a failure even at that). I fell into teaching English as a Second Language because I needed a job, and there it was. I did not ache to be a writer. I sometimes ask myself what my life would have been like if I hadn't been gay, and this is what I see: a teacher or mid-level bureaucrat, married, two children, right of centre politically, content rather than happy.

For a period in the 1990s, I did become a teacher, of journalism at Ryerson University in Toronto. I was also, and had been since 1987, a working prostitute, the revelation of which provoked a scandal that convulsed the school for months and eventually led to my dismissal. I wasn't content. My life was in disarray, and my future was threatened. Yet I was happy. My life was in disarray but remained congruent with my ideals as a teacher, journalist, and activist.

Serendipity can sometimes seem like an organizing force in my life, but my career was shaped and served by words. Sometimes savaged by them too. Here are more.

Marathon
. . . .

ACCORDING TO MY MOTHER, the first words I spoke as a child constituted a full, syntactically correct sentence. There was no earlier
dalliance with monosyllables. Till then a silent child, I stood up one
day in my crib and announced, "The man in the moon is a cowboy."
The tale seems apocryphal. Surely, like most children, I must have
tried out words like "apocryphal" or "asymptote" before hazarding
something so complex as a reflection on the occupational status of a
lunar personage. Still, I like the story. Mother claimed the sentence
was a phrase from a song she used to sing to me. I like the sense
that music, one of the consolations and challenges of my life, had so
early an impact. It pleases me to realize that I was already entranced
enough by words to want to weave them together and to have done
so correctly the very first time. The story also makes me seem
precocious, perhaps pretentious, and a little bit ridiculous — ways
I like to think of myself.

The first words I remember speaking to my father were said as
I stood, bewildered, on a tabletop in a dimly lit room in a house
I'd never seen before. "Who is going to undress me?" I said to him.
"You, maybe?" He would tell this story occasionally when I was
older, secretly pleased that for once I had turned to him rather than

to my mother. He didn't realize that I wasn't hoping that he would be the one to undress me and prepare me for bed. I was dreading it. Even as a three-year-old, I feared him.

I was standing on the kitchen table in an ill-furnished two-storey shingled house at 3 Armour Street in Marathon, Ontario, a town that was then little more than a wound in the bush on the north shore of Lake Superior. I, my mother, and my infant brother, John, had just arrived by train from Bathurst, New Brunswick, where both John and I had been born (I on July 10, 1944) and where my mother's family lived. My father, who was from Nova Scotia (I never did establish how he and my mother met), picked us up at the station. He had moved to Marathon some months earlier to take a job in the pulp mill that had opened in 1946, planning

Me in droopy drawers in Penn Lake, near Marathon, 1949.
Photo: Gerald Hannon

to earn enough money to bring his family to him. The town, with its promise of jobs, attracted many Maritimers, working-class men willing to take a chance on a remote outpost. Educational credentials were not important — my father, I believe, had completed grade nine; my mother, grade six. Of that first night I remember only the dimness of the room, my wariness in the presence of my father, the sense that my mother was bustling about, preoccupied, perhaps impatient, probably forgetting that she'd put me down on the tabletop and left me there while an issue of greater moment claimed her attention. I had no sense of where we were, but, except for short vacations with relatives in the Maritimes, I would live there at 3 Armour Street, and then next door, at 1 Armour Street, until I was eighteen years old.

When I was twenty or twenty-one, at university, I began an epic poem modelled on Byron's *Don Juan* and based on my life. (I did mention "precocious, perhaps pretentious, and a little bit ridiculous.") I wondered in one of the stanzas how much space

My mother Yvonne Hannon and me, Marathon, 1945. Photo: Gerald Hannon.

should be devoted to one's childhood years — and this at a time
when childhood years were about all I had:

I won't say much about my early youth,
That Charlie Dickens stuff is such a bore,
But stick like Holden Caulfield to the truth
About my later years: now, do I hear a roar
From the psychologists' camp, who think I'm most uncouth
To leave out all that Freudian, formative lore?
Well, Freud's a name that trips a poet's tongue,
And he says little of interest to the very Jung.

I was clearly showing off that I'd read lots of books and knew
about Freud and everything.

Even then, I feared boring the reader: every childhood is a web
of ecstasies and terrors. The proportions differ, that is all. I feared
particularly to produce yet one more boy-growing-up-in-the-bush
story, ur-Canadian, featuring much in the way of boreal flora and
only moderately ghastly fauna. I feared being able to engage the
reader's sympathies — I was desperate to be cool and brittle and
sophisticated because I had come to know I was not, never had
been, and, frighteningly, might never be like the people I was beginning to read about and to meet.

For a child, though, there is no such thing as cool and brittle
and sophisticated. There is only the world, and as a child I could
not imagine that any people anywhere lived differently from me.

Perhaps that is not so true anymore. The lives of children and
young adults are media-saturated. I grew up before that time. There
was no reason for me to imagine that other towns were different
from Marathon or that the world wasn't mostly bush. There was no
television, just two available radio stations, and my family had little

interest in books or magazines. I saw pictures of other places at school, but they had no more connection to reality than the movies I saw on Saturday afternoons at the Strand Theatre. I knew there were cowboys and deserts and oceans, men who could fly and monsters from outer space, ships at sea and orchestras that played for men and women in fine clothes, men and women who ate in restaurants and drank cocktails and danced. They all seemed equally real to me. Or, perhaps, equally unreal. Miss Carr, my grade one teacher, wrote in the report card that would graduate me into grade two, "Gerald does quite good work, but often seems to be dreaming."

Marathon was not much older than I — a new town for a new pulp mill built on a remote and sheltered bay that floated the booms of logs that the mill would turn into a kind of crude cardboard and provided safe harbour for the ships that would take that cardboard to market in the United States. The mill itself was large, frightening, noisy, smelly. The town was drab. But everything else was very beautiful. I wouldn't have understood the reference then, but it was like living in a Group of Seven painting. Everywhere was up from Marathon, everything was higher — the Precambrian shield swelled around me the moment I turned my head. Snow mountains had shadows edged in pink and blue that vanished back into shadow when I looked too closely. The night sky crackled with the swirling oceanic greens of the northern lights, and I walked among them with the snow squeaking beneath my boots and my head high, awed and reverential no matter how often they appeared. Summer days sometimes disappeared in fogs so thick that the town seemed wrapped in swaddling, and all was hush, and I thought I was the only face on earth until another face suddenly appeared and I could laugh about it. Wherever I walked, I might be the only one. Sometimes, when I walked far from town, I would tell myself, "Every step I take now is the first step any human has ever taken on this land." At the time it didn't occur to me that those first steps had been taken by Indigenous peoples, some of whom still lived on a reserve not far from town.

I pride myself on being very urban now, on having expunged every trace of bush, but once upon a time it was everything to me. The forest — though we always called it "the bush" — was everywhere, the town just a rough space that had been crudely hacked from it. The bush began, in my earliest memories, right in the backyard of our house and stretched uninterrupted from there north to Hudson Bay. Almost every waking minute not spent in school was spent in the bush. I knew it deep in my senses — I could, as a child, smell a clearing before we came to it in our sometimes reckless, raucous wanderings. The air carried the signs of it forward, carried them into me, the smell of rocks warmed by the sun, of vegetation different from what we were clambering through. Most often, this happened on the Mountain.

That's what we called it. It was at one end of our street, one of those great peaks of the Precambrian shield, a looming presence that stopped the town dead in its tracks. And it was the Mountain, I was convinced, that hid the sun when it slept — after all, I could see that the sun slipped down behind it each night. I was sure that if only we could reach the top at the right time in the evening we would find ourselves at the edge of a cliff, and there below us, in some great, swirling, unimaginably huge whirlpool of fire, would be the sun, biding its time, waiting for day. I persuaded other boys to help me hunt. We would gather and begin the climb, but it was steep and thickly treed and provided so many opportunities for play and adventure that the gathering dark would finally drive us back. One day, much later, we would reach the top, but not while we were still young and ignorant enough to believe we could hunt the sun to its lair.

We found the world, though. Perhaps, better put, we created it. Because there was little reason to think that the world was anything but an endless unravelling of trees and lakes and rivers, we made it ours by naming it. The lakes and the rivers already had names. We named the rocks.

We named them because they anchored the thread of narrative we wove through our childhoods. We named them because adults would never come to find us there, would not even care to know of their existence, and that made them ours. We weren't particularly imaginative — there was Cave Rock (it had a cave). There was Ten Foot Rock (we guessed it was ten feet high). Sometimes we strove for more. There was Paradise Rock, almost unfindable on a side of the Mountain we explored less often, rising from a deep split in the rolling wave of granite that seemed to be the world's very floor, hidden by trees, carpeted in moss, so hushed and lonely and sun-dappled that even noisy boys would sit and whisper. There was the Ice Pick, a cave that even in the grip of summer held black slabs of the previous winter's ice. We could chip away at it. Hold it near our faces. Smell the tangle of spruce and dank in it as we crouched there in the dark. There was Bum Rock and Cub Rock and the Rock Cut and the Rock Pile — the naming of each a matter of debate among us, though once settled the name was fixed forever.

The other constant was water.

"And Marathon looks on the sea" — that's not quite true,
Although I always thought of it as ocean.
Superior: sometimes an opaque, Wedgwood blue,
And you forget there's such a word as motion;
A child may lift his head and see that view
And feel, perhaps, his first poetic notion

Slide through the shifting sandbox of his mind,
Where castles fall, and toys are left behind.

That's me, channelling Byron. I was serious in that stanza. Superior was a presence, visible from every part of what we called downtown, which consisted of the Strand Theatre, the Everest Hotel, the Rec Hall, the Toronto Dominion Bank, Chapples Department Store, and the police/fire station. Above them all, at the top of the hill and on opposite sides of the street, stood Holy Saviour Catholic Church and Trinity Anglican.

Superior is a lake that breeds monstrous storms, and it kills people. In winter, it piles mountains of ice along the shore; they creaked and groaned beneath us as we climbed them. In the summer, we swam in it, though we were not so foolish as to swim anywhere near town. An open stream of frightening chemical waste flowed downhill from the mill into the water, coating it with a thick layer of brownish foam and sludge. The trees on either side of that stream died, made a ghost forest for us, but we never played there. We walked far down Pebble Beach to a place we called the Black Lagoon in homage to one of our Saturday afternoon movies. Once, that rocky beach (Pebble was a misnomer) was carpeted with monarch butterflies, thousands and thousands of them, all facing the water, their wings sending a slow sigh among the boulders, waiting for some mysterious signal that never seemed to come. Any quick movement startled clouds of them around us, the world a giddy and silent whirl of orange. Then they would settle again, on our heads and shoulders if we didn't move.

More frequently, we walked inland, away from Superior, which was always very cold, to Penn Lake. It was warmer, not so dangerous, probably less than an hour's walk from home. And it had the raft.

We found it one summer, apparently abandoned, down at an end of the lake far from where most people would go. It was too big and too well built to have been made by kids, but we never discovered who made it. It became ours, though, and we guarded it jealously. We would push it into obscure little coves, cover it with branches so no other boys would find it. Head out early in the morning so we would be the first to lay claim if we thought we had left it not that well hidden. Once we laid hands on it, we poled out into the middle of the lake, maybe a half dozen boys, and floated there the day long, very Huck Finn–ish, naked much of the time, often flat on our stomachs with our faces pressed close to the water's surface, fishing for the small perch and rainbow trout we could see weaving below, giving up and plunging in ourselves when they ignored us, as they often did.

I see those images, but they are like silent movies. What did we talk about? What do boys talk about? Comic books, for sure.

Me (centre) in drag in a Marathon school performance. I always liked to perform.
Photo: Gerald Hannon

Squabbles, provocations, dares. Where best to re-enact the Saturday afternoon movie, which we always did on the way home from the Strand. We argued about who would get to play which character. Perhaps we talked of school sometimes. Never about sex — which I don't think existed for any of us, even as a topic — or our families or religion. I know for sure, though, that after the age of twelve or so, I began to talk to the other boys about Giuseppe Verdi's opera *Aida*.

One day, my grade eight teacher brought a record player to class — something I couldn't remember her having done before — and set it up at the front of the room, telling everyone to listen to the record she was about to put on. Until then, almost all the music I had heard in my life consisted of songs sung by Bing Crosby. My family owned a record player that played only 78 rpm records. I didn't actually know at the time that other kinds existed. My father listened to Bing Crosby over and over, especially when he was drunk. I often heard the songs that the Happy Gang sang on the radio at lunchtime when I came home from school. Sometimes my mother sang to herself.

Now, at school, Miss Kenzie puts on her record. The music starts. The other children sit politely and look bored or interested or curious. Something different happens to me. It is as if the air has suddenly coloured, as if the world has stumbled and caught its breath, and I hover there in the moment with it, afraid to breathe. The music is like nothing I have ever heard — grand, purple, almost frantic in its excitements. It goes on and on, so much longer than a Bing Crosby song. Then it's over. Miss Kenzie tells the class that it is the "Triumphal March" from *Aida*. Everyone writes that in their notebook.

I wrote it down too, and I became obsessed with the idea of owning it.

I went to Chapples Department Store, which had a small section in the basement that sold records. There it was, on a shelf, a box set featuring an Egyptian bas-relief sculpture on the cover. It did not strike me as odd at the time that, among the few dozen records on sale in a small department store in northern Ontario, one should find a complete recording of Verdi's *Aida*. It was a recording, and stores sold records. Made sense. What did strike me was the price: $13.98, so wildly expensive that I could not even begin to think of asking my parents to buy it for me. I did, however, have a paper route — I delivered the *Star Weekly* — and I began to save. I can't remember how long it took to save that much money, and I would periodically go to Chapples to check that it was still there, take it off the shelf and hold it, always worried that someone else would snap it up before I'd saved the full amount. No one did, and I finally had the money, and *Aida* was mine.

There was only one problem — I couldn't play it. Our family record player could play only 78s, and the box contained three long-playing discs. It also contained a booklet, which provided some historical background, a story, and parallel columns of text, one side in English and the other in what I finally concluded must be Italian, given that the notes said that Verdi was an Italian composer. I hadn't realized that *Aida* was an opera, wasn't even sure what an opera was, but I was desperate to hear it and frustrated that I could hold it in my hands but still couldn't listen to it.

I solved the problem by becoming an always available baby-sitter to any family that owned a record player that could play long-playing records, which remained my only way of listening until I received a portable record player as a gift when I went away to university. I remember putting on the first record and sitting down with the book in my lap to listen. I was completely puzzled — instead of the transfiguring march I remembered, the music began softly and continued so until voices made an appearance. I quickly figured out that they were singing the Italian text, and that the English was a translation. I'm not sure I got as far as the "Triumphal March" that evening. I can't even say I was hooked. The experience was too new — people singing instead of talking to each other, singing in another language, the music not a tune, exactly, not a ditty, certainly, approachable but difficult to hold on to, to keep in my head. I'd never heard music before that wasn't completely there for the listener the moment you heard it.

I ached for babysitting jobs, and I put the records on the moment the adults left the house. I eventually began to sing along, would one day be able to sing along with every character and do great chunks by memory. I babbled on endlessly to my friends about how wonderful it was, but no one evinced the slightest interest. They seemed devoted to the pop music broadcast from the Lakehead — I realized I should be as well. I was starting to sense that there were popular kids and not-so-popular kids, and I was clearly beginning to be relegated to the latter group. But, really, the music mostly bored me, though I would regularly sit myself down beside the radio and suffer through the Top Ten broadcast.

I did not own another complete opera until I left Marathon. I did eventually own a second disc, *Four Gems from Carmen and Pagliacci*, which I also played over and over. One day in my early teens, I tuned into the CBC on a Saturday afternoon and discovered the Metropolitan Opera broadcasts. It became the most sacred day of the week, the day I lived for. I was often banished to the basement because my father could not bear the music. If he was on night shift and sleeping during the day, I'd have to huddle with the radio, down beside the coal bin, the speaker close to my ear and the sound turned down. I didn't like everything I heard — Wagner, not surprisingly, was a tough slog — but I listened to everything, each afternoon building to that climactic moment when announcer Milton Cross would say, "As the great gold curtain slowly falls" over the sounds of a packed theatre cheering madly. Opera became as important to me as the bush.

I WAS BORN IN 1944. The 1950s were famously repressive. There was no sex education of any kind in the schools I attended. I remember asking my mother where babies came from — the question quite rattled her, and she didn't want to tell me because, she said, if Daddy found out, he'd kill her. I persisted, and she ended up taking me with her into a closet. We stood in the dark among the coats and jackets, the wire hangers tinkling together if we moved, and she whispered, "Daddy puts his birdie in Mommy's belly." That was that. I didn't find it disturbing or unsettling, just incomprehensible. Our scoutmaster, on whom boys could rely in some towns as a guide to matters sodomitical, restricted himself to regular installments of his (and our) favourite game, "Fireman," which required that we strip down to our underwear, lie down in the dark, and pretend to be asleep until the fire bell rang. The boy who got dressed most quickly was the winner. Although I was an altar boy from the age of eleven or twelve until I was eighteen, Father Greengrass, the pastor of Marathon's Holy Saviour Catholic Church, showed no undue interest in any of his charges except to indicate during mass, sometimes gruffly, that we should pour him *all* of the wine. (The realization that he would soon turn it into blood and then drink it I did find unsettling.)

Mrs. Fownes, his housekeeper, was also the town librarian. I discovered the library in my early teens and became a devoted patron. The collection was very small, but a bookmobile servicing the isolated communities on the north shore would periodically bring in new titles (and considerable excitement). Word would go around —

"The bookmobile's in town!" — and my friends and I would rush down to the small room on the third floor of the Rec Hall and face Mrs. Fownes. I liked her, but she was a gatekeeper, and I hated that. I would collect the books I wanted to take home and bring them to her desk. She would examine them one by one, sometimes bestowing on me a sharp little glance, and she would make two piles: the books I was permitted to borrow and those I was forbidden to read. It was a public moment, a little shame-inducing, and probably has a lot to do with my fierce distaste for censorship. As a result, I read a great many boys' adventure stories. As I got older, science fiction and certain detective novels were permitted. I became particularly fond of G.K. Chesterton's Father Brown stories, and for a time Rex Stout's Nero Wolfe was a favourite. I do not recall reading anything that mentioned sex. The library had a small shelf of oversized art books, and for some reason Mrs. Fownes had no problem allowing me to take home Dante's *Divine Comedy*, though she must have realized that the text was quite beyond me and that it was the Gustave Doré illustrations of naked sufferers in hell that I wanted to ponder. Still, she allowed it. Perhaps it would have seemed a bit much to her librarian's soul to deny someone access to one of the masterpieces of Western literature. So it was, ironically enough, that Virgil became my guide as well as Dante's to those pleasures, still fledgling, that had placed the sodomites, my forebears, in the seventh circle of hell — a little lower than murderers.

Not that I would have known then what a sodomite was. And sensual pleasures were indeed fledgling, though I very much enjoyed looking at the pictures that so horrified Dante and Virgil, without quite knowing why I kept going back to them. I'd often been nude with other boys while we were growing up, and I had taken no interest in their bodies, but Doré was showing me adult bodies, grown men. (Burning in hell, perhaps, but buggers can't be choosers.)

There were certain moments, though, when I did notice my friends. I remember waking up once, in my early teens, beside a boy who had slept over. It was early, and the blinds on the windows were yellow and glowing, and everything in the room glowed too. Richard was asleep. The bed was small, but so were we. I was half nestled up against him, and we'd kicked the covers off during the night, and when I turned toward him I saw his wiener sticking out of his pajamas, and it was hard. I'd never seen anyone else's boner before, and though he was a little younger than I, he had a bit of hair around the base of his penis, which was larger than mine. I lay there in the yellow light and stared, desperate to touch it, not knowing why. When I was thirteen or so, again at a sleepover, a friend tried to teach me how to masturbate, though I didn't know the concept, had never heard of such a thing, and was quite wary and suspicious. I was a very credulous child, often the butt of practical jokes, and that a wiener might be useful for something other than peeing seemed a bit of a stretch. Still, Brian seemed to quite enjoy manipulating his penis, and though I didn't join him that night (fearing that it was a joke, I evinced a haughty disdain for something so childish), I did try it on my own later. The stroking felt rather nice but also seemed a lot of work for not much effect. I also nourished the vague sense that there must be something sinful about it, though Father Greengrass had never forbidden it. To forbid the act would have meant having to name and describe it, a prospect I'm sure he felt too mortifying to contemplate. As I got a little older, I tried again. Eventually, I had an orgasm, which terrified me. Though the pleasure was intense, I was sure I'd hurt myself somehow, but I was too embarrassed to speak to my mother. I couldn't even bring it up with the friend who'd tried to teach me years before. (Clearly a sexually precocious lad, he used to encourage Taffy, his cocker spaniel, to lick his penis when we were playing in the bush. Brian was a Protestant. Since by my lights he was going to burn in hell anyway, there seemed little reason for him to avoid sin.) Because he hadn't ejaculated that time at the sleepover, I figured he must have been doing it correctly, and I, an inept, must have burst some internal vessel. Still, it was a risk I would take again and again, even though all on my own I concluded that because it was pleasurable, it must be sinful. I somehow decided that God would not be quite so terribly upset if I didn't actually ejaculate, so I allowed myself orgasms if I could simultaneously squeeze the muscles in my penis the way you do when you stop peeing midstream and thus retain my "vital bodily fluids," as I would one day hear them described in the film *Dr. Strangelove.*

Such ignorance must seem odd and scarcely believable today, yet in those days I would discover there were similar experiences, even within my circle of friends. Robert Trow, who would eventually become my lover, was five years younger than I. He grew up in Toronto but did not discover masturbation or orgasms until sometime in his late teens or early twenties when he ejaculated spontaneously while looking at the penis of the man standing next to him at a urinal. My friend Philip McLeod, twenty-two years my senior, never masturbated until after he'd had his first orgasm, in his mid-twenties, the result of certain oral attentions having been lavished upon him in a Montreal park.

Though I was ignorant, I had intimations that there were aspects of adult life that were very important, so important that they were masked or spoken of in code. Jokes that were incomprehensible to me would convulse the adults.

My parents were not exactly social, but occasionally they had parties. When I was quite young, I would be in bed, asleep, when guests arrived. But sometimes my parents would wake me up, and I'd be brought downstairs in my pajamas, clutching the stuffed toy dog I slept with for so many years. I'm not sure why. I think I was an amusingly dozy child (friends still find me astonishingly slow), and I have a sense I was put on display: there was much laughter, and eventually I would be taken back to bed. But it continued, even into my early teen years, though a new element was added by then if Mrs. Millette were over, as she often was. I liked her — red hair always done just so, very French Canadian (as we said then), her husband one of the chefs at the Everest Hotel — but at these parties what everyone found funny was her being flirtatious with me, and my confusion, and the way it always ended, with me running in fear to the stairs and her catching me in the stairwell, pulling me down on my back, and crawling on top of me, saying seductive things in her earthy French accent, trying to kiss me. I can still picture her drunken face coming down to mine, the luridly painted lips, the haze of perfume, the laughter. I didn't like it. But I always admired her dresses. Classy satin numbers no one else would have dared.

We were forbidden to enter our parents' bedroom. So of course we did — even I, the good little boy, though guiltily, because I was still decades away from realizing that it was disobedience that got us out of that boring hellhole, Eden. We didn't sneak in often because it really wasn't that interesting. Just a bedroom, with a double bed, a dresser, a closet. My younger brother John sometimes stole small change from the top drawer of the dresser. Sometimes I would find a magazine, "men's magazines" I think they were called, precursors of *Playboy*. They did not interest me much, though I surreptitiously read a few of the stories — they seemed often to be about American soldiers who were stranded on tropical islands during the war and who met whole tribes of women. The women would teach them pleasurable things, though it was never clear to me what those things might be. The women often took their clothes off when they taught, though, which I thought most peculiar. None of my teachers did that at school.

One afternoon, when I was eleven or twelve, I spent time in the closet, though it had never seemed like a very promising area for exploration. Way at the back, behind some boxes, I found a pile of magazines. That surprised me. Until I discovered the town library, the only reading matter I had access to in our house was the occasional men's magazine or *Reader's Digest* and the weekly town newspaper, the *Mercury*, which included the *Star Weekly*. But here was a whole stack. The ones on top were about weightlifting and strength and had lots of pictures of men in bathing suits lifting heavy barbells or posing in ways that showed off their muscular development. My father had never shown any interest in sports of any kind. I had rarely seen him lift anything heavier than a case of twenty-four. So these magazines didn't make much sense. The ones further down in the stack were even more mysterious. They were smaller — brochure size, more or less. They had almost no text in them — just pictures, and just of men, but those men were often completely naked. You could even see their bums. You never saw their wieners — an artfully placed arm or a small Greek column or a slight twist in the body ensured that. If they faced you directly, they would be wearing a funny little pouch thing — not something I'd ever seen anybody wear. Sometimes a few paragraphs of text near the beginning would talk about the healthy male body, how it was important to exercise, and how these photographs illustrated the virtues of adhering to a healthy diet and a program of frequent exercise. Daddy did neither.

The pictures fascinated me. I can't really say why, since I don't recall associating them with a sexual thrill of any kind. Perhaps it was just the nudity — as groups of boys out alone together, we would usually swim nude, but I don't recall ever seeing a nude adult. I put those magazines carefully back the way I found them. But I went back, time and again, to look through them. They were my introduction to masks, to hidden stories.

When I was a little older and a little taller, I climbed into our attic with a friend. That was forbidden, of course, but since access could be gained only by someone tall enough to stand on the rim of the bathtub and lift away the boards that closed it off, my parents didn't much worry that I'd disobey. Eventually, I was tall enough. I knew clambering into the attic was dangerous — not only was I disobeying a parental injunction, but a misstep could put my foot through the drywall that constituted the ceiling. That would be hard to explain. Still, it was terra incognita at a time when all too much terra in my life seemed way too cognita. One day, when for some unfathomable reason both my parents were out of the house, Brian (he of the masturbation lesson and the cock-licking cocker spaniel) and I stood on the tub, lifted the boards, and climbed in.

There were boxes of Christmas decorations. I knew they'd be up there — I'd stood in the bathroom and handed them up to my father — but there was also a cardboard box I didn't recognize. It seemed to be full of letters, which was not very intriguing, but I grabbed one of them at random and opened it. A small curl of hair fell into my hand. I let it sit there. The letter was from my mother to my father — I recognized her handwriting — and I can't remember how it began, but I very quickly was reading aloud this sentence: "Here's a curl from my pussy to wrap around your prick." Brian was shocked and amused. I was mortified. I quickly replaced my mother's vaginal curl in the envelope and put the envelope back into the box, and we carefully lowered ourselves back into the bathroom. I never revisited the attic.

Years later, in 1977, when my father died, my brother John returned to Marathon to help my mother clear out the house and settle the estate. She told him to be very careful going through their effects because he might find photographs, and if he did he mustn't look at them. He must put them aside, she said, and they would destroy them.

He did find photographs. He tried not to look, but they were of my mother and father having sex. Of course, he should have disobeyed and looked at them, one by one. Of course, he should have saved them. He didn't. He allowed her to destroy them. They burned the letters too.

This drives me kind of crazy. Those photos and documents were archival, with respect to the sex lives of two very ordinary people, one of whom had died and another of whom would live another twenty-five years but could have no complaints concerning privacy violations after that. We don't have enough such material. That an ill-educated, churchgoing woman like my mother would dare to write dirty talk is revelatory. It thrills me to think that Fred and Yvonne Hannon might have had a loving, passionate marriage, at least for a time. Their relationship, as I remember it, segued from my father's maudlin doting to his simmering rages to his sudden drunken explosions into violence, a constant counterpoint being my mother's anxieties and attempts to protect us. Yet, early in their married lives, she could write him sexy love letters. She could snip off a curl from her pussy and mail it to him. They were, at some point, not the people I thought I knew.

MINE WAS NOT A happy family. I wonder if Tolstoy was wrong or just hadn't visited a pulp mill town in northern Ontario. There, many families seemed unhappy, and all unhappy families seemed unhappy in precisely the same way: because of drink and ignorance and domestic violence. A typical scene: in the kitchen, my father, drunk, slouched beside the table, beer at hand, always a beer at hand, always Red Cap, unfiltered Player's cigarette hanging from his lip. The air is blue from smoke. My mother: probably doing dishes. He's goading her, his voice slurred, rough, but not yet loud. Maybe it's that she tried to take his plate away before he was finished. Or maybe it's that she didn't take his plate away fast enough. Or can't she see he needs another beer? Or the food, sitting there in front of him, untouched, is cold now. Is she going to heat it up? Does he have to beg? What does she do all day anyway? Back when I still saw, still heard, I would hear it, see it, slowly building, my mother's sullen silences the only punctuation until maybe, finally, she would snap something back at him, and I would have been praying for her not to, please don't say anything, please don't say anything, because I knew then I would hear the chair shoved back, the lurch from the table, the smack of flesh on flesh, the screams, the begging, my mother on the floor, maybe, or backed up against the sink, holding her face, cowering, whimpering. It didn't always end there. Sometimes it reached me. Or my brother. Or both of us.

And I? I am at the dining room table, doing my homework, only a few feet away from them. Until my brother yells at me, right at my elbow, dragging me back to seeing and hearing, I had only a vague sense that something was happening somewhere in the house. The shell I made was working. I would get my homework done.

As a child, I often found myself unable to sleep unless I shaped all the bedclothes — sheets, blankets, pillows, even the clothes I'd taken off — into a four-walled fort. I wanted the walls to be just higher than I was. When they were, I curled up in the middle in my pajamas, and I slept. I was often awakened, though, by the sounds of my father shouting or my mother screaming. If it went on long enough, I would get up and go downstairs, always clutching the ratty yellow stuffed dog I slept with, afraid I, too, might be beaten but hoping it would stop if I appeared. Sometimes it did. It is a skill, oblivion. I have never lost it. I think sometimes that it is one of the reasons I am a good journalist — I have to make myself see, even today. I can never casually look about me — looking is always an act, willed, fresh, no longer frightened but rarely mechanical. I tell myself that I see things other people miss. I tell myself that I can still concentrate so intensely that the world will disappear. Others have noticed. At my first job, in an insurance company, I once looked up from some project I was working on at my desk to discover several of my colleagues had perched themselves on the desk across from me and were pelting me with paper clips. They said it had taken a long time for me to notice.

My brother John is about two years younger, more impish, the one likely to get into trouble, cannier than I, more likeable than I, but not as good at school. At home, he never taught himself how not to see. The price, for him, was delinquency, arrest, reform school. Eventually, when I was about eleven, another brother, David, came along. I think David, the only child left in the house after he reached the age of seven, did learn, as I had learned, how not to see. But I don't think he always remembered how to switch back.

I loved my mother. She was high-spirited, at least in the early years, and loving, holding us in her arms, reading books to us that I would bring home from the library. She did her best to protect us — she would yell at my father to restrict his beatings to our backsides. Daddy seemed to prefer the face.

We got a new kitten, once, for my brother and me. Playful,

frisky, we loved it. Then one morning, we couldn't find her. She was nowhere in the house. Mother was subdued, said it must have got outside somehow, disappeared in the bush, we might not be able to find it. We looked, and we didn't, and we were heartbroken. Later that day, my brother and I were playing in the basement, and I noticed a strange mark on the cement wall, higher than we could reach. We pushed a chair over, and I stood up and touched the spot. It was sticky and left a red mark on my hand. It was blood, and there were bits of fur stuck to it. And then we saw that it wasn't the only mark — there were smears and bits of fur on the adjoining wall. We ran upstairs and told Mom. She looked anguished and guilty. She sat us down and said we wouldn't understand, but Daddy had found the kitten trying to kill John in his sleep last night, that the kitten had crawled onto John's chest while he was sleeping and was going to smother him. So Daddy had had to kill the kitten. That he'd had to take it into the basement and kill it. Maybe we'd get a dog.

I have too many stories like that.

I'm fourteen, maybe fifteen, in bed, reading. My father suddenly lurches through the door, sits at the end of my bed, drunk, smoking. He doesn't say anything. I don't even look up. Then he slurs out, softly, not at all angrily, "I don't think you can feel pain." I say nothing. He turns, lifts the covers off my feet, takes the cigarette from his mouth. "Maybe you'll feel this." I keep reading. He brings the cigarette close to the sole of my foot. "You can't feel pain," he's mumbling softly to himself, doesn't even seem that aware of me anymore, his head lolling loosely, the cigarette wavering closer. I don't flinch, don't stop reading, though I can feel it now. I don't flinch, don't stop reading. Then it's almost against my flesh, and it hurts, and I bite my lip, but I don't flinch. Don't stop reading. He stops. Puts the cigarette back into his mouth. Doesn't say a word. Lurches out of the room. I keep reading.

So much violence. I didn't like it, but I think I was saved from trauma because it seemed normal. There was no one to tell me that life shouldn't be like that. If I went to school with a black eye, I'd have some silly explanation that no one believed but everyone accepted. Many of my friends had similar experiences and didn't complain.

Violence and a kind of simmering brutality were so all-pervasive that I once tried to talk my mother into killing my father. We would do it together, I told her, and the world would understand and forgive. On another occasion, I persuaded her to help me pour all the beer in the house into the sink in the basement. She must have suffered for that, though he did nothing to me when he got home. He sat alone in the living room and smoked and glowered. That did not bode well, at least for Mom. My brother did fight back once. I can't remember the provocation, but I do remember, even though he was still just a boy, that he managed to knock my father to the floor and was astride him, and I danced around them, shouting, "Kill him, John. Kill him!" I too fought back once, though it was a reflex action, and I was ashamed of it because, though I saw nothing wrong with parents beating their children, it somehow seemed against nature that a child might reciprocate. This is what happened: when I was in my early teens, I borrowed a pen from my father and did not return it properly to its case. He brought the case to me to show me what I'd done. I might have said something flippant. He began punching me in the face, and I, without intent, without forethought, purely reflexively, reached out and grabbed a beer bottle off the table and brought it down on his head. He fell to the floor, blood streaming down his face. My mother was hysterical. I wish I could say I felt good about what I'd done, but I didn't. I felt mortified; I felt

I'd sinned, the black eye I bore for days afterward the visible manifestation of the stain on my soul.

But he never struck me again.

SUMMER VACATIONS WEREN'T ALWAYS spent in Marathon. When I was a boy, my mother, brother, and I twice visited our relatives in Bathurst for weeks on end. (My father couldn't get that much time off work.) On one of our car trips, I overheard the adults in the front seat talking about how long it would be before we reached the ferry that would take us across some impending river. I understood them to be speaking of a "fairy," never having heard its homonym, and I became very excited, pressing for details as to whether we would cross on her back or whether she would bear the car in her arms. There followed a meretricious, and no doubt amusing, debate among them as to which it was likely to be. Every few miles, I asked again how close we were. We finally arrived, and I think it had been settled that we would be carried over on the fairy's back. I was crushed to discover that a ferry was nothing more than a boat capable of transporting an automobile. There was much amusement at my expense. No one had taken the trouble to explain what a homonym was — the perfect teaching moment, gone for good.

I was older than I should have been to have believed in fairies. I was always older than I should have been, or, perhaps more appealingly, I was always younger than my chronological age, at least in terms of credulity and practical knowledge of the world. So much of what happened around me seemed inexplicable and wondrous.

Credulity is a wonderful trait for a journalist. Even today, I begin by believing every word uttered by every subject I ever interview. I expect it shows in my face. I suspect it makes subjects want to tell me more and more. I get so excited by what they tell me. I don't do it as a strategy. It's not a trick I've devised to get subjects to open up. Only later, when I read my notes or listen to the tapes, do questions begin to surface. Skepticism, that other essential journalistic trait, makes its belated appearance.

THERE CAME A SUMMER when my Marathon friends lost interest in the bush. They would sometimes half-heartedly join me for our usual games and forays, but soon they made it clear that they would rather hang around downtown, either at the Rocket Lunch in the Rec Hall or at the cafeteria in the Everest Hotel, where they would meet and talk to and flirt with girls. (There was also the all-male pool hall, a known asylum for bad boys, which I sometimes dared.) I had no interest in girls as playmates, couldn't really interpret the language of flirtation, and was disappointed that girls showed no more interest in *Aida* than my boyfriends did.

There was a girl, though, who was interested in me. Eleanor was several years older than I. She evinced what was for me a deeply embarrassing predilection because it began when I was a boy of eleven or twelve. She would attend the Saturday afternoon matinees at the Strand, find out where my friends and I were sitting, and bring me candy she'd bought from Mrs. Cummings at the concession. I would shrink into my seat and try to refuse, while my friends giggled and poked me. Eleanor was oblivious, and she wouldn't leave until I took the candy.

When I got to high school, she became more or less a permanent feature of grade nine. I'm not sure she ever made it to grade ten — in those days, students could fail, and did, and remained in a particular grade until they passed or quit in frustration. She finally became my girlfriend, though it's probably more accurate to say that I finally became her boyfriend, that pathway having been paved via some considerable expenditures on candy. She asked me to a Sadie Hawkins Day dance. Of course, I had no other offers. All my friends were going, so I accepted. Marathon's stupidest girl and Marathon's smartest boy were now a couple. (Academically speaking, I'd been first in my class pretty much since public school. I was diligent about homework, obedient, and respectful — something of a suck, I suppose.)

We remained a couple, in a strangely desultory fashion, throughout my high school years. She was good-natured, perhaps a touch raucous in her vivacity, not beautiful but on the safe side of plain. I liked her mother, whose somewhat sardonic view of our relationship I can appreciate more fully today. I can't much remember her father. She had no siblings. The family lived in a better, newer part of town and owned a television set, that being something of a trophy in those days (we didn't have one), though reception was intermittent at best. (For a period, there seemed to be one television for the town, set up in a room at the Rec Hall. Occasionally, one could see dim pictures on it.) I do remember going to her house to watch my first opera — Gluck's *Orfeo*, part of the CBC Festival series, a much-anticipated thrill vitiated somewhat by her absolute lack of interest and unquenchable capacity for mindless chatter. I recall actually wanting to hit her, if that's what it would take to shut her up. I would see other shows in the Festival series at her house, but *Orfeo* was the high point.

Eleanor introduced me to what would now be called mild petting. By then I must have seen enough movies to realize that kissing was something men and women did, and at school dances my classmates would, for the slow songs, clench as tightly as decorum and the teachers would allow. Sometimes, when I was at Eleanor's house, her parents would go to bed and allow us to stay up for perhaps another hour. Soon after they had left the room, Eleanor would make it clear we should start necking, and we did. I found it exciting — mostly, I think, because it was clandestine, and because it was new to me, and because I had a sense that doing it made me part of the world, connected to what other boys and girls were doing. Eleanor knew the limits, though. She would allow me to touch her breasts, but only through her clothing. She never touched me below the waist. I assume she would not have allowed me to grope her, had I shown the slightest inclination, which I did not. She did permit full body contact, if we were stretched out on the chesterfield, and did not object to an erection, though I recall that it once escaped from my underwear and abraded rather painfully against the zipper on my pants.

We remained an item until I graduated from grade thirteen. (Having achieved a grade of at least 80 percent, I became the first child of Marathon to be named an Ontario Scholar.) I went on to the University of St. Michael's College in Toronto. She quit school to follow me, having been accepted as a student at a hairdressing academy in Richmond Hill.

I had long ached to leave Marathon. The violence and baseness of life at 1 Armour Street were testing even my talents for obliviousness. My brother John had vanished from our lives years before — apprehended so frequently for petty crime that he was finally consigned to reform school. (Where, I knew not.) David I loved and had some sense I should protect, but he was six years old, and I was seventeen. I detested the idea of abandoning my mother, but, like most teenagers, I was sufficiently selfish to put that thought to the back of my mind. I had to leave or go mad. University was to become my escape route. I had chosen St. Michael's College because it was a Catholic school, and I was still an altar boy and, for a young man, somewhat disconcertingly devout. A friend a year or two older than I, also an altar boy, had gone to St. Michael's the year before and spoke positively of the experience. To prepare, I sent away for a University of Toronto calendar, but I found it largely incomprehensible. I tried to work it out with my mother, but the dizzying array of courses on offer puzzled us both. Because I had always been good at math and sciences in high school, and because I imagined, thanks to their portrayal in Superman and Batman comics and film serials, that scientists led lives that were exciting, significant, possibly mad, but never boring, I gave up on the calendar and wrote a letter to U of T saying that I would like to take mathematics, physics, and chemistry. My marks were good, and I was accepted. I turned eighteen that summer, in July.

I wanted to leave Marathon, but more than anything I wanted to be in a city. The idea of *city* had become talismanic to me. The world I knew may have been mostly bush and lakes and rivers, but on trips to the Maritimes, the train would stop in Montreal, and we would have to spend hours in the station waiting for a connection to Bathurst. My mother would warn us that this was a city, that it was dangerous, that we should remain close to her in the station and on no account exit onto the street. If we did, she said, we would turn a corner and be lost to her forever. I was an obedient child, but this was difficult. I was thrilled by the bustle and clamour, by the sight of hordes of people who appeared not to know each other, by the traffic, human and vehicular, I could see outside the doors. I begged for permission to just step outside, but it wasn't forthcoming, so I pressed my face against the glass and drank it in, staying there until it was time to catch the train.

Toronto, I was sure, would be different. (It then featured, I had discovered, the tallest building in the British Empire.) I was preparing myself, that summer of 1962, for university and what I was sure would be a new life, a city life, a life with other smart people, a life that featured opera and tall buildings and busy streets and something else that glittered at the back of my mind, never brought to the level of consciousness but always there — the sense that in a city, a city with thousands of men, there might be another one like me.

WAS I A HOMOSEXUAL then? In a way, most certainly. In a way, not at all. It's difficult to be something if you do not know that that something exists, if you have never seen the word *homosexual*, if you do not have a name for the inchoate feelings with which you are struggling. The concept hovered in the air. At school, it was said that you were "a fruit" if you wore green on Thursdays, and though there was much giggling and teasing if someone inadvertently broke the rule, it was never quite clear what a fruit was. The older brother of a friend of mine was reputed to be one. Boys seemed to avoid him, but he was somewhat slow, and I wondered if being a fruit meant you were a little bit stupid — which I wasn't. When I masturbated, I didn't fantasize. Even to fantasize, one has to have some notion of what the possibilities are. One of my best friends had a large, uncut penis, and the sight of it excited me, but it somehow didn't occur to me to think of it when I jerked off. If I ached for anything, it was for wrestling sessions with Nick, a boy with whom I snared rabbits in the winter, a boy not cool and brittle and sophisticated but who filled some atavistic need in me, a need for close male friendship that trembled on the edge of violence. We invented the Game.

In the Game, one of us would attack the other at any time, without warning. We had to fight until one of us gave in, really gave in, really lost and lost badly, at which point the winner grabbed the loser's crotch and squeezed. That was Nick's idea. Later that summer, we added knives to the Game, Bowie knives we'd persuaded our parents to buy.

The day came, hot and buzzing, deep in the bush, the two of us alone. One quick move. Nick was on top of me, and we struggled, twisting together on the forest floor, he with his knife, and I? Too late, knifeless, taken by surprise, on my back, he full-length on top of me, pushing the knife with all his might toward my heart, and me holding on to his wrist, pushing him back. There was no pretending in the Game. We had sworn to each other we would not pretend. We had sworn we would come within a hair of killing. He pushed down hard on the knife, but I was slowly able to move the blade, only an inch above my heart now, toward my shoulder. I was weakening, and he knew it. Nick was thinner, wirier than I, but he was on top. He had gravity on his side. The tip of the blade touched my flesh. We were both shirtless that day. This was where the Game was supposed to end. He had won. He was close to killing. But it didn't end that time. He kept pushing. His eyes were dreamy, and I could smell the Brylcreem he used in his hair. I could feel his belly, slippery, pulsing against mine. The tip of the knife pierced my flesh, but I didn't really feel any pain, even as he continued to push, and the blade went in further. I sensed the blood trickling down toward my armpit, saw that Nick's eyes were still half-glazed and dreamy, smelled the stuff he used in his hair, felt his smooth belly taut against my own.

The scar is still there, almost invisible now, some fifty years later. The smell of Brylcreem, though, should I ever encounter it, still provokes erotic fantasies. I carry it from a time when life began each day puzzling and brutal and sometimes kindly in its intermittent magic.

I still have a photograph he took of me that summer, just before my eighteenth birthday. I'm emerging from a cave at the Rock Pile, have a bewitching resemblance to *MAD* magazine's Alfred E. Neuman, and am not wearing a shirt. That I should appear to be naked was my idea. Nick found that peculiar, but he went along. He was unusually shy about his body — I think we went skinny-dipping together only once — but I somehow wanted to take with me to the city an image that suggested something intimate and untrue about our friendship, that we were casually naked together, innocent and guileless enough to take each other's photographs.

Ours was not a friendship anyone might have predicted. He was a few years younger, an age difference that represented a social chasm in high school, but one I risked bridging, partly because he loved the bush when most of the boys my age had lost interest. He seldom laughed; he had crafty, vulpine good looks and a simmering temperament that found release in our extraordinary games. He came close to ending my friendship with another boy, one who was more congruent with my developing tastes and affectations.

Steve was my age, sickly and bespectacled, a chess devotee who taught me the game. I enjoyed it, but he always won (early evidence that strategy would not be a strong suit of mine). He had a languorous, drifting manner, read as much as I did, pressed Mary Renault's *The Last of the Wine* on me and asked leading questions about it. (Like many young readers, I didn't detect that the male-male relationship it described was anything other than a deep friendship. Steve did, though he kept that to himself.) He had a giggly sense of humour, much like mine, and was "artistic," involved like me in Teenantics, the teen summer drama group that so enriched our lives. He would eventually direct a play, *Sing a Song of Sixteen*, in which I played Henry, the young male ingénue. Started by a young man from Toronto with a summer job in the mill, the Teenantics organization gave me my first taste of theatrics, of stage lights, costumes, makeup, music, and dance. It drew in almost all the town's young people, perhaps not as significant an achievement as it seemed at the time (the high school counted only some one hundred students). It thrilled me — it seemed a glimpse of what would surely be waiting for me when I left for the city.

My friendship with Steve went back further than that with Nick, and we often walked together to and from school, a ritual that became complicated and then untenable when Nick entered the picture. He wanted to walk home with me as well, but it soon became very clear that he and Steve didn't get along. They quite despised each other. Steve was in most ways the kind of friend I wanted, but he couldn't provide the reckless sense of danger that Nick exuded. Steve would never have wrestled with me in the bush or suggested we fight with knives. It seemed I might have to choose between them, but they quarrelled one afternoon as the three of us headed home, and Nick punched Steve in the face. It was vile of me not to have ended my friendship with Nick on the spot, but I didn't. He won the right to walk home with me, and we continued to trap and grapple in the woods. I would reconnect with Steve years later.

THE SUMMER OF 1962, Nick photographed me with my shirt off. It was the longest summer I would ever face. It seemed as if September were inching away from me rather than approaching. I had been ready for weeks, at least sartorially — my mother and I had sat down together with the Eaton's catalogue and finally settled on an olive-green suit, chosen mostly because it featured three pairs of pants, which made the thirty-dollar price tag seem a little more palatable. I had won every scholarship Marathon had to offer, but they did not cover the cost of tuition — which at $466 a year now seems very inexpensive — and residence fees on top. I was too young to work at the mill that summer and had no money of my own. My parents confessed that they didn't have the money either, but my Aunt Rita, my father's sister, came to the rescue with a gift. I'd had no idea how close I'd come to not being able to go to university at all. Many, many years later, it occurred to me to thank her.

I left Marathon by train. It was a long trip, more than twenty hours. I was leaving my family, my friends, a land of extraordinary physical beauty, and the only home I knew. I didn't care. I imagine I hugged my mother at the station and shook hands with my father, but I don't remember anything but the desire to part from them. Our house was near the tracks, and for years, the sound of trains at night had conjured up a world of people who were not locked into lives like mine, people who read books and stayed up late, people who left home and asked questions, people who didn't look back, people who laughed, and people who had secrets. I would get on that train, I thought, and first I would be like one of them, and then I would be one of them.

I arrived at Union Station in Toronto and exited through the doors that led onto Front Street. I looked up, staggered back a few steps in consternation, pressed my back against a wall to support myself. I was looking up at the Royal York Hotel. It was the largest building I had ever seen. I thought it terrifyingly, threateningly huge.

I knew I'd come to the right place.

2

St. Mike's and the City

WHEN I GOT MY marks at the end of my first year at St. Mike's, I had failed every subject except Religious Knowledge. The only surprise was that I had barely passed even that, though to fail that subject in those days would probably have necessitated an auto-da-fé in the college quadrangle, bad PR for Holy Mother Church. I had simply given up partway through the year, stopped going to classes, didn't hand in any work. I floated aimlessly about for the last few months of school, dutifully sat and wrote my exams, then left the room sick with the certainty of failure. The truth was, I really wasn't smart enough for what was reputed to be one of the most difficult degree programs the university offered, and for me it was a brutal truth. I was used to being smart, to being the smartest, the high school student others turned to for help, the valedictorian, the student who would return to Marathon trailing clouds of academic glory. My failure was so mortifying that I decided to hitchhike home rather than take the train. I knew it would take longer, and I didn't care if I had to spend the night in the bush on the way; I half-hoped I'd be mauled by bears. In the event, I got picked up by a fellow student returning home to Sudbury, spent the night with him and his family, and reached Marathon unmauled.

Not only was I not so smart, I had to wonder if perhaps I wasn't quite as ready for city life as I'd imagined, and that suspicion deeply depressed me. For all my attempts at fitting in as a city boy, I almost certainly would have come across as a hick — I recall, after many failed attempts to make a phone call, asking an incredulous fellow student to teach me how to use a rotary dial telephone; importuned once for a loan by a street person, I showed that I was no fool by having him sign a receipt, and I enriched my hick status later by displaying the receipt as proof that I knew how to handle myself. I wrote my mother a letter about the elevators in the Sidney Smith Building on campus — not only were they the first elevators I'd been on, but you didn't have to push a button to reach your floor. One's finger had only to graze the surface of each floor marker to see it light up. That was so cool. I subscribed to hick standards of hygiene, and I must have been a very smelly boy. In Marathon, I had bathed once a week, by parental decree, but I saw no reason to be quite so particular in Toronto, where there was no one to enforce the rules — until once, sitting on the toilet in residence, I noticed that my balls were black with caked-on lint. I decided to shower. I grew to rather like it.

I found the university's size and bustle exhilarating, but I also found it intimidating. The library didn't have a Mrs. Fownes to tell me what books I couldn't read, but it was never very clear what books I should be looking for or how I should find them once I knew. My fellow students seemed to think my interest in opera even more peculiar than had my friends in Marathon. I had the great good fortune, however, of having the late Father Owen Lee as the prefect on my floor in residence. He would one day write several highly regarded books on opera in general and Wagner in particular. At the time, I thought of him only as the one person with whom I could discuss this thing I was passionate about. He was unfailingly kind, making office time for me, tolerating my callow views — I didn't much like Wagner then and worshipped Puccini, my endless blatherings about the man to my fellow students earning me the nickname Pooch, which stuck with me until I graduated. I would one day, years later, have occasion to interview Father Lee for an article I was writing. I asked if he remembered me. He did, but allowed that he could not approve of the direction my life took after I graduated.

Academic failure was a first for me. There were a number of other firsts that year: I would see my first opera on stage, *Madama Butterfly*, starring Teresa Stratas, from the last row in the top balcony of the O'Keefe Centre; taste alcohol for the first time, lemon gin stolen from my roommate's drawer, the effects of a few mouthfuls such that concerned fellow students found me giggling on a bench in Queen's Park; and, most devastatingly, fall in love. I would also, by some current definitions of the term, be sexually molested, though that is not how I thought of it then. I didn't know how to think of it then because, as with homosexuality, I didn't have the words or the concepts.

Even though I wasn't sure at the time what to think or feel, the incident clearly had an effect on me. I've never forgotten the man's name, sometimes find myself Googling him, was startled once, sitting in an office waiting room, to see his photograph in a magazine. (I recognized him instantly, though more than forty years had passed.) I didn't want to name him while he was alive because I didn't want him to get in trouble, but I was startled the morning of February 19, 2018, to see his photo in the "Lives Lived" obituary page of *The Globe and Mail*. Thomas Allen Patterson died September 4, 2017. He seems to have led a good life, filled with much charitable work overseas. This is what he did to me.

Shortly after arriving at St. Mike's, I reported for the compulsory physical the university required. The doctor, smiling and friendly, asked me to strip naked and stretch out on my back on an examination table. I did what he said. I'd been to the doctor as a child, but I'd never had a physical and had no idea what to expect. He began, with his stethoscope, to listen to my heart, but he so positioned himself that one elbow kept grazing my penis. Every slight move he made meant that he was in gentle, rubbing contact. It didn't take long for me to get an erection. He didn't say anything, just took it in hand and began to jerk me off. He chatted on, asking general health questions, never letting up even when he asked me to stand before him, perhaps he was checking my eyes, his face close to mine, but one hand was always down there, stroking my cock. This seemed to go on forever — I was in the examination room much longer than the previous student. He wanted me to ejaculate, I could tell, but I managed to will myself not to. Finally, he told me he was finished and I should get dressed. I went to class in a paroxysm of shame and uncertainty, barely able talk to my friends or look them in the eye.

I'd somehow heard of homosexuality by then and figured out it meant fruit. I was ashamed because a man had given me an erection, because I'd been wondering at some barely conscious level whether I might be a fruit and that erection seemed to suggest the answer was yes. Oddly, I felt no hostility at all toward Dr. Patterson. For all I knew, what he'd done was a routine part of any medical examination at the university. To have questioned it might have made me seem a hick yet again. (Perhaps, I thought, I was supposed to ejaculate for the exam, and he was being kind in not admonishing me.) There was certainly nothing sleazy or surreptitious about how he went about it. He was lively and light-hearted throughout. Only when he was standing beside me, his face close to mine, his hand pumping away, did I get a sense, from his slightly ragged breathing, that he might be excited as well.

Society doesn't look very kindly on such behaviour, which is why I didn't want to identify him while he was alive. The punishment would certainly have been out of all proportion to the seriousness of the infraction. Perhaps he shouldn't have done what he did; on the other hand, the event kick-started me thinking about homosexuality and gave me a first taste of what it would be like to have a man jerking me off. I'd have to wait six years before that happened again. Now that YouTube has made everything visible, I often find myself searching for medical instruction videos, particularly ones that coach young doctors on how to examine the male genitalia. Masturbating the patient seems not to be a standard feature — I was just lucky. Dr. Patterson gave me my first sexual experience of any kind; it resonates still, more than fifty years later.

University, in those days, seemed almost designed to stimulate homoeroticism. St. Michael's in particular was intent on keeping boys and girls apart — residence buildings for both sexes were strictly off-limits to the opposite sex. There was a curfew at Elmsley Hall, the men's residence in which I found myself, which I would occasionally violate. I was used to curfews, though — the siren on the water tower in Marathon blew at 9:00 p.m. each night, and kids were expected to be off the street and at home. Hart House was closed to women (the athletic facilities wouldn't be co-ed until 1975), which made the building a rich source of homoerotic shame, pleasure, and embarrassment. First-year students were required to pass a swimming test — failure meant compulsory swimming lessons, which I did not want to have to take. I enjoyed being in the water but had been a dog-paddle kid, never having learned to swim properly, so I was worried about the test, which required you to swim two lengths of the pool. I would have been more worried if I'd known that I'd be taking it naked in the presence of dozens of other naked boys. When we arrived, we were told to strip and line up single file. This meant that your penis was almost touching the ass of the man in front of you, and some stranger's penis was close to grazing yours. I struggled not to get an erection, stared straight ahead, didn't dare to move even slightly until it was time for the queue to move one man up as someone far ahead of us plunged into the pool.

I passed the swim test, passing the don't-get-a-boner test as well, but what intrigued me most was that it was clear that everyone swam nude all the time in the Hart House pool. Occasionally, one would see some guy in a bathing suit, but it was rare and seemed perverse. (I wonder if most boys, like me, grew up swimming nude, so it seemed natural to continue doing so.) I became a frequent visitor to the pool's observation gallery, pretending to myself that I was interested in what good swimming technique consisted of but ashamed of how long I would linger there, telling myself just another five minutes, realizing suddenly that a half hour had passed, and I'd still have to force myself to leave. I would occasionally run into other boys I knew from St. Mike's. It would be excruciating for both of us, having to pretend that we were somehow sportif when it was perfectly clear that we weren't and that there could be only one reason, really, why we spent so much time looking at naked male bodies. I suppose the good side to a topic's being unmentionable is that it is, well, unmentionable.

When I met the eyes of those other boys, along with the shame and the embarrassment, I had a sense for the first time that there were other men like me.

I WAS OLD ENOUGH to work in the Marathon pulp mill that summer of 1963, the summer after my glorious first-year failure. I was intent on returning to St. Michael's in September — not, obviously, in math or science — and I needed the money. I would get it. I was offered the dizzying amount of $2.22 an hour — a figure I would chant to myself as I walked down the street because it seemed so ridiculously high — but it would mean shift work, just like my dad did. The midnight shift, known as the graveyard, was the worst, but I didn't care. I wanted the money.

I didn't last very long at the first job they assigned me — I had to stand, with a pike, beside a conveyor belt carrying massive logs toward a huge, spinning blade that would turn a whole tree into wood chips in seconds. If the logs began to gang up, I was to use my pike to break up the traffic jam. I couldn't do it — I was skinny and not very strong — and it took only a few logs falling off the belt and hurtling down the stairwell for the boss to realize it would be safer for everyone if I were moved to another part of the mill.

I wish I could say that the experience taught me a new respect for my father and the other men who sacrificed their youth, their health, and sometimes their sanity so they could feed a family, but it didn't. Back then, I thought that they were fools, that they could have done better if they'd read books, like me, and listened to opera, like me, and stayed in school, like me. I feel differently now. I'm not surprised that many of them were alcoholics. I'm not surprised that many of them drank on the job. The mill was a dark, satanic place, a cramped and towering (yes, both) universe of noise and smells and stupefying labour that seemed to lead to nothing more than an endless sheet of white cardboard rolling out of the machine room, to be cut and baled and shipped away. They spent their lives making cardboard. They drank and they smoked and they swore and got drunk on long weekends and raped their wives and beat their children and maybe, sometimes, howled and wept. And then they went back to work. I think I understand a little of my father now. Still, it took me a long time to stop hating him.

I can't remember if I continued dating Eleanor that summer, but she evaporated out of my life about then. I can't remember if I still hung out with Nick, though I do recall longing for him at St. Michael's and writing him long letters, which he occasionally answered. I have a sense that we did meet that summer, but that nothing was the same between us. He seemed part of my old life — not that my new life was anything like what I'd envisioned — and I did not feel I could look back. We were awkward with each other. The friendship ended, in the way of most adolescent friendships, without regrets, tinged with embarrassment, cauterized by a slightly shaming sense of relief.

I had decided to take philosophy and literature when I returned to St. Mike's, on no other grounds than that they were subjects as far removed from science as I could imagine. I had a feeling, from the few arts courses I'd had to take in first year, that these were more suited to my temperament, tastes, and talents. What do I remember of the academic portion of the next three years of school? Not much. I believe that St. Thomas Aquinas claimed a large part of the curriculum (not surprising at a Catholic college), but the only element of his philosophy I remember is that small people can be pretty but not beautiful. I found *Middlemarch* an unbearable chore. (I would adore it later in life.) I clearly encountered Holden Caulfield, since he made his way into my *Don Juan* pastiche. I worshipped Gerard Manley Hopkins. I loved Byron and Pope. (I am now very good at writing doggerel.) I took a Classics in Translation course and became obsessed with Aeschylus's *Oresteia* and the *Bacchae* of Euripides. I took an opera appreciation course, which, no surprise, I aced. I wrote a play, *A Tinkling Symbol* (now lost, just like many Monteverdi operas, but perhaps not quite so unfortunately), which received an honourable mention in a university playwriting contest. (I do wish I had it — from what I remember, it was drenched in incident that would now read as homoerotic.) I acted in a play — the Messenger in Jean Anouilh's *Antigone* — performed on the small Stratford-style thrust stage that was once a feature of the Colonnade building on Bloor Street West. Most importantly, I took classes in philosophy from a Mr. D., and I fell in love.

Mr. D. was young. He taught in a way that both scandalized and entranced me. He seemed interested in what his students thought, not in how much they had memorized. I thought it ridiculous that anyone should care what I thought. I was nineteen. I wanted injunctions, not exchanges. He was thin and handsome and intense, and he launched right into Big Topics like the existence of God, which I thought both flirted with impropriety and, well, might also just be the kind of question I should be asking if I were serious about philosophy. I was still an altar boy then. I served mass at St. Basil's Church on campus, just as I had at Holy Saviour in Marathon. The priests in the confessionals at St. Basil's would ask me if I had "sinned with myself." I guessed what they meant, but given that they did not bother going into lusciously explicit detail, I felt I could imagine some other solitary infraction and legitimately say, "No, Father." I could tell by their tone that they weren't always convinced.

I was seduced by the force of Mr. D.'s relentless questioning, by his skepticism, but most of all by his glee, by his obvious pleasure in the examined life. He wasn't afraid of asking the wrong questions; he revelled in it. He might have paid a price — he wasn't on staff the following year, and there were dark rumours that he'd run afoul of the college authorities. I began to feel that perhaps I should question things too. I began by asking myself why it should be so important to God that I attend mass every Sunday, why I should be guilty of a mortal sin, and therefore consignable to hell for eternity, if I did not. Was it not enough that I should be devout on my own terms? (There I was, channelling Martin Luther, about four hundred years too late, and not even aware of it!)

I decided, one day, not to go to Sunday mass, a decision over which I agonized. I had attended mass every Sunday from about the age of seven, and as an altar boy would regularly be assigned weeks when I had to serve every day, early in the morning before I went to school. I liked my cassock and my surplice, the incense and the bells, the Latin, the singing at High Mass, the Easter and Christmas services with their arcane rituals. I wasn't especially fervent, but I was dutiful, and I believed everything I was told. Now I was going to risk hell because, ironically enough, a professor at a Roman Catholic college had made me want to not believe everything I was told, had made me want to question authority.

I thought it wise, though, to take out hell insurance. That first mass-less Sunday, I went to chapel, knelt, and prayed for much, much longer than I would have spent in church. I asked God to understand, to forgive, to read my heart, to balance the books in my favour. I was alone, and the room was silent, and it began to dawn on me, giddy-makingly quickly, either that day or the next Sunday, that I was talking to myself, that I had more evidence for the existence of Santa Claus, who could be counted on to visit the Strand Theatre in Marathon each year at Christmas, than I did for God, who at best would send His mom to Fatima or Lourdes but never to Marathon, though I'd sat in the empty church there, praying for a sign, staring at her statue until I thought, maybe, I saw her hand move. But, no, I never had.

That statue's torpor didn't make me lose my faith. It was seeing myself from the outside, seeing how absurd it looked to be mumbling into the empty air in a dimly lit room when a real world lay just outside the doors, a real world that did not come with pre-packaged answers. As soon as I could, I told a priest at St. Basil's that I would no longer be an altar boy, and I never went back to mass. Today, I see the Roman Catholic Church as an evil empire, but I don't regret having been raised in it. Culturally, it's a motherlode, and a touch of evil can be a salutary thing, rather like a vaccination.

One other incident, a trivial one, contributed to my decision to abandon Catholicism. I had, all of my life, respected the priesthood. Father Greengrass, in Marathon, may have been occasionally grumpy, but he was a kind man and once treated all his altar boys to a trip to Sudbury, which was very exciting because, though Sudbury seemed not to qualify as a city, exactly, we all got to stay in the Nickel Range Hotel. Father Lee, my prefect, was an opera boy's dream come true as a mentor. I didn't know any others.

I was broke most of the time at school. My mother would occasionally mail me a five- or ten-dollar bill she'd managed to save, but I wanted more, so I took a job as a waiter in the priests' dining room in Brennan Hall, employment that also meant access to leftovers of a higher quality than the meals served to the students. I would arrive, put on my starched white waiter's vest, set the tables (learning, in the process, that the blade of the knife must always face the plate), and, when the priests had taken their places, serve their food. (There were two students helping the Portuguese women on staff, and, for a time, my colleague was Philip Marchand, a wisp of a young man, pale, smart, slightly standoffish, who would eventually become the book columnist at the *Toronto Star*.)

The only priest we were afraid of was Father Iverson. There was a crazy priest who mashed all his food together with a fork and then refused to eat it, but he was harmless, and we got used to him. Father Iverson watched us. Father Iverson took note. Father Iverson had an acerbic wit. (If I'd been older, I'd have been more delighted with him than afraid.) One evening, as I passed by his table, Father Iverson said, "Come here, boy."

I approached and stood beside him. I thought perhaps his table needed something. He turned toward me, reached up to me from a seated position, and began to unbutton my waiter's vest, slowly, one button at a time. I had no idea why he was doing this; I feared he was going to undress me in public. Though he said not a word, the room grew silent, and all the priests turned to watch. There was nothing I could do but stand there and blush and feel his fingers moving slowly down my chest, undoing button after button. When he reached the last, and my vest was open, he said, with great gravity, "You did your job badly. The buttons were misaligned. Be more careful next time." Everyone laughed, and I went back to the kitchen, mortified and humiliated, to button my vest properly.

It's odd how an incident so trivial remains so vivid in my memory. As an adolescent in a deferential era, I was used to feeling powerless, and no teenager is a stranger to humiliation, but that it should be priests, a roomful of them, seated and silent and watching me blush, that it should be a priest's hands unbuttoning my vest, all of that somehow combined to push the incident beyond the trivial and helped push me out of the Church. (Tellingly, I still feel the need to capitalize that word.) I don't want to suggest that Father Iverson was making a sexual advance, though today that would be a fashionable claim to make. I think he was enjoying the exercise of the power he had. He could do what he wanted with me, within the bounds of dining hall propriety, and we both knew it. There would be something exciting, if not necessarily sexually so, about that.

I WAS, BY THEN, desperate to be in love, more so than to have sex, whatever that might be like. It was becoming very difficult for me not to think of myself as a homosexual. I looked at guys all the time, spent hours in the pool observation gallery at Hart House, started getting a hard-on in the showers one day when the whole U of T football team suddenly took over every showerhead but mine. But I was adept, by this point in my life, at not seeing, not knowing, not thinking. I knew and didn't know, didn't allow myself to know. I had a special way of dealing with the tension of knowing and not knowing. Periodically, when I made the daily trek from St. Mike's across Queen's Park to classes on the main campus, I would stop among the trees, away from other students hurrying by, and I would say, softly to myself but out loud, "I am a homosexual." And then I would keep walking. That was all. Somehow, the saying of it purged it from my mind, if only briefly. Mind you, I still had a fairly dim idea of what being a homosexual was all about. I had heard of Oscar Wilde. But then one of the nuns who taught us at St. Mike's mentioned him one afternoon. "You will hear rumours about Oscar Wilde," she said. "But they are vile. And they are not true." I found out much later that Wilde had converted to Roman Catholicism on his deathbed — turns out that nun was simply standing up for one of her own.

I had met Frank Cavallo in 1962, my first year at St. Michael's. He was one of the American students, a boy my age from Bergen-field, New Jersey, with whom I would be hopelessly in love for the remainder of my university career, though I didn't fall for him right away. In fact, I'd barely noticed him that first year because I was so in love with Lou, another American and Frank's best friend. Lou, I am sure, scarcely knew I existed. I spent the summer fanta-sizing about my reunion with Lou, imagining ways I could impress him and become his best pal, hoping we might be taking some of the same subjects so that there would be classes to bring us together and topics to talk about.

When I arrived back in September 1963, I didn't see him among the mass of returning boys. I did see Frank, though, and asked, as casually as I could, about his friend. Lou wasn't coming back, he told me. His marks weren't good enough. Frank's marks were apparently not stellar either, but he had been accepted. It seems strangely mechanical, but I simply plugged Frank into the place in my heart I had created for Lou. After all, Lou had chosen him as a friend. He must have qualities. So I fell in love. And, as happened so often in those early days, I fell in love with a straight boy.

Frank was slim, with a prominent nose, a weak chin, and a rose-bud mouth; he was smooth of face and body and had, as I would eventually discover, a very large cock. (He lived up to the English translation of his Italian surname.) More important to me, a nerd *avant la lettre*, was that he was cool. He was American, which in my mind almost guaranteed coolness; but, beyond that, he had an easy confidence bolstered by a hint of swagger, owned a guitar, could lean back in a chair, beer bottle in hand, cigarette dangling from his mouth, and sing the pop songs that everyone but me seemed to know. More than that, he had a circle — boisterous, loud, beer-drinking boys, bad boys who could drink and party all night, boys who invaded construction sites under cover of darkness and climbed half-finished apartment towers, boys who could show me a drowsy midnight city at our feet and yell it into submission, dazzled by the wind up there and the danger.

They became my circle too. I so wanted not to be a good boy. I so wanted to be cool. Perhaps the fact that I was known as Pooch meant that I was actually more of a mascot. But that didn't matter. Everyone had nicknames. (Frank was either Hoseman or Clothes-man, depending on whether his penis or his fashion sense was being extolled.) I was suddenly friends with SuperDon and the Bod and Father Norm and a host of other guys who took Frank's friendship with me as sufficient bona fides. We had reached an age where the restrictions imposed by St. Mike's seemed unbearable.

My closest friends at St. Michael's College, circa 1964. I was hopelessly in love with Frank Cavallo (left), who was straight.
Photo: Gerald Hannon

We wanted to be loud. We wanted to be up late. We wanted to study as little as possible. In 1965, after two years in residence, Frank and I decided to move out and get an apartment on our own. We found a place in a row of slum houses on Charles Street at Bay, where the Manulife Centre now stands. It had only two rooms — a kitchen and a bedroom. There was a toilet in the basement, but no tub or shower. It was close enough to St. Mike's to allow us to sneak back into residence and shower there. I can't remember what it cost, but we managed. There was a problem, though — it had only one bed, just a mattress on the floor in the room that wasn't the kitchen. We looked at the bed, and then at each other. "I guess we sleep together," Frank said.

That would not happen today. It's impossible to imagine two twenty-year-old straight guys blithely deciding to share a bed for a full academic year. It's as difficult as imagining dozens of uncomplaining naked teenage boys, tightly lined up single file, waiting to take a compulsory swimming test. Today, many young men seem to avoid public shower rooms unless there are individual curtained stalls. Today, there's gay out there. It's increasingly accepted, but that doesn't mean straight men are casual about being mistaken for gay.

The world is different, too. There's more student housing. There are student loans. If you've always had access to cash and had your own room in a nice, clean house, it's unlikely you'd settle for a slum room with a shared basement toilet and a double bed with another guy in it. To us, though, before there was easy money and credit cards, before boys were squeaky clean all the time, and most especially before there was gay out there, those things seemed a small price to pay for freedom and independence.

We moved in. It took an hour or so — we had no belongings other than clothes and books. Those two rooms would soon become party central for what today would be called our posse. SuperDon dubbed it the Hogan (the traditional home of the Navajo people, which I didn't know until the advent of Wikipedia). We partied. We studied some of the time. I kept up my job serving the priests and sometimes picked up extra cash by washing dishes at the seminary on St. Joseph Street. We could stay up as long as we wanted.

When it came time to sleep, Frank and I would get undressed, put on our pajamas, and climb into bed together. And so began a year of tortured bliss.

I was sleeping with the man I loved. It was a dream come true. It was also the most exhausting, debilitating, crazy-making, heart-breaking, lust-provoking, rage-inducing, tear-stained thing I would ever do. Can you go for a whole year without sleep? I'm sure I came close. We'd get into bed, leaving as much space between us as a double mattress would allow (we were still straight guys, after all), and, before long, Frank would drift off. I could tell by the change in his breathing. I, on the other hand, was wide awake, calibrating possibilities. Should I move closer? Could I touch him? Would he feel it? What if I just turned over and accidentally brushed against him? Surely there'd be no problem if my foot touched his foot? I would almost stop breathing if he turned over in his sleep and pressed his body against mine — I was afraid any slight movement I made would send him back across the bed. Often, that's how I might finally fall asleep: our bodies accidentally pressed together, his warmth seeping into me, the regular cadence of his breathing finally echoed by my own.

There was one night of perfect bliss and perfect torture. I'd turned over, facing him. He was asleep. When I was drifting into sleep, he turned over, facing me. Our faces were suddenly inches apart. Our lips were just a breath away from a kiss. I didn't kiss him. But I lay there and stared at him and felt his breath mingle with my own, and I was perfectly miserable, and I was imperfectly happy. There was another night like that. Had we been drinking? I can't remember. We were in bed, it was late, and we were both officially asleep. We weren't pressed against each other. Suddenly, he took my hand in his and began to stroke it. That was everything I'd dreamed might happen, but I panicked. Was this another of the many practical jokes he and others had played on me? If I responded, would he scream, "Faggot!" and punch me out? What if he had been dreaming that he was in bed with a girl, and I went along with it, but he woke up and was totally grossed out? What if he really wanted me?

I pushed his hand away and turned my back to him.

We were strangely awkward with each other the next day. When it came time to go to bed, Frank told me he thought he'd sleep on the sofa that night. There was a miserably uncomfortable, ratty old couch in the room as well. Sometimes, when a buddy got too drunk to make it home, he'd sleep there. We never did. That told me he knew what had happened. That told me he was mortified, but I didn't know why. Because he'd meant it to be a joke, but I'd thought he'd meant it seriously, which meant I thought he was queer? Because he had meant it seriously, thinking me queer, but I turned out not to be? Because he was dreaming of a girl, and my sudden rejection woke him up and made him realize what he'd done?

He slept on the couch that night, and possibly the next night as well. Then, the night after that, he crawled back into bed with me as if nothing had happened. I didn't say anything. I was simply happy that the sofa was a wreck. It meant that if he wanted to sleep at all, he had to sleep with me. Happiness is sometimes brought by cheap, uncomfortable furniture.

Though there was no "gay" back then, what was out there was "queer." I began to hear about queer from my friends, from the Hogan boys. They'd discovered that St. Joseph Street, between Bay Street and Queen's Park — the southern border of St. Mike's — was a cruising area. If you walked that block slowly, late at night, cars would slow down, and the drivers, always men, would catch your eye and smile. If you smiled back, the car would stop, and the driver would open the door for you. The guys had figured out the scene and gamed it. They'd get together, party, drink a lot of beer, and piss into plastic bags or fill them with water. When it was time, they'd head out to St. Joseph Street, each carrying a bag, stand somewhere along that block, the seminary at one end, Carr Hall at the other, and wait. A car would come by, slow down, the boys would smile, the car would stop, the door would open, my friends would lean in and then swing the bag full force into the interior, drenching the driver and the whole front seat. They'd scream, "Faggot," slam the door shut, and saunter off. There was no need to run. No faggot in those days would go to the police, not with a story like that, not when it might seem clear that he'd been trying to pick up boys. Homosexual acts were illegal and would be until 1969. So those men drove home; if they were married, they would have had to explain why they and the car were drenched.

My friends would come back to the Hogan with those stories. There was much drunken laughter. They tried many times to get me to join them, but I never would — as opaque and unthinking as I was, I knew it would be wrong. (My decision not to be one of the boys is one of the few things from those years that I can hold on to with pride.) I don't imagine that made them think I might be queer. Queer was alien. Queer didn't hang with you, laugh with you, drink with you, share a bed with you — and there I was, doing all those things, so I couldn't be queer. Eccentric, gullible, weird, maybe. But not queer. Years later, when we were both in our sixties, one of those boys would turn up at my door. I didn't recognize him. I was a sex worker by then. He'd booked a session, and I took all comers. The sex was a challenge — he still had the remnants of a hockey player's body, but he was pushy and demanding and couldn't get hard. When he was getting dressed, he said, "You don't recognize me, do you?" I didn't. And then I did. Doug. Loudmouthed, hockey-playing, beer-drinking Doug. The Hogan boy who'd discovered the fags on St. Joseph Street; the Hogan boy who'd led the first piss-bag attacks. I never told him I remembered what he'd done — his life seemed punishment enough. Married with kids, with a passion for sucking cock he could rarely indulge. I didn't want to have sex with him again, but we settled on a contra deal. I'd let him suck my cock if he prepared my will. A lawyer, he understood a bargain, and he accepted. I can tell you the exchange rate — four blow jobs bought me a will.

There was one other queer world we all knew about. On the

infrequent occasions when the smelliness of our wardrobe dictated a laundry session, we would go to the King Koin Laundromat at 575 Yonge Street, not very far from St. Michael's. The door opened into both the laundromat and a stairwell to an upper floor. If I were there late enough, I'd see men climbing those stairs, men in a flurry of sweaters and giggles and devastating pronouncements, men who might look through the window at me and arch an eyebrow, men who might then turn to their companions and smile. Somehow, that all meant queer. I don't know how or why — there were no models I was aware of — but it meant queer to my Hogan buddies, and so it meant queer to me.

My friends dared me once to go up those stairs. It was the perfect dare. None of them would do it, and if I did, I'd not only satisfy my curiosity but also gain some marks for bravery. I demurred for a short time, of course. (One shouldn't seem too eager to experience something quite that sick.) Then I started up the stairs to encouraging shouts of "Go, Pooch!" from my buddies on the sidewalk. The small anteroom at the top of the stairs was empty, except for a woman sitting at a desk. She was clearly selling tickets, and there was a door, covered with a beaded curtain, next to the desk. In my memory, it glowed red behind that curtain, and music and laughter carried out into the anteroom, and I was afraid, and I so wanted to go in, and she looked at me and said, "Can I help you?" I don't think I said anything. I was tongue-tied. I looked pleadingly at her, but she shook her head, and I turned and hurried back down the stairs. My buddies laughed when I told them what had happened. Many years later, I would discover that I had entered the Music Room, one of the city's first gay clubs, and that the woman at the desk was Sara Ellen Dunlop, only eight years older than I but already devoted to trying to create a new world for gay men and lesbians. (Also a founding member of the band Mama

Quilla, she died of cancer in 1978.) She was tough. She had to be. The ArQuives, Canada's LGBTQ+ archives, notes, "She was very protective, and put her body on the line by blocking the entrance to gay and lesbian bashers; on one occasion, she fought a gang of motorcycle hoods who tried to trash the club." She would have been wary of any face she didn't know coming up those stairs, though I doubt she thought I was a queer-basher. I'm sure I just looked too scared and too young. In photos from that period, I look like I'm in my early teens. I remember being stopped by police one night on Bay Street when I was nineteen or twenty and feeling very adult. "You're out a little late, aren't you, kid?" the cop said, leaning out the car window. A few years earlier, I would have been mortified and apologetic. This time, I was angry. I was beginning to rebel.

In the summer of 1964, I went to New York City and then, from there, to Mexico. Manhattan still lured, even more so because the World's Fair had opened in April. I had little money, but I did have a connection: Frank lived in New Jersey. I could stay with him and commute. I'd dreamed of such a trip since high school, but I remember little of it. Yes, I was dazzled. Yes, I got lost. (Frank had recommended a map. I didn't think it was necessary — the streets form a simple grid, I told him.) I remember most how it ended — on my last day, Frank's father drove us to the Port Authority Bus Terminal in Manhattan. I said goodbye to them, got on a chartered bus filled with other students, and left for Mexico.

At St. Michael's College that year, I had joined a group called the Conference on Inter-American Student Projects (CIASP). It was a Roman Catholic version of CUSO (Canadian University Students Overseas), a non-politicized vehicle for naive young people who wanted to do good but felt it unnecessary to begin at home.

After a gruelling three-day bus trip, we arrived at Tamazunchale, a small town on the Moctezuma River in the Sierra Madre Oriental mountains northeast of Mexico City. That was the jumping-off spot for the village of Pisaflores, at the time accessible only on foot after a five-hour walk, but at least it was downhill. Pisaflores (the name means "stepping on flowers") was itself the jumping-off spot for a number of ranchos (small farming communities scattered through the mountains, also accessible only on foot). Some students were to remain in Pisaflores and help build a school and a rough road into town; others were assigned to different ranchos, though their mandates were often unclear.

Two other students and I were chosen for La Escondida de San Rafael (St. Rafael's Hideaway), one of the smaller villages (I doubt it had more than 150 people), about a three-hour walk from Pisaflores, mostly uphill. After a few days of rest in Pisaflores, we left for La Escondida, guided by men from the town, who also carried our luggage. The climb was exhausting, but the countryside was breathtakingly beautiful — verdant forest alternating with corn-fields seeming to defy gravity, they grew on such steep slopes. As we climbed, we would suddenly burst out of the trees and gasp at the panorama of the Pisaflores valley spreading below us. I saw trees I'd never seen before, flowers I'd never seen before, insects that seemed the very definition of exotic. I was almost giddy with glee — I felt safe, I liked the two students I was with, and we seemed to be living one of the boys' adventure stories I'd grown up with.

We were to start a school from scratch — La Escondida had never had a teacher. We would eat what the Mexicans ate, supple-mented by a food box that arrived weekly. We would be guests of the Torres family — Don Francisco and his wife, Dona Hermelinda, and their five children (three adult daughters and two boys, both of them intellectually challenged, the younger one, a child, severely so). I came to think of the Torres family as a second family, and

I spent summers helping set up a school in rural Mexico, mid-1960s. Here I sit (centre) surrounded by the kids. Photo: Gerald Hannon

I loved them deeply, staying in touch by mail for years, though eventually, to my shame, I let the connection evaporate. In a way, they and the other students I was teamed with began to liberate me from my past. I came to them without a history — to them I was Geronimo (the name assigned to me by the local priest, who had trouble pronouncing "Gerald"). I was not Pooch, not the feckless, naive, opera-loving hick from northern Ontario that seemed ever to be my role in Toronto. In La Escondida, I was Geronimo, the one my fellow students came to depend on because my Spanish was usually better than theirs (we'd had access in Toronto to an oral lab course, and, no surprise, I was more diligent than most), and that gave me a leadership role I found surprisingly easy to take on.

I discovered that others listened when Geronimo had ideas about how to teach. Geronimo had confidence, confidence that a group of young Canadians who'd never taught before could start a school without desks, without paper or pencils or a blackboard, and that's what we did, requisitioning supplies from Pisaflores, creating makeshift desks out of boards and sticks, finally even getting our hands on a map of Mexico and a small blackboard. Toronto's Gerry could never have done any of those things. (Not that they were worth doing — I eventually came to see the whole experience as cultural imperialism.) And Pooch? Not a chance.

Pooch was waiting for me, though, when I returned to Toronto. It's also clear, in retrospect, that Pooch was going mad.

I'd begun experimenting with marijuana, introduced to it by a fellow student, a woman whose interest in me extended to the corporeal, but, as before, I played dumb. I liked getting high, but it frightened me too — sometimes, the giggly pleasures it induced would be shadowed by endlessly circulating images and memories: every little awkward moment, every social clumsiness, every failed attempt to be clever, every minute I'd stolen from study to watch the naked boys at Hart House, every casual, brief contact with Frank in bed, every time I'd said, "I am a homosexual" to the indifferent trees in Queen's Park. Those thoughts would crowd in, grinning and derisive, one after another, new ones always at the ready, and every one of them tinged with shame for both what I was in my secret life — a homosexual — and what I was to the world: a fool. I was a pathologically credulous young man, the butt of many a practical joke. The most elaborate almost destroyed my friendship with Frank.

One day, at the Hogan, I received a piece of mail from an organization calling itself the Solar Society. It was a nudist group, and the letter, on convincing letterhead, invited me to become a member. I was intrigued and felt a little special — no one else I knew had received such a letter, and I began to imagine scenarios where, if accepted, I'd be innocently in the company of many other naked men. The application form struck me as oddly detailed —

among many other attributes, it asked for my penis size, both flaccid and erect. I consulted with the Hogan boys about why such information might be necessary, sought advice on the proper way of measuring one's penis, and talked the whole matter up with friends and acquaintances both male and female, particularly after I was interviewed by a young female representative of the Solar Society and saw my acceptance as imminent.

A classmate took me aside one day. She told me that there was no such organization, that this was an elaborate prank, that everyone knew about it and found it very funny, but that she thought it was mean and, well, she wanted me to know.

I was waiting in the Hogan when Frank and SuperDon and some of the boys came in from class. We fought, Frank and I. Flailing, punching, grappling on the floor, our bodies twisted together more intimately than they'd been in bed, and yes, I thought of it that way, held that in my mind along with the desire to hurt him, giddy with the drama of it, with being out of control, with being too far gone in violence to stop. It was me and Nick again in the Marathon bush, me and Nick without the knives, me and Nick but not a game, not a game this time, and it soon became clear to everyone in the room that someone should step in. SuperDon pulled us apart. Frank turned from me, thinking the fight was over, but I sucker punched him in the mouth, and we plunged back into it, fuelled now by rage and shame and pain. I can't remember why it stopped — we were probably pulled apart again and shoved into separate rooms. My punch had loosened one of Frank's teeth and fractured a cheekbone — he needed dental work and had to wear a cast for two weeks. I found out later he hadn't even been one of the ringleaders.

It's a cinematic cliché that young men who fight each other violently become, or remain, friends. Frank and I remained friends.

I kept going crazy. The swirling cloud of shame that sometimes disfigured my dope sessions began to happen even when I hadn't smoked up. I could feel it coming, but by then it was too late. I was gone. There were times when I would run if Frank tried to come near me. I would call him the devil. When we got together many years later, he said he had tried to calm me by playing the overture to *The Marriage of Figaro* over and over, and I'd conduct it, in a kind of antic trance, and then slip back into some incoherent, lost-boy state that frightened him. I remember none of this, though I've no reason to doubt it — his knowing enough to try to rescue me through opera has the ring of truth.

I was found one night, naked and in tears, crouched on the floor of a shower stall in Elmsley Hall. I'd sneaked into the building (I was no longer in residence). As I stood there under the streaming water in the dim light of that curtained stall, I saw myself as others saw me: hapless, foolish, virginal, witless ... I saw too what they couldn't see, but what I feared one day they might — that I was sick. A pervert. Those thoughts and images swirled round and round, crowding one another, a vortex leaving no room for anything else, and I somehow knew that this time I'd lost. That this time I wouldn't surface bright and cheerful, and there was nothing for it but to slide down the wall to the floor and weep. Students found me there, moaning. I heard them asking me questions — I couldn't bear it, pushed myself deeper and deeper, beyond questions and answers and reasons. I don't remember much after that. I awoke the next day in a bed in St. Michael's Hospital. A nurse was giving me a sponge bath. She told me they wanted to keep me under observation for a few days, but I begged to be allowed to leave. She agreed, reluctantly, on the conditions that she would first make an appointment for me with a psychiatrist and that I would promise to meet him. She did. I made the promise, and

I kept it. The psychiatrist was a soft-spoken South Asian man at the Clarke Institute of Psychiatry on College Street. He asked me some desultory questions, and then, apropos of nothing that had come before, he said, "Are you a homosexual?" I said I was not. He nodded and wrote something in his notebook. That was the last I saw of him. I didn't keep the next appointment.

3

Graduation and First Sex

I GRADUATED IN 1966 with a general B.A., philosophy major, English literature minor. At the beginning of that final school year, Frank and I had moved out of the Hogan and into an apartment on Irwin Street with Hogan boys the Bod and SuperDon. Significantly, I can't remember the sleeping arrangements. I wasn't sharing a bed with Frank — that was all that mattered, and that then unacknowledged disappointment blurred the year in my memory. The few photographs I have are the only evidence that our boisterous undergraduate behaviour hadn't much mellowed and that I was still getting drunk too easily and experimenting with drugs and frightening my housemates with inexplicable flights into a dazed or antic withdrawal. I don't remember a thing about my studies or the marks I achieved. None of that seemed important. I had no plans, other than the vague feeling that postgraduate work should be next. There was nothing I wanted to do. There was no one I wanted to be.

I didn't stay in Toronto for graduation. I returned to Mexico and La Escondida with CIASP, Geronimo trading places with Pooch. The Canadian students in the nearby rancho El Rayo cooked up a graduation ceremony for me, complete with a handmade B.A.

and a handcrafted mortar board. Mexico had its usual salutary effect. I had work to do, and I was good at it. The villagers loved me. Anything homosexual seemed so far off the map that it scarcely registered, though before returning to Toronto I did travel the country for a week with another CIASPer, Michel, an alluring Montreal francophone whose hip, *de rigueur* dark glasses shielded a sunny, open temperament. We tried to pick up girls in Mexico City. We found a remote Pacific beach, borrowed horses from a friendly peasant family, rode for miles, swam naked in the surf — that last my idea, of course. I developed a system that gave me something of what I wanted from him — whenever we booked into a hotel or inn, I always asked, because my Spanish was better than his, whether a room with a double bed was cheaper than a room with twin beds. It almost always was. "We can save a little money," I'd tell him, "if you don't mind sharing a bed." He never minded, guileless straight boy that he was.

I returned to Toronto and registered for graduate school in philosophy. It seemed my only option — there was nothing I actually wanted to do. After two, perhaps three, classes, I withdrew. The lectures concerned the pre-Socratics (Thales, Anaximander, and Anaximenes), and I couldn't face the prospect of weeks of study devoted to ancient Greeks who had come to the conclusion that everything is made of water. Or made of air. I was floundering, directionless, and I needed a job.

It wasn't difficult to find work in those days, but it took a kindly gentleman in an employment agency to explain why I never got a second interview. It had to do with the way I dressed. I was very proud of the business outfit I'd pulled together: a bright orange shirt splattered, blood-like, with crimson splotches; a crimson tie with multicoloured splotches; purple pants, in a rather heavy velour fabric; and a wide black leather belt. (I still have the photos.)

It's 1966, I thought. *This is how people dress.* "You're a smart young man," he told me. "But you'll never get a job unless you dress … well … for business." I'm not known for listening to sage advice, but this time I did. Not long after a sartorial makeover, I was hired as a computer programmer trainee by Zurich Life Insurance, with offices then on Richmond Street, just east of University Avenue. I had no experience, of course. No one had computer experience then, but I'd done extremely well on the tests I'd had to write. ("Among the highest marks we've registered," I was told). Suddenly, I had a job.

It didn't last very long — I would quit in less than a year. Things I remember: being scolded by my boss for letting my hair grow to Beatle length. He insisted I get a haircut, and, reluctantly and probably sullenly, I did. Computer hard drives the size of oil drums in a special air-conditioned room. Writing code on paper and being eager for the delivery of the punched cards that would allow me to test my program. Colleagues pelting me with paper clips to see how long it would take me to notice. An office washroom with a shiny stainless steel bar near the ceiling. In it, you could see reflected the penis of whoever happened to be standing at the urinal while you were seated in the nearest stall. Once I had that little epiphany, I made a point of always sitting down to pee.

Marijuana Mary, or so I dubbed her.

She was a secretary in my department. She was chubby-cute and giggled and favoured what I came to think of as a Carnaby Street look. She lived in Yorkville, then ground zero for young druggies who wanted cheap accommodation, and she made it clear that she could get me high. It was just as clear she wanted my body. She was very forward in ways that strike me now as quite progressive but seemed not very ladylike at the time.

"When are you going to have me over to spend the night?" she'd ask, a giggle at the ready.

"Every day next week," I'd say, keeping the joke alive while fully aware she'd made a serious proposal. She even turned up at my door once — I sat with her on the porch steps and chatted, but I didn't invite her in.

I have to give her marks for persistence — she began inviting me back to smoke up at her place, a room in a house on Hazelton Avenue. Back in Marathon, Eleanor had put her faith in candy, but the stakes were higher now. I would accept, turn up, get high, then excuse myself and go home. Even I began to see this as pathetic — she was throwing herself at me, and I was this namby-pamby milquetoast — and besides, if I just went through with it, I'd have a story to tell Frank and SuperDon. That was the important part — I'd finally have a sex story for the Hogan boys. So the next time she said, "Why don't you stay the night?" I did.

She went to the washroom, and I got undressed and into bed. When she returned, I was lying flat on my back with the blanket pulled up high enough to cover my mouth (a childhood ritual of solace that continues to this day). She got into bed beside me. Seductive until then, she was suddenly, inexplicably shy. I was expecting her to take the lead, so I lay there, unsure of what the next move should be, and soon, I was asleep.

When I awoke the next morning, I had my usual matutinal boner. She noticed. Everything happened very fast then, and it didn't take very long. She drew me onto her and guided me in. I still wasn't entirely sure what it would be like down there. It felt warm and soft and cushioned, and I thought, *Wow, this feels great,* but the main thought in my head right then wasn't at all about what I was feeling — god knows, even less about what she might have been feeling — but the way I was going to tell this story to the guys, how I'd finally gotten her alone in her place and really fucked her. What I neglected to mention was that really fucking her lasted about half a minute.

We didn't talk much when it was over, but she did say, "You know, I guess I'm wrong, but I was beginning to think you were a homosexual."

What I was thinking, as I walked home in the bright morning sunshine, was this: *I'm twenty-two years old, and I'm no longer a virgin.* What I wasn't thinking was this: *I'm twenty-two years old, and I'm still living a lie.*

DID I LAST A full year at Zurich Life? I don't think so. The work was challenging, but the computer staff was entirely male. I didn't fit in with either the jock or nerd tribes, and, I suppose, I eventually saw every one of their penises reflected in that washroom's shiny metal bar. I didn't want to have sex with Mary again. I'd been frightened by a false-alarm pregnancy in the wake of our one encounter. I did want to go to Expo 67, the World's Fair in Montreal commemorating the hundredth anniversary of Confederation. I wanted to take my mother and my brother David to Mexico. I quit my job. I went to Expo 67 on my own and, like everyone, was dazzled and suddenly proud to be Canadian. I took my mother and brother to Mexico the way I'd done it — by bus and on foot, though I made some concession to my mother's age by securing a burro for her to ride when it came to the steep climb up to La Escondida. And then I was back in Toronto, jobless and directionless.

For a period, I did supply teaching in high schools, though I was not credible as a teacher. Though I was twenty-three, I was often mistaken for a student — I suspect there was something unformed and adolescent about me. I remember running down the hall once, late for the class I was to teach or, more properly, babysit, and being brought to heel by another teacher who took me for a grade twelve student breaking the no-running rule. Every time I said, "But I'm a —" he'd cut me off with, "Enough out of you, young man," until I was finally able to spit out, to our mutual mortification, that I, too, was a teacher.

By then, I'd moved in to a large apartment on St. Nicholas Street with a group of young men I knew only casually from the neighbourhood. I was assigned to share a bedroom with Ken, the one I did know passing well. He was slight and cute in a baby squirrel sort of way, though with something of a cat's languor in his slow, easy, considered movements. He had the most alluringly confiding voice — everything he said sounded like a confidence he was sharing. The room we were assigned was very small and narrow, with two single beds parallel to each other and about a foot apart. One very hot summer night we were both trying, not at all successfully, to fall asleep when he suddenly reached across the divide and touched my arm.

"Gerry?"

"Yeah?"

His hand caressed my mattress, making a slight, whispery sound.

"I'm worried about something. Can I ask you to do me a favour?"

So soft, so pleading.

"Sure."

Long pause.

"I think my penis is too small. Would you take a look at it and tell me what you think?"

Barely audible. An aching whisper.

I didn't, though just his asking gave me a boner. I told him that I'd read that penis size wasn't important to women, so he should stop worrying. He didn't insist. I, convulsed with regret and shame, and he, I guess, with frustrated lust, pretended to fall asleep in that cramped, sweltering little room. We might have managed. Ever since the Solar Society, I'd feared that almost anything might be a prank, that I'd say, "Sure, I'll look at your penis," and he'd yell, "Fag" and tell all the other guys in the house and say he couldn't share a room with me anymore, and I'd be asked to leave. I moved out soon after anyway — thanks to Frank's having to retake an English course, he was unexpectedly, and thrillingly for me, back in Toronto.

We rented a third-floor apartment at 609 Yonge with big windows overlooking the street. It was one large room, incorporating a small kitchen. The washroom, which featured a bathtub, was on the second floor. To my initial dismay, there were two beds, though that was maybe for the best because it also meant the end of a particularly excruciating form of torment. Still, Frank and I did sleep together one more time. The heating system broke down one frigid winter night, and though both of us were shivering in our beds, I would never have said anything because ... well, because I was gay. Because I didn't want to come across as a sissy. Because I didn't want to come across as too eager to sleep with him. Frank had no such problem. "Come on, Pooch," he said. "We're both freezing. Get in bed with me." And so, cuddled together under the blankets, we slept. Even I did.

The building at 609 Yonge Street is still there. I can stand on the west side of the street and look up at those windows, now opening onto high-end office space, and think, *That's where I went crazy for almost the last time, and that's where my life began to change.*

How do I write about being there and not being there? If I don't remember, did it happen? If my best friend was there and watched and remembers and tells me years later, did it happen? If it means I was still humiliatingly in love with him, did it happen? If it means

I don't want to think about it even now, even if it did happen, did it happen? Did I noisily burst into the room one night, late late late, Frank asleep, me drunk or stoned with a girl I knew, a girl I liked, both of us giggling and high and trying or pretending to be quiet? Did we sink to the floor, sink to the floor when my bed was right there, and start making out? Did Frank wake up and start watching? Did he see her pull my pants down and start sucking my cock? Did he see her fingering herself? Did he see me start to drift in that way that meant I wasn't coming back, and did he see her, see her sucking my cock, and did he hear her, hear her begging me to fuck her? Did I finally surface and turn to him and say, "Would you be a good friend and fuck her for me?" Did she say, "Will *someone* please fuck me?" Did he fuck her? Did I sleep through it? Did he fuck her while I slept, and did I miss seeing his hard cock? Did she leave before I woke up? Did she never speak to Frank again?

I have some letters from her, still. One, dated June 7, 1968, is mostly cheerful and chatty, and then there's this: "I had to burn the letter you sent. It would have been great for blackmailing purposes."

I NEEDED A JOB. My bridges were burned at Zurich Life. They made that very clear when I asked for my job back. I spent days searching, in a desultory fashion, through the newspaper employment sections, but it was Frank who spotted the ad, sometime in February 1968. The Toronto School Board was hiring teachers of English as a Second Language. No experience necessary. The only qualification seemed to be that applicants have a B.A. I went for the interview and sat in a room with other hopefuls until it was my turn to be questioned. I was asked if I had a B.A. I did. I was then asked if I could start on the following Monday. I could. The interviewer told me I would receive a week's training, that the hours would be 4:00 p.m. to 10:00 p.m., and that I would be paid $30 a day. If that was satisfactory, I had the job. I'd never harboured ambitions pedagogical, but I needed work, the money was good, and the hours were perfect. I accepted.

Ed Jackson was one of the many hopefuls in that room waiting for an interview. He would be hired as well. I didn't notice him or anyone else, but he took note of me. He would tell me later that I stood out — in that group of energetic young people eager to put their best foot forward, I looked solitary and still, dazed and lost. That makes sense to me now — he was seeing Pooch.

When we began teaching in March 1968, I was twenty-three, he a year younger. Meeting Ed is undoubtedly the single most important event in my adult life. Everything that followed was different from what went before — within the next two years, I would be able to say, "I'm twenty-five years old now, and I'm living ... if not exactly the truth, at least less of a lie." I would develop a new circle of friends who knew nothing of Pooch; I would have sex with two men and two women; I would meet Jews for the first time; I would see my first bit of gay porn, absolutely enthralled but evincing what I hoped was a sophisticated disdain. (It was a short, silent, black-and-white Super 8 film from Sweden, European centre of all things lascivious in the mindset of the day. We watched it at Ed's on a home projector borrowed from the library. I can still picture the queenlier of the two men fastidiously wiping his fingers on a precisely folded towelette after having applied some lubricant, my amusement a sign that I was beginning to understand camp.)

Ed and I have known each other for more than fifty years, and we are still close friends.

Ed was the kind of person I had always wanted for a friend but had never found. The man I had in mind (and it was always a man) would be sensitive, artistic, verbally playful, and smarter than I. (In other words, a particular brand of homosexual.) The Hogan boys had helped me become less of a goody two-shoes, but it was their rambunctious energies I admired and wanted to emulate. Delicacy and refinement they could not provide. Delicacy and refinement they would have found suspect. (I don't want to suggest that all those boys were louts. SuperDon in particular was creatively fond of neologisms and would go on to write poetry and become an ardent naturalist and a much-loved high school teacher and family man.)

Ed, if not exactly delicate and refined, had a manner more fluid, more careful, more considered, and more self-conscious than my Hogan buddies. It could suggest an almost aristocratic disdain, though he grew up, the younger of two boys, on a farm not far from Fredericton, New Brunswick. His early schooling came thanks to a one-room schoolhouse where his mother was the teacher. His childhood years as the much-loved youngest child of a sturdy, warm, and hard-working farm couple were as idyllic as mine were tormented. His parents went so far as to sacrifice for their children the rural life they loved, moving to Fredericton when it came time for the boys to enter high school, his father having no choice but to take a menial job as school custodian. Much earlier than I, Ed sensed he was a homosexual and knew what that meant. He went to the University of New Brunswick, also in Fredericton, and while there began an affair with another student, a young man his age who would wound him grievously. ("So," the fellow said after telling Ed the affair was at an end, "what are you going to do about your homosexual problem?")

I introduced Ed to Frank — my new best friend to my old best friend. I had a sense it wouldn't work, and I was right. Ed's sniffy disdain was amply reciprocated — Frank warned me about him. Nothing too direct, at least not at first. But the general tenor was that Ed wasn't exactly manly, was he?

And he wasn't. Too slim, a little sinuous, likely to accessorize, no interest in sports, a master of the raised eyebrow. Ah, but he knew stuff. He knew stuff I wanted to know. Not that much about music — not, at least, about opera. But he knew more about art and literature and history than I did — even had oversized art books in his collection. Better yet, he was happy to talk about it all. Even better, he liked talking about other people. Straight boys don't gossip — at least they didn't back then, and even now it isn't much of a manly sport. That you could analyze other people, and do it wickedly and amusingly, was new to me. I pestered Ed, called him frequently, hoped for invites. Our teaching hours — four until ten — meant we stayed up late, sometimes with the other teachers in late-night blab fests, but often I managed to get myself invited back to his place. He had rooms on the third floor of a house on Tranby Avenue, north of Bloor Street and Avenue Road. We'd talk for hours and, probably at my insistence, listen to records. I was past *Aida* but still pushing opera on people, and that year I think I wanted everyone to listen to Strauss's *Der Rosenkavalier*, to wallow with me in its giddy-making lushness. I would sigh over that final trio. I hoped he would too, three female voices in a love triangle, after all — such a hint. Then I'd notice that it was too late to catch the subway. Gosh! Already? So I'd ask to crash there, with him. I'd noted that his bed was somewhere between a single and a double.

I knew, at the buried level of knowing I allowed myself, that Ed was gay. I knew a sleepover might unlock that knowing. I don't know how many sleepovers I'd talked him into, but sometime that summer came this particular night.

It was very late, and we were stretched out together in that little bed. The lights were out. We were in our underwear. We kept chatting for a while, low murmurs, until we began to drift. Then Ed said, "I have something I want to talk to you about."

I knew this was the moment. I knew what Ed was going to tell me. I had my speech all prepared. "That's no problem," I was going to say. "I still want us to be friends. There's no reason at all why we can't remain friends."

Then he said it: "You should know that I'm a homosexual." He was right on script.

I got ready to make my speech.

Before I was able to start, he added, "And I think you are too."

Way, way, way off script.

"Me? Why?" I asked. Ed put his hand on my tighty-whities and pointed out that I had an erection. He gave me a blow job later, which I allowed on the condition that I wouldn't have to reciprocate, or kiss, or anything icky like that. What was most important to me, though, wasn't the sex — even though by then I'd been chaste for almost two years. What was most important was that I got to raise every objection to homosexuality that I'd ever heard — and hear them shot down.

It's unnatural.

No, it isn't, and the reasons.

Well, you don't find it in the animal kingdom.

Yes, you do, and the examples.

The Bible condemns it.

Well, Jesus never does. And it's not at all clear the Sodom story means what we all think it means.

It's gross.

If it's so gross, why do you have an erection?

Men shouldn't be effeminate.

Why not? And anyway, not everyone is. Most homosexual men are not. (Ed could be very persuasive. He would eventually get into his bed, for a one-time blow job, a big, butch, handsome, guitar-playing, straight colleague of ours at school.)

And then I heard about Philip, his landlord, who lived on the first floor. I'd met him a few times, guessed he was a few years older than we (it turned out he was almost twice our age): a very handsome man, funny, not manly in the super-butch sense but not at all effeminate. Philip, too, was a homosexual, I was told. More than that, he was Ed's lover. They'd been together for several years.

I heard so much I wanted to hear that night, though I didn't hear myself admit that I too was a homosexual. I would claim bisexuality for some time to come — that time-honoured transitional stage for nervous queers. I even had real girlfriends and had real sex with them. But the friendship with Ed, and later with Philip, shaped my life irrevocably, and not just with respect to sexual politics. I still had too much of the bush about me, even then, some six years after leaving Marathon. Ed would note, in his quietly acerbic way, that I ate by pushing food onto my fork with my fingers. (I still do when I'm alone or with close friends, even though he showed me how to do it properly, with a knife. You'd never guess, when I'm eating in public and following the rules, that there's rarely a dirty knife in my apartment.) He also made a point of informing me that just because an article of clothing featured buttons, it was not strictly necessary that every button be fastened. (Such a relief. I have a photo of myself at eighteen, pajamas buttoned tightly right up to the neck and tightly at the wrist. That went on until Ed and I met.)

I should have figured out all those sorts of things long before, but I had never taken a good look at myself. I had taught myself not to see.

FRANK LEFT TORONTO LATE in the spring of 1968. There was no reason to stay — he'd passed his exams, was about to graduate, and had been drafted into the American army. Every previous parting, even if only for the summer, had been devastating for me (nothing captures such moments better than the film *Brokeback Mountain*), but this time, I knew, we'd probably never see each other again. He was American. I was Canadian. He was straight. I was gay (not that I allowed those thoughts to surface). He seemed not to mind America's involvement in Vietnam and never considered being a draft dodger. I wasn't exactly politicized but was likely to sympathize with that decade's hippie ethos: make love, not war. Still, I was in love with him.

I don't know why we decided to go swimming at Hart House. Was it my idea? That would make sense. I knew it would be one of our final moments together, and I knew we'd be nude. I can't recall that we'd ever swum there together before, but, my idea or Frank's, that's where we ended up.

The pool, as usual, was full of naked guys. Frank and I splashed about and shoved each other around in the water and hung off the side of the pool and chatted, and I tried to be high-spirited, but I was miserable. I don't think I showed it. I tried not to. When we decided to leave, I got out of the water first and then watched as Frank reached up to the deck and lifted himself out. His cock was semi-erect. Very quickly, I became semi-erect. We walked together to the showers. By the time we got there, we were both fully erect, but neither of us acknowledged it, and we stood there, side by side, showering and talking, pretending we didn't have boners. Though I didn't think for a moment he was gay, it was a lovely and agonizing way to part. Days later, he was gone.

I was depressed and wretched. And then I wasn't. I was young; moods changed quickly, and I was meeting new people. Ed became my closest friend, but he and the other teachers constituted a circle, and this time, unlike the Hogan boys, it wasn't one I'd inherited. Because of our working hours, we were like actors/models/

waiters — young people sleeping when the rest of the world trudged off to work, just starting to party when the rest of the world was preparing for bed. They liked me — I could be quick with a quip, and people thought I was funny. Suddenly, too, I was meeting other homosexuals. Fellow teachers Wayne and Richard, the former stolid and manly, the latter screechy with a passion for silver cutlery and candlesticks, were gentrifiers before the term existed and had dared to buy a Victorian mansion in Cabbagetown, then a very sketchy neighbourhood, which gave their party or dinner invites a frisson of possible danger. There was Arley, so effeminate that I once quipped, as after-dinner mints were being passed around, that the candy also described the way Arley left the table. There were lovable eccentrics: Julian, short, thin, pale, and Scottish, utterly devoted to researching voles and the raptors who preyed on them. Ross, who nicknamed me Virtues, occasionally performed naked yoga when he visited and categorized his friends and acquaintances as either Apollonian or Dionysian. (Curiously, given the nickname he'd given me, I fell into the Dionysian camp.) Paula, his sometime girlfriend, witty and sardonic and straight out of an E.F. Benson novel. The three of us would sleep together just once — chastely, if you don't count the giggling. Lydia, our favourite, married but steeped in the romance of being a homosexual's best friend. Marsha, who shared with Ed and me a passion for cryptic crosswords and with whom we tried to create a puzzle where every solution was an obscenity. Mel, the second man I would have sex with. He wasn't among the original group that had started at the same time as Ed and I — he was a Torontonian studying at Oxford, home for the summer and needing a job.

Mel was Jewish, as were fellow teachers Sheila and Bernice. They were my very first Jewish friends. (Marathon had none, and, not surprisingly, neither did St. Michael's College.) That made them

Ed Jackson and I taught ESL to new Canadian adults, late 1960s. Here we are with fellow teachers: I'm standing (centre, with tie), Ed is kneeling (left front).
Photo: Ed Jackson

exotics, though Mel didn't need what to me was then an arcane religion to qualify as a hothouse plant. Corpulent while still being prancy-nimble on his feet, he could surround and absorb you the way an amoeba absorbs a food vacuole, drawing you out while drawing you in, eager to talk, not quite as eager to listen (even while soliciting your opinion on everything from *Carmen* to Caravaggio), flagrantly seductive, shameless in his appetites, intimidating on almost every count. We might leave teaching at ten and return to our respective abodes, but my phone would ring at eleven or later, and it would be Mel. The conversation would go on and on and on, and sometimes it would be closer to a Melvinian monologue than a conversation, a monologue occasionally interrupted by the phrase, "Gerry. I need to know. How *are* you?" His letters, handwritten or typed, consumed every sheet of paper in its entirety, the margins left, right, top, and bottom filled in by hand, often with gaspingly intense injunctions as to which operas, featuring which performers, I should buy. He knew at least as much about opera as I did, and much more about classical music generally. He was writing a novel. He could play the piano and was busy composing a musical based on *Gone with the Wind*. Ed remembers that he once played selections for us, describing the stage action as the music poured forth, announcing dramatically, after a particularly Wagnerian chord, "This is where the negroes come in."

I can't remember how we ended up in bed. I didn't find him sexy, but he was impressive and smart and knew everything, including what he wanted, which was me, and I'd never been wanted quite like that before, and that made me want him, made me want him wanting me. Somehow, we seemed to feel the need to give our physical flailing the lineaments of a grand passion, as if something so new to both of us must be Love and must therefore feature poems and long, turgid letters. I believe my poem actually rhymed; his, fashionably, did not. The relationship looms large in my memory, but it lasted the summer only. He returned that fall to Oxford, where, a year later, we reconnected.

I continued to seek out, or rather fall into, relationships with women. Perhaps that is why my life was shadowed still by the paroxysms of shame that had not long before put me in hospital. I remember struggling against the vortex as I was out walking with Ed one night, fearing that I would be lost yet again and he would see it happen, but I somehow managed to surface before the only option was to surrender and sink to the sidewalk in tears.

Fourth sexual experience, sort of. Sheila: handsome, strong, politically astute. I liked her. She invited me back to her apartment, and we started to kiss, and then she took off my pants, but nothing she could do would make me hard. I was mortified, almost as much by the fact that I was wearing bright red bikini underwear as I was by my lack of tumescence. I was so eager to leave that I didn't even fully dress — just pulled on my pants and left, straggling down the street with a wisp of red underwear protruding from my back pocket. A few weeks later, when she and I and some other teachers were joking about how some people's last names lent themselves to unfortunate pronunciations or double entendres, I chimed in with, "There isn't much you can do with 'Hannon,'" only to hear Sheila dryly observe, "There *certainly* isn't much you can do with Hannon." It stung, of course, but I couldn't help but think, *Touché!*

Our ESL students were also a rich source of erotic fantasy and, at times, fulfillment. They were mostly young adults. In 1968, my first year as a teacher, many were from Czechoslovakia, fleeing in the wake of the Russian invasion. They were educated, sophisticated, and eager to learn — the highly regarded pianist Antonin Kubalek was one of my students, though it was another Antonin who drew my attention. Tall, thin, and friendly, with, perhaps not surprisingly, some resemblance to Frank, he often asked to come home with me after class because he wanted me to teach him how to dance, North American style. By then I had rented a large room on the second floor of 95 Burnside Drive, just north of Bathurst and Davenport. The landlady was Nancy Tyrell, known to all as "Twiddles," a senior instructor in the ESL department and the woman who had taught us newbies how to teach. When Antonin was over, I'd put on records, not too loudly because this was a rooming house, with Twiddles in a room just across from mine; next to her was crazy Claire, with her vanishingly small smile and her absolute conviction that men might try to break through her window and into her room. After I'd calibrated the volume just so, Antonin and I would dance. Always fast dances, never cheek to cheek. Sometimes, when it got very late, I'd say he could sleep over if he wished. He declined often, but sometimes stayed. I had a double bed.

I decided one night, when we were in bed together and about to fall asleep, to ask whether he would like to have sex with me. I'd concluded that his willingness to stay over meant he might not be averse to the idea, that it might be his way of sending a message, of being flirtatious. I was wrong. Once he understood what I was suggesting — which, given his language skills and the novelty of my proposal, took a while — he professed to be appalled, albeit in broken English, the whole scene becoming terribly awkward when it became clear that it was too late for him to return home and we'd have to spend the rest of the night in bed together. Which we did, he pressed against the wall, simmering silently, and I apprehensive that our easy student/teacher friendship was over and that he might tell his classmates or complain to the administration. The Hannon Dancing Academy closed its doors for good that night. He was cool to me ever after but, as far as I could tell, never spoke of the incident to anyone. It might have been difficult without implicating himself to some degree. ("So you went to Mr. Hannon's rooms late at night for dancing lessons, and then you agreed to sleep with him? And you're accusing him of trying to seduce you? Uh-huh.")

Blanche was also Czechoslovakian and might even have been in the same class as Antonin. She, in a rather roundabout way, became my girlfriend. (There was no sense that students should be off-limits to teachers — many were our age and eager to socialize, if only for the chance to practise English in real-life situations.) Blanche, however, wanted Ed. She'd corral him after class or ostentatiously seek him out and chat him up when students and teachers headed out to a tavern. She was quite beautiful — photos show a passing resemblance to Elizabeth Taylor — and she was smart, picking up her new language more quickly than most. There was no reason for a red-blooded male to be as standoffish as Ed felt compelled to be, so we constructed one. It was a prank, really, and mean, though I suppose at the time it just seemed practical.

By that time, Ed and I were hemi-semi-demi "out" to a select group of teachers who we had concluded would be simpatico. Paula was one of them. She was also a woman who could turn reading a book or opening a door into a performance, so the three of us, with much giggling, devised a scheme. She would turn up, flamboyantly dressed, at our next pub party with the students. She would yell out, "Edddyyyy!" from across the room when she spotted him, make for him like a heat-seeking missile, sweep him into her arms, and linger there in a long and passionate embrace. All went as planned. Paula was magnificent. Ed was doting. Blanche was crushed. I can't remember if she asked me to dance later that evening or if I, feeling sorry for her, led her onto the dance floor. In any case, it became apparent, then or shortly after, that I would become Blanche's consolation prize.

I WAS ALREADY ADEPT at seeing and not seeing, knowing and not knowing, but that year I would put that talent to the test: I was suddenly beginning to grow and develop as a gay man while living the sketchy outlines of what I imagined it was like to be a straight man with a girlfriend. Except I wasn't straight. I wasn't even bi. I slept periodically with Blanche. She occasionally wondered why it didn't happen more often — she told me, significantly, that she had a girlfriend whose boyfriend wanted sex almost every night. She introduced me to her family. She introduced me to her monkey. I've no idea how she ended up with Marco, but it couldn't bear the sight of me and flew into her arms in a gibbering rage whenever I visited. Most extraordinary of all, I took her to Marathon to meet my family as if this were a real courtship and we were soon to be married. I know that visit happened only because I have the photographs:

my father touring us through the mill and pointing out to Blanche some piece of machinery; my mother standing with her arm around Blanche somewhere out in the bush. I have no memories of the trip whatsoever. I was astonished to find those photographs. As far as not seeing and not knowing goes, that Marathon excursion was something of a triumph.

In the interstices of my time with Blanche, I was cruising men and being cruised. One incident stands out in my memory, but it's best described in a letter written by Ed's partner Philip McLeod to a friend of his then visiting Paris. It's no exaggeration to say that Philip's many letters taught me how to write — I tried to emulate his style: parenthetical, allusive, alternately witty and silly, playful with both words and ideas, and as likely to quote Auden or McLuhan as he was to describe the friends, colleagues, and tenants who made up a world that alternately amused, depressed, and sometimes frightened him. (He was a veteran of World War II, had landed in

Philip McLeod was Ed Jackson's partner and an early writing mentor to me.
Photo: Ed Jackson

Normandy shortly after D-Day, and had never quite lost the apprehension that circumstances might one day bring a fascist party to
power in Canada. He was fully aware of how the Nazis regarded
homosexuals.)

I don't know how this particular letter came into my hands, but
it's an amusing description of what Ed and I imagined might be
one of the accomplishments required of a developing homosexual
(hosting a dinner party) and shows how fractured and obsessive my
social skills were at the time. The letter is dated September 8, 1969.

*On Saturday night, Edward and I drove over to Gerry
Hannon's house — Edward and Gerry have decided to prepare
fine meals on alternate weekends. Gerry began the series and
I was invited because of my rigorously exacting palate. We
dined on a card table in Gerry's room — it was covered with
old Spanish lace generous enough to wipe your mouth on if you
didn't mind a few lesions. First course was ice-box cold soup,
then an intermediate dish of moulded gelatin populated with
tidbits of fruit. Then Gerry went downstairs and brought up
the nucleus of the meal: Brazilian something or other ... it had
capers in it ... it also had a number of (you would ordinarily
think) inadmissible ingredients, but whatever they were they
were effectively disguised by a dense surround of mashed
potatoes. Edward provided the wine. I supplied the carping. I was
unblushingly hypocritical and praised the repast ... After supper
was over Gerry played the first act of Otello at full volume —
he contrived nonetheless to be heard above the singers and the
orchestra ... Edward sat by on the sofa in a state of lugubrious
stoicism. I noticed to my astonishment that Gerry knew word for
word everything that was sung in the first act, and with his hand
he directed the orchestra and hummed the orchestral phrases.*

I think that one half hour of Otello may have deafened me
a little ... I decided at 10 o'clock that I had better leave. Folk
music was taking over. Edward and Gerry and Co. [another
friend had turned up] went into Saturday night orbit: they
went to Letro's, but the place was full. They went to La Trique,
but the place was empty. They finally came to ground at a table
for four beside the washroom door at the St. Charles. Gerry
was puzzled all over again that boys would want to walk THAT
way — apparently there were quite a number of egregious pansies.
Earlier in the evening Gerry with a certain air of may-I-have-
everyone's-attention-please-for-an-important-announcement,
said, "I've decided that I AM homosexual!" The affirmation
scarcely raised us from our torpor. A few weeks ago a Negro boy
had ingratiated himself with Gerry on the trottoir near where
Gerry lives. He went back to Gerry's rooms and made some
unequivocal overtures. Gerry said to him, "Are you gay?" The boy
acknowledged the fact and a long chat ensued but nothing other
than facts was spilled, but that episode was the basis of Gerry's
Saturday night disclosure. He told Edward that he is attracted to
boys who look rather stupid — a clear case of narcissism, surely.

Stupid? I'd said no to sex with a cute boy who'd followed me
home. I'd turned down the chance to assess the size of another boy's
penis. I was going, with friends, to gay bars and making fun of men
who were effeminate. I was announcing I was gay, yet I was having
sex with Blanche and taking her home to meet Mommy and Daddy.
When Ed asked me to pose for naked Polaroid photos, I did. I was
exchanging love letters with Mel after his return to Oxford. I began
ingratiating myself with Marlene, another ESL teacher, who was tall
and lusciously creamy and blonde and whom I liked and with whom
I wanted to have sex — or so I told myself. I believe I asked her once,

on the eastbound platform at the Bathurst subway station, if she'd consider it. Possibly surprised that I'd asked in the same tone of voice I would have used to comment on the late arrival of a train, she said no. Not much later, in England, we would have an affair.

Through all of this, through all those two-plus years, Ed and I had been planning a trip to Europe. That had long been a dream for both of us, but it wasn't to be a two-week excursion. We were to live abroad for at least a year. Perhaps we would find work; perhaps we'd settle in for much, much longer. I talked him into beginning our European tour in Mexico — Ed knew me as Gerry, of course, and had glimpsed the hidden Pooch, but I wanted him to meet Geronimo, the assured and competent one who knew the Sierra Madre mountains and the language and had his very own Mexican family who loved him. I wanted to show him how beautiful the country was. Ed had never considered going to Mexico and wasn't excited by the prospect, but he agreed.

We left Toronto by Greyhound Bus, with tickets for the border town of Nuevo Laredo, Mexico, late on the evening of September 2, 1970. We had already purchased airplane tickets to Europe — Icelandic Air, from New York to Luxembourg. (It then advertised the cheapest fare and included a necessary touchdown in Reykjavik, though Luxembourg was the only mainland European country to which the airline had access.) Our luggage consisted of two huge metal-framed orange backpacks with bedrolls attached. I have a photograph of Ed, staggering under the weight of his, in the backyard at 46 Tranby. He'd also arranged for Philip to ship a suitcase (or, as Philip put it, a valise) to be picked up when we reached London. Earlier that evening, Ed had burst into tears while taking his final Toronto bath — he was leaving Philip, his first real relationship, and the first real circle of friends he'd ever had. I didn't weep, though those new friends meant as much to me. I was cruelly and stupidly happy that leaving would mean an easy end to my relationship with Blanche.

Mary Ellen and Sean, a married couple with whom we taught and who knew the score, drove me and Blanche to the bus terminal at Bay and Dundas. Philip drove Ed. All six of us stood there, awkwardly making conversation among the panting buses. Mary Ellen gave us a funny homemade going-away card and a £5 note to spend in England. Finally, it was time. Blanche, stalwart until then, started to cry and threw her arms around me. Ed and Philip didn't hug. Perhaps they shook hands. Ed and I got on the bus, took our seats, and stared out the window at the unlikely entourage we were leaving behind. And then the bus pulled out. And then we both cried.

A Year in Europe
· ·

WE DIDN'T WEEP FOR long. We had barely passed the Toronto city limits before we'd become giddy with a sense of being irrevocably on the road, feeling that everything from this day forward would be different, that we might never return, that we might die in the Sierra Madre, shot by bandidos, and lie forever in an unmarked grave, that we might cut a swath through London society (those clever, witty young men from the colonies), that we'd be immersed in the storied glories of European civilization, that our guides would be amenable boys with charming accents and, as Baron von Gloeden had recorded, significant penises (we'd done our research), and, less fancifully, that we might … just might … meet men … have sex or even, maybe … it could happen … a romance.

That exuberance wore a little thin over the next three days as we lurched, mostly sleeplessly, through the American Midwest, discovering "Greyhound America," the company's promotional motto celebrating the undistinguished towns and unwelcoming mid-size cities on our route to the Mexican border. In Chicago, we were unsettled by the superfluity of heavily armed, porcine police officers. In San Antonio, we were underwhelmed by the Alamo. (It became quite clear why Americans thought it necessary to conjure an injunction to remember it.) We arrived in Laredo, Texas, around midnight on September 4, too weary to reflect on whether the famous "streets of" merited a cowboy's lament, spent some four hours traversing customs, had our passports stamped in Nuevo Laredo in the early hours of September 5, got on a bus for Monterrey, arrived later that morning, booked into a hotel, killed an extremely large cockroach ("A most un-Canadian intruder," Ed sniffed), spent a day exploring the city, boarded another bus for Tamazunchale, and, finally, arrived in that region of Mexico where I, Geronimo, felt at home.

From there, after a short bus ride to the Pisaflores turnoff, we walked. Hours downhill to the Moctezuma River, which we crossed in the usual flat-bottomed boat, though this time it transported, besides me, Ed, our backpacks, and our boatman, a very large and not very happy cow. We walked to Pisaflores and spent the night there, sleeping on the cement floor of the building we CIASPers had built only a few years before. We left at dawn and walked three to four hours to La Escondida, with Ed, if not exactly in tears amid the alien corn, certainly sweating profusely. The Torres family received us with their usual courtesy and generosity. The rancho held a celebratory huapango dance. We went to the forest pools for a naked swim with the local boys. And then, after less than a week, we left for Mexico City, where I fucked a man for the very first time.

I fucked Cuauhtémoc, named after an Aztec emperor executed by the Spanish. Cuauhtémoc, a young man to whom I had a letter of introduction from a wealthy older friend who travelled frequently and had a taste for lithe young foreigners. Cuauhtémoc, whose face somehow combined aristocratic Hispanic delicacy and the prizefighter bluntness of an Olmec warrior. Cuauhtémoc, who turned onto his stomach on my hotel bed, grabbed my cock, and guided me in. He was slim, with smooth, soft skin, and I lay on him for a while without moving, knowing that if I started thrusting I would come very quickly and wanting time to relish this, my first homosexual fuck, dizzy with the sense that a part of my body was actually inside another man. Shamingly, I feigned bisexual nonchalance when I told Ed, who'd been considerate enough to absent himself from our shared room for an hour or so, claiming that it was really no different from fucking a girl. He reported this in a letter to Philip, who responded, "I was delighted that Gerry penetrated so deep into the body politic. I was struck that it should have been an experience no different than those he had with Blanche ... it raises the delicate question of whether he was letting himself in via the right aperture."

WE'D SPENT ALMOST A month in Mexico and on the road, with the bus trip from Mexico City to New York a particularly gruelling segment. We stayed at the YMCA for a night or two when we reached Manhattan, where, just a year before, on June 28, 1969, the Stonewall Riots had birthed the modern gay rights movement. The Stonewall Inn had not yet become a place of pilgrimage, but I must have been aware that history had been made there, if only because Ed knew. He remembers that we looked about for street posters announcing meetings we could attend, but we weren't successful. And we had a plane to catch.

Ed and I landed in Luxembourg, after a brief stop for refuelling in Reykjavik, on October 5, 1970. We spent no time in Luxembourg — it was Europe, for sure, but in our minds it wasn't part of the mythology of Europe. It had no character. (It still doesn't.) We wanted to reach England, the mother country, the nation responsible for the fact that every world map in every Canadian school was coloured mostly pink because pink meant part of the British empire. We took a train and then a ferry, and two days later, on October 7, 1970, we landed in Dover.

I hadn't experienced culture shock in Mexico, but England, which I expected to be just like Canada but with a classy accent, frequently infuriated me. Their money, transitioning at the time from the archaic — pounds, shillings, crowns, and other obscurities — to a decimal system, was mostly incomprehensible. As was their accent — not everyone sounded like the erudite characters on the British radio show *My Word*. The food was horrible. The rooms we could afford were dark, cold, and damp; what heat there was emanated from electric grills that had to be fed the country's idiotic coinage. Milk seemed to be served at room temperature, a savagery that once drove me to shout at the waitress who brought it to our table. Ed was more adaptable. Eventually, I, too, adapted. It was difficult to remain crabby when each day meant a museum or a gallery or an opera at Covent Garden or Sadler's Wells or a play in London or Stratford by the Royal Shakespeare Company, the very things we'd fantasized about in provincial Toronto. ("So it's every night to the theatre," I would write home to Philip later that year, "our 23rd consecutive evening tonight; a performance of Andy Warhol's *Pork* — his first play, the amusing moments of which will probably seem side-splitting in contrast to the vapid drone of most of it." I clearly felt no obligation to actually see something before jumping in with some smart-ass critique, though I think that assessment turned out to be more or less on the mark. What I most remember is that two cute young guys in the play were frequently nude and had their pubic hair dyed yellow and pink.)

Our ex-pat Canadian friends helped ease us into British life. When we visited Oxford, we stayed with Mel and his then love, Juliet (they would marry in 1972). Brilliant and troubled, she knew something of Mel's voracious sexual appetite; she would tell me later, by letter, that she would not have minded if Mel and I had slept together during that visit. (We didn't, though I had the sense he was enmeshed in a web of semi-secret, semi-tormented same-sex flirtations.) High-strung, thin, a cleverly meandering letter writer, Juliet had few illusions about her precarious mental state, writing to me the following year, "I refuse to feel belittled by being told that imagination, hope, despair etc etc equals chemical because it follows that the reverse is true, so bully for the little chemicals (says she, stuffing a handful of jolly pills into her face). Crazy perhaps, quite likely in fact ..." She had a breakdown that year — I remember visiting her in hospital, bringing as a gift a copy of the then recently published *The Female Eunuch*. (An unwise choice, it turned out. The cover illustration, a woman's body draped like a dress on a hanger, quite unsettled her.) In her fragility and wit, she reminded me of Virginia Woolf. A few years later she justified that assessment by killing herself, modelling her exit, alas, on Anna Karenina's, not Woolf's.

In London, we crashed with Marlene, who had moved there with a teaching job. The affair that had been budding in Toronto came to fruition in her flat in Brixton, though it was stymied, at least at first, by my not surprisingly recalcitrant penis. It's difficult, so many years later, to justify or even explain why I so frequently found myself in bed with women when I was so frequently not up to the task. I wasn't bi, except functionally from time to time, but I liked women, was mildly fascinated by their genitalia. The vagina had turned out not to be the perfectly round, comic-book bullet hole I'd imagined it to be — I recall, in bed with Marlene, asking if she'd mind me spending some time just staring at her pussy. She didn't. So I stretched out and stared. It became a real affair — the last heterosexual fling I would ever have — and it stretched over a good chunk of that year in Europe. (She would visit us in Spain, and I remember a feverishly excited fuck in broad daylight on a hilltop, my pants pulled down and her skirts lifted, the air scented with the wild thyme we'd tramped over, our orgasms segueing into giddy laughter.) I was also a bit of a jerk — impatient with her when she couldn't climb a hill as fast as I could, incredulous when she wasn't eager to show off by running down a flight of stairs as recklessly as I. Disappointed, in other words, that she wasn't a boy.

I think I must have been aching for romance, and, thoughtless, desperate creature that I was, I simply swept Marlene up in that need. "… you desire 'to climb into my eyes,'" she wrote me once, "to know everything about me and to see things as I see them. And I suppose it is this desire on your part that makes me yearn for your lovemaking. With other men I have felt affectionate or sisterly or, on occasion, like a piece of machinery but never have I been able to be so totally uninhibited. You said once that you liked making love to me because I so unashamedly enjoyed it. It is the most exquisite of dances — soft and gentle warm. No limits."

I LEFT ENGLAND MUCH the way I'd left Toronto — leaving behind a woman who was on the verge of falling in love with me, a woman I cared for, a woman I'd at least passively deluded, a woman from whom I was happy to part. On November 16, 1970, Ed and I boarded the *Monte Ulia*, a freighter carrying 114 passengers, with stops in Spain and the Canary Islands of Tenerife and La Palma. The passenger list noted the presence of Sir Edgar and Lady Newton, though we spotted no one with a bearing sufficiently aristocratic to qualify for those titles. Actually, we spotted fewer and fewer people over that three-day voyage — the ship plunged into a raging North Atlantic storm, and the dining room hosted fewer and fewer voyagers as *mal de mer* took its toll, until finally even the obese gentleman who dined alone, always on several helpings, failed to show. Ed and I had had the foresight to take preventative medication, and though we slept little in our tempest-tossed narrow bunks, we didn't get sick. On November 19, the seas calm, we landed in the Galician city of Vigo in northern Spain.

We would return to England, after travelling through Spain, Italy, and Greece, on July 14, 1971, and fly back to Canada on September 11. In all that time, I had had sex only with Marlene. Ed wanted to have sex with me, but I pushed him away. I remember the incident — we were in bed together somewhere in Spain, working together on a cryptic crossword puzzle (a nightly ritual), when he became physically playful in a way that left no doubt as to what he had in mind. I pretended, in my long-practised way, that I had no idea what was going on, that he was just being silly and kittenish, until that wasn't possible anymore and I had to say no. That made him angry and me sullen. (Ed recently pointed out that we don't hug, the way everyone else on the planet does, and he traces that aversion back to that year when we were intimates in every way but physically.)

And why did I say no? I found him attractive, loved his company. He'd introduced me to gay life and, along with Mel and Cuauhtémoc, was one of just three men with whom I'd had sex. We were together, hour after hour, day after day, month after month, so why not? That year-long closeness partly explains why not. Ed seemed perfect for me, and I feared that if we became regular sex partners, we would become lovers, and if we became lovers a door would close — we'd be together forever and ever because we were perfect for each other, and my gay life would be settled and shut down before I'd even begun to explore it. That wasn't a rational response. I'd seen how Ed and Philip had constructed a life together that made provision for both conjugality and liberty, but my only other model was the fetid relationship that had trapped my parents in a life of mutual loathing. Perhaps that's why I so frequently fell in with women — I knew those relationships could have no future. They might not be good, but they could never go bad, at least not the way Mommy and Daddy's had. You had to really care to cause or suffer that much pain. I might end up wounding, but I'd be safe from hurt. Safe from love too — though I avoided thinking about that.

That year, then, was an homage to onanism, though Ed would have sex with Mel when we returned to England. A late night. Much talk. Juliet asleep. I can't remember if Marlene and I picked up where we left off, but I suspect we must have. Today, of course, one would seek out gay bars or baths or community centres, but in 1971 it wasn't easy to find other gay men, particularly in Spain, a country still in the iron grip of a fascist government under General Francisco Franco. We'd decided to spend the winter there — it was cheap, relatively warm, and largely untouristed. We rented a two-bedroom house with a large, enclosed back patio for $75 a month in the tiny fishing village of Benajarafe, about forty-five kilometres east of Malaga on the Costa del Sol. We were the only non-natives. It's a tourist mecca now. The Mediterranean was across the road from our front door, its beach dotted with colourful boats and often peopled by locals repairing their fishnets. A goat-herd wandered by daily with his charges and would milk a nanny for a small fee, if we supplied the jug. That near-Arcadian environment seemed to put us under some obligation to develop artistically. I wrote poetry. Some of it was good, most of it perhaps too clearly derived from Gerard Manley Hopkins and W.H. Auden, my poet heroes at the time. I sent some to Philip for comment — he replied that he found my poems "awful, artificial and amusing," pointing out that Christopher Wren's design for St. Paul's Cathedral had been commended in exactly those terms. We tried to teach ourselves to draw. (We favoured figure studies and drew each other's penises.) We dressed up like Roman senators and photographed each other. We read aloud from an English translation of Dante's *Divine Comedy*, losing interest after we'd left behind the picturesque horrors of hell. We wrote long letters to our friends in Canada and read each other's before we sent them, trying to outdo each other in wit and descriptive powers. We waited breathlessly for aerogramme letters from Philip, who outdid us both in elaborating the comedy and sometimes the pathos of a life devoid of dramatic incident.

We used our house as a base from which to explore the rest of the country. It felt, sometimes, as if we had Spain to ourselves. Though Malaga was heavily touristed, the rest of Spain seemed empty. Ed photographed me nude in the mountains above El Escorial, apparently straining to push a huge boulder down on the building where Spain buried its kings. We were virtually alone when we visited the Alhambra in Granada, its reflecting pools thinly coated with ice. We often wandered the hilly region behind Benajarafe, never encountering another soul. (Ed photographed me nude there as well, brandishing a wooden spear, like a scene from *Lord of the Flies*.) When we did meet other travellers, either in Spain or during the rest of the trip, they would inevitably be straight couples or sports-loving boys on a lark, and we knew any conversation would lead to talk of girls or to questions we wouldn't want to answer — "the playacting I'm beginning to loathe," as Ed put it in a letter to Philip. We would be polite but distant with them, and they would get the message. Consequently, Ed and I were everything and all to each other — not the healthiest of intimacies.

From a letter Ed wrote to Philip from Florence, dated March 26, 1971:

Gerry and I had one of our arguments today, arising as
always from eating. My dislike of his atavistic eating habits (a
fixation no doubt revealing my insecurities) and his obstinacy
about changing them — the only things he is ever adamant or
opinionated about concerns filling his face — lead to irrational
clashes (I must accept that he will never be able not to eat
without burying his hands in his food, pushing everything on his
fork with fingers, blowing, like a hurricane, on soup whether hot
or not) … I feel guilty about these sudden attacks of viciousness.
He just never initiates an idea or likes discussion: any argument
stated confidently enough wins him over. He admits it,
admirably, and I can see the need, the almost aching need, for a
creed (pagan, outworn or otherwise) that he can memorize and
obey unquestioningly.

The poems I wrote during those months are almost amusingly
obvious about how desperate I was for something to believe in, a
desperation that looked back longingly at my Roman Catholic past
and its puerile certainties. On December 14, 1970, I completed
a poem I called "Star Chamber," the opening lines of which are,
"Old church men knew the answer:/Proud heretics were bent upon
the rack;" and went on to declare, "… love, true love/Could well
be forced, since heart must bleed/Before it hears the soul." (To
this day, Ed loves to quote that opening line whenever it seems I'm
stubbornly in the grip of some absurd ideology.)

ON JULY 10, 1971, we celebrated my twenty-seventh birthday in
Venice. We ate at a nice restaurant. I was miserable — I felt my
youth had ended, that one could claim to be in one's twenties until
the age of twenty-five or twenty-six, but at twenty-seven one was
hurtling toward thirty and the torpor of middle age. And what

did I, soon to be a man no youth could trust, have to show for all those years on earth? Not much. A general B.A. Modest success as a teacher. A clutch of largely derivative poems that revealed rather too much about my tepid intellectual life. The ability to draw a more or less believable penis. An almost monastic chastity, scarcely alleviated by the three men and three women with whom I'd had sexual congress. It wasn't quite enough that Europe had delivered much of the culture and the magic I'd yearned for — we'd sat, Ed and I, almost alone, on the Acropolis of Athens on a fresh April morning; we'd tented in an olive grove on Corfu, picked kumquats off the trees, and swum naked one night in a phosphorescent sea; been the solitary campers on the bright blue eye that is St. Paul's Bay on the island of Rhodes, staring up each morning at the Acropolis of Lindos; had seen our tents flattened by a storm on the far western tip of Crete and had fled, like Ulysses, to a cave for shelter. We'd been to Naples, Rome, Florence, Venice. We'd visited Madrid, Toledo, Seville, Granada. We'd seen paintings, buildings, sculptures. But our year was coming to an end. We were almost out of money, and we would soon have to either return to Canada or find work in Europe. On July 14, we left Venice and flew to London.

We seem to have put off thinking by going to plays every night — that was the period of our twenty-three consecutive performances — though, on August 10, I wrote to Philip:

> *Life seems such a limbo, only there seems no hope of a harrowing, and returning to Canada gives the illusion of action, or of having decided something finally ... It is the exception for me now, Philip, to feel relaxed; I generally move in a state of stomach tightening or throat constricting tension. I feel totally powerless in a condition of emotional aridity and intellectual stasis: I don't know anything. I'm supposed to have studied*

philosophy but I couldn't name four philosophers with even a two-sentence evaluation of what they believed. I don't want to work. At all. Yet I feel moved in the direction of math teaching the way most university grads decide to enter English teaching — it seems the least objectionable of alternatives, and I don't really relish a life of poverty, grinding or otherwise ... My plans now are to work for the coming year — supply (my god) teaching — then enter university next Sept, hopefully here as an undergraduate (the measure of my desperation) or in Toronto in a makeup year or two. But in what?? Tentatively math, but I intend to dabble prodigiously in every subject I have ever found vaguely interesting during the coming year. Perhaps I'm a latent linguist? A closet carpenter?? A repressed radiologist???

The letter ended with that touch of humorous whimsy, meant to convey that I was basically okay, but I wasn't. Perhaps a week later, in my desperation I answered a newspaper ad seeking someone to teach mathematics in a small private girls' school. I was interviewed over tea in their Victorian-era parlour by two elderly ladies. We didn't talk about math or my qualifications — the subject seemed to baffle them, so we made polite chit-chat about the weather and Canada and other far-flung outposts of empire. Tea over, they smiled and offered me the job. I accepted.

I should have left their rooms in a state of elation: I had a job! I could stay in London! I left in a state of even deeper misery: I had a job teaching math to girls who'd probably hate the subject and, by extension, me. I'd have to stay in London — where my sole personal/romantic/sexual connection would be a woman, a woman I liked and admired, a woman who'd guided my clumsy lovemaking to focus not just on my pleasure but on hers ... but a woman nonetheless, and I wanted to fuck with men.

I walked the streets until I came upon an outdoor phone booth. I called the school. One of the ladies answered. "Hello," I said, "I'm sorry, but I can't. I can't teach math. I can't teach girls. I can't." They were, understandably, rather starchy in their response, and I no doubt made it difficult for any future job applicants from the colonies, but I felt my spirits lift as I walked, now jobless, away from that phone booth. It seems I had chosen, if only by default, to return to Canada.

It was undoubtedly on another walk with Ed that we noticed posters advertising meetings of the Gay Liberation Front. We attended one. Ed remembers. I don't. It wouldn't be hard to reconstruct such a gathering, though — it would have taken place in some grubby hall or church basement, been mostly male, young, almost entirely white, loosely disorganized, ostentatiously collective in its decision-making, and, for all that clumsiness, exhilarating. People our age and even younger were talking openly about homosexuality. Talking openly about their lives, without looking over their shoulders to see who might be listening. We'd always been careful — we'd learned that from Philip. Even in letters, we were careful — Philip tended to refer to "that e.i.t." (that "ever interesting topic") or use circumlocutions so convoluted they would put all but the most diligent off the scent. Here was a roomful of people who didn't seem to care. More than that, they were planning a public demonstration for August 19, just three weeks before we were to return to Canada. People were to gather outside St. Paul's Cathedral and march down Fleet Street to protest the way British tabloid newspapers handled gay issues, which ranged from ignore to deplore. After some soul-searching, we decided to join in.

I've been in more demonstrations than I care to count or remember since then, but that first one? It was like losing my virginity — clumsy, painful, scary at first, and then the quick, fierce, billowing certainty that though I might not yet be quite an adult, I certainly was no longer a child, no longer the one to be patted on the head and told everything was okay, no longer the one to be put early to bed, no longer the one who's told, "You won't understand, this is not for you," no longer the one to be spanked or slapped or humiliated when I got it wrong. Still the one to blush, though, and that's a good thing. Still the one to weep. Now the one to stand and stare and question. Now the one to stake a claim. The closet kept me young, but only in the worst ways.

How long did it take, that day, to grow up? Perhaps an hour. Ed and I arrived at the advertised meeting place, near St. Paul's Cathedral, in lots of time and wracked with uncertainties. Would the police be there? Would there be violence? What if only a handful of people turned up? What if our pictures appeared in the papers? What if, what if, what if? We hovered near the cathedral doors, watching the crowd slowly gather. We sat on the steps, perhaps hoping to pass as weary tourists. More people arrived — clearly there'd be more than a handful of us, but still, what if …? We stood off to one side, backing away from anyone who came too near. We had to talk ourselves into it. St. Paul's, "awful, artificial and amusing," welcomed us inside, and we entered Christopher Wren's miraculous building. The street sounds dimmed. We stood in the half-light and talked in a whisper. We told each other, "We have to do this, we have to go back outside, we have to march."

We were shivering when we left the church and stepped into that day's light. Not many minutes later, we were shouting, shouting slogans we'd thought we could never say in public. They weren't poetic or clever, though Ed remembers one that made us both laugh: "Ho, ho, homosexual! The ruling class is ineffectual!" But that didn't matter. What mattered was that we had shouted out our darkest secret, replaced it with a swelling brightness that blossomed in our hearts and eyes and voices. A book by Lisa Power, *No Bath But Plenty of Bubbles: An Oral History of the Gay Liberation Front 1970–1973*, describes us marching to the *Sun*, the *Daily Mirror*, and the *Daily Express*, handing out leaflets and "using the newspapers' own hoarding placards with gay slogans superimposed to get the message across that the tabloid press was sexist and anti-gay and contributed to prejudice."

Another demonstration, this time organized by the Campaign for Homosexual Equality, took place nine days later, on August 28, beginning in Hyde Park and marching to Trafalgar Square, but we were visiting Mel and Juliet in Oxford at the time, and we missed it. In the wake of that Fleet Street demo, though, Ed and I had begun talking incessantly about working to make gay lib happen in Canada. We were unaware, when we returned on September 11, 1971, that the country's first public gay demonstration had already occurred. Coincidentally, it happened on August 28, the same day as the London march to Trafalgar Square. Inconsequential colonial news didn't play in Britain, of course, but some one hundred gay men and lesbians, many of whom would soon become my friends, had marched in the rain, rallied on Parliament Hill, and delivered a list of gay rights demands to the government of Pierre Trudeau. We would read about it, not long after, in a fledgling paper called *The Body Politic*.

5

The Body Politic: The Beginnings

THE FIRST ISSUE OF *The Body Politic* that I bought was dated November/December 1971. It cost twenty-five cents, the price of a glass of draft beer. I made my purchase at a gay dance at Holy Trinity Church in downtown Toronto. I've no idea what day that purchase happened, but I'm fond of anniversaries and want one, a date I can cite for the moment I first picked up the publication that would consume my life for the next fifteen years. I would find out later that that first issue was delivered from the printer on October 28. Any gay dance would have been held on a Friday or Saturday. So I'll pick a Saturday a few weeks later, in November. Let's say November 20, about two months after I had returned to Canada, desperately unhappy, my life unmoored in every way but for an urgent, overriding desire to replicate what I'd felt as I left the protective embrace of St. Paul's Cathedral and began shouting out to the world that I was a fag. It was too early then for me to care, except abstractly, about social justice or equal rights or political change — I simply wanted to feel that good, that free, that alive, over and over again. And there I was, on November 20, 1971, dancing in a church! With other men! In a church! Feeling good and free and alive and frequently in lust, though still a little shy about showing it, and deciding to part with twenty-five cents for a copy of *The Body Politic*, handing the money to Paul Macdonald, a corpulent, hippie-esque fellow with shy, skittish eyes who would be a housemate in the communal life soon to come. He handed me a folded tabloid newspaper, the cover photo showing a handful of people, men and women, standing beside a bus bearing a sign, only partly visible, that said, "Gay Rally Ottawa." On the back, there was a photo of two women kissing in front of Toronto's new City Hall, though the image was so overexposed it could have been two men. Or, for that matter, a man and a woman.

I would soon meet and know everyone in both those photos. My life, after the doldrums of Europe, seemed suddenly and wildly over-oxygenated — just two months back in Canada and I was already a member of the Community Homophile Association of Toronto (CHAT, which had organized that dance after forming less than a year earlier). I would soon join the more "radical" Toronto Gay Action and would soon get fucked for the first time, that honour going to John Scythes, then the scion of an established Toronto family but in no way epicene. On the contrary, he had the hard, sculpted body of a manual labourer (which is mostly what he did), owned and lavished attention upon a green 1948 Packard, and had a voice, an unstoppable voice (hand him a topic, any topic, and he could go on and on), not a mellifluous voice but a grating, droning voice that could cut through sheet metal and that was, if you were in lust (and I was), so very much, totally adorable. Still, that first fuck? It hurt like hell. No condom, of course. Back then, they seemed something of a punishment for being straight, although I'd never used one in any of my hetero trysts, relying upon the women with whom I had sex to do whatever it was they did to not get pregnant.

Shortly after I returned, I met with Blanche. I owed her that.

She'd been my girlfriend. She'd wept when we'd parted, and I'd sent her, at most, two postcards during that year in Europe. She was surprised to hear from me, but she agreed to meet. We met in a restaurant, and I told her I was a homosexual and we could no longer see each other and it had nothing to do with her — it was all, all, *all* about me — and she said, "But can't we be friends?" and I said, no, we couldn't, that I wanted nothing to do with my previous life, and she was part of it, and even if I agreed to be friends we'd see each other once or twice and then it would be over so why not just end it now, here? I suppose I had logic on my side, but I can't help but feel, looking back, that I was a complete asshole. It's a feeling I often get, looking back. Not *always* an asshole, though. Sometimes just socially clumsy.

As with my first sex with a black man, picked up at a dance at Hart House organized by the University of Toronto Homophile Association. We'd danced and flirted, and when it became clear we were going back to my place together, I asked him what country he was from, hoping that I'd be *in flagrante* with an exotic from some obscure African nation. "Canada," he said, a little pointedly. Not one to let a conversational gambit slip by, I brought up the fact that I'd encountered other black Canadians, lovely gentlemen who'd been porters on the trains out of Marathon, which turned out to be less offensive than it would be today — Toronto was a very different city then, mostly white. And, as a conversational gambit, it more or less worked — he told me, without indignation or embarrassment, that his father had worked out of Halifax as a train porter.

Sexual opportunities suddenly seemed everywhere, in contexts more appealing to me than the few mostly scuzzy, straight-run gay bars I'd begun to patronize. Even CHAT, which focused largely on maintaining a counselling/distress phone line, could be ripe for cruising. That wasn't supposed to happen, of course, particularly not in a counselling context, but I remember, as a volunteer counsellor, meeting with a chubby-cute young man who began by telling me he wasn't gay. In fact, he was getting married the next day. He had trained as a butcher and been offered a job in a small Ontario town, but he didn't want to marry and leave the city without having tried homosexuality. This would be his last chance. What did I recommend? I suggested several bars or baths where he might pick someone up and enjoy a quickie. "I want to have sex with you," he said. "Please have sex with me."

The "please" made the difference. I'm a sucker for politesse. Actually, I suppose, I'm a cocksucker for politesse. What I did next would have been very unprofessional if I'd been a professional, but I wasn't, so I said, "Come home with me," and he followed me back to my apartment. I still remember how he trembled as he undressed and how he very, very gently lowered his naked body onto mine and, after hesitating for just a moment, kissed me.

When we finished, he said, "Thank you very much." I asked him whether he'd enjoyed it. He had. I asked whether he might seek other homosexual encounters. He thought not. On a whim, I asked his name and, guilelessly, he told me. His surname sounded like "Deeth," so I asked how it was spelled and he said, "It's D-E-A-T-H" without the slightest trace of self-consciousness or awareness that others might pronounce it differently or be amused or shocked or terrified. I'd had sex with the butcher, Death. On the eve of his wedding. I felt ready for anything.

I WAS EAGER TO be a part of *The Body Politic*, even though that first issue had perplexed me. It wasn't because of the way it looked — that the design was a clumsy mishmash simply meant that it was counter-cultural and not a glossy, soulless, consumerist rag. It was even less professionally put together than *Guerilla*, the anarcho-lefty tabloid that in some ways helped birth it. (For a detailed history of the connections, personal, political, and rancorous, see Rick Bébout's online history at rbebout.com, and for wonderful period photos and anecdotes about *Guerilla*, see Peter Zorzi's memories of decades of gay activism at onthebookshelves.com.) What perplexed me was its non-hierarchical organizational structure and its penchant for analysis and dense political writing. (Poet Ian Young, an early contributor, delighted in referring to *The Body Politic* editorial collective as "the body politburo.")

I'd never been "political." I'd done my duty as a citizen and voted, but I'd never felt the urge to volunteer for a party. My background was working class, but I wanted out. I wanted better. I did not have a class analysis. (I recall an early meeting of Toronto Gay Action, during which I referred to "the lower classes." There was some throat-clearing. "What?" I asked. An awkward silence followed, and then someone said, "We say 'working class,' Gerry.") Because of my Marathon background and my up-close view of social inequities in Mexico, I felt at some gut level that the world was not structured fairly, but the most I'd thought to do about that was to spend part of my summers helping "the poor Mexicans" by teaching them skills they were most unlikely to need.

(Friend and *Body Politic* colleague Ken Popert once asked me how I might describe my politics. "Liberal, small 'l', I suppose," said I, knowing that Ken would describe himself as a Marxist. "That probably puts me in the category of 'useful idiot' as far as you're concerned," I added. "No," he said, after a Popertian pause, "I've never thought of you as useful.")

Of course, I knew that in 1969, the Trudeau government had brought in changes to the Criminal Code that had decriminalized certain acts usually associated with homosexuals — but that was politics as I knew it then, politics from the top down. It was the way the world was supposed to work, and though I was grateful that it had happened, it neither excited nor inspired me. As for politics from the ground up? I had heard of the Stonewall Riots in New York, but I knew nothing of the years of quiet, letter-writing activism by men like James Egan, or of the formation, in 1964 in Vancouver, of the country's first homophile organization, or of the arrest and imprisonment in 1965 of Everett George Klippert for repeated, consensual sex in private with adult males — a scandalous injustice that partly motivated the 1969 Criminal Code amendments. Ed had been more fervent than I about contributing to the gay struggle. The University of Toronto Homophile Association had formed in October 1969, before we left for Europe. Ed had been eager to participate, but we worked evenings teaching ESL and couldn't get involved. I can't recall that I was particularly interested — I had my new circle of teacher friends, many of whom knew I was at least gay-ish. They accepted me. That seemed enough.

Still, politically ignorant and naive as I was, I had the sense that I'd have to become political if I were to get involved with *The Body Politic*. To that end, I tried to invest it with an allure that electoral politics never had for me — the allure of the revolutionary, of Cuba and Che, of crystal-clear ideals and bright-eyed fervour for social justice, of the willingness to mount the barricades, face the firing squad, and stare death in the face — which was all very well until I realized that becoming political mostly meant attending meetings likely to be overpopulated with long-winded ideologues.

We devoured that first issue of *The Body Politic*, Ed and I. It was literary, or at least had literary pretensions — it contained a review of E.M. Forster's novel *Maurice* and a review of the 1971 film *Sunday Bloody Sunday* — which had built-in appeal for a couple of smarty-pants young men who'd spent a year in Europe, written poetry, read widely, and drawn penises. A meeting of the collective had been advertised, and we decided to attend together.

The meeting took place at Jearld Moldenhauer's apartment at 65 Kendal Avenue. Jearld is justly celebrated as the paper's founder and has the distinction of being co-founder of the University of Toronto Homophile Association and founder of the gay bookstore Glad Day Books. (He claims that history fiercely — he's Cerberus at the gates of Hades if you try to challenge it.) That night, even ignorant of the fact that he was the one who'd called us all together, what struck me most was that he liked opera, a passion I'd shared with no one but Ed and Mel until then. He owned what to me seemed a huge collection of recordings, including some, by composers like Janacek, I'd never heard of. He was thin, of average height, and had the *de rigueur* long, lanky hair of the day, a crafty, knowing look, and a voice always on the edge of a dismissive cackle. When the meeting ended, he said that if anyone wanted to stay longer and talk, they'd be welcome — what I didn't realize at the time was that it wasn't a general invitation, though it sounded like one. He had his eye on the cutest boy in the room, which wasn't me. Everyone left but me (perhaps everyone understood but me). I tried to turn the conversation to opera (with the background hope that we might have sex — I found him geekily attractive), but he was sullen and uncommunicative to the point of rudeness, and I soon enough took the hint and left.

"What is one to say about Jearld Moldenhauer?" I wrote in the tenth anniversary issue of *The Body Politic* (January/February 1982). That question is as hard to answer today as it was then. Now, one might hear it put more crassly as, "What to say about Moldy?" or, depending on your history with him, the rather nastier "about Moldy-bore?" What to say is a challenge because he kick-started so much that he should be an admired elder statesman, turned to for his opinions, anecdotes, and memories and celebrated for his unflinching commitment to his vision of gay liberation. (That he also became rich as the proprietor of Glad Day Books doesn't detract one whit from his accomplishments.) He's not treated as an elder statesman, though. I think it's fair to say he isn't much liked. Perhaps likeability is an irrelevant category. Does one ever "like" a *monstre sacré*? Along with writer Scott Symons, he's the closest I've ever come to meeting the real thing. (The difference would be that Symons would have nominated himself for the distinction; Jearld might acknowledge it with his usual high-pitched cackle and twitchy self-consciousness.) I saw him as often abrasive, tactless, insensitive, impatient, and close to predatory in his pursuit of young men. These were young men who sometimes found through him the quick, sharp break with the past that lifted them out of their frightened, reflexive hesitations about accepting their sexuality. Others felt enjoyed, then used, and then abruptly dropped. Some grew in sophistication and knowledge. Some fled back into the closet. "I know I wasn't really close to anyone during the entire history of the paper," Jearld wrote in that anniversary issue. "I'm not saying that my personality is in any way an easy personality to get along with. I've always been a very sexual being and I've always been very forward, and people have a difficult time dealing with that kind of openness."

I would see another side of him years later at a party he co-hosted on December 29, 2013, in the Parkdale mansion he then co-owned with John Scythes. (He also has a home in Fez, Morocco, where he spends much of the year, mostly alone, I understand, except for the birds in his aviary. He is particularly fond of parrots.) He had aged, was slightly paunchy, had thinning hair, had to keep adjusting the hearing aid in his right ear. He was also benign, reflective, a little sad somehow, and warmly anecdotal — not the Moldenhauer I was used to, though there were flashes of the bristly, Salome-obsessed opera queen of old: he and Scythes burst into "Niemals, Tochter Babylons, Tochter Sodoms" as some guests were on their way out. There was something valedictory about the evening — he'd invited a cross-section of the aging activists he'd been associated with in his youth (not always amicably) and a selection of young men, some of whom had worked for him at Glad Day Books. He'd spent the day cooking a lavish spread. At the door, when we parted, I thought we might hug. We'd never hugged. We didn't then, either. The moment passed.

At that first meeting back in his apartment on Kendal Avenue, though, only his rudeness rankled, and that wasn't until the end of the evening. I was mostly immersed in observing and assessing the others in the room. There was Paul Macdonald, who'd sold me that first issue and who would always be the movement's ultra-leftist, and his friend and roommate Herb Spiers, an American import, a founding member of the collective, hunky even before it was hot to be hunky, a doctoral student at the Ontario Institute for Studies in Education, and the possessor of a significant penis he had no qualms about brandishing. (Several photos of Herb naked would appear in *TBP*, though usually in a comic vein. There were so many anxieties at the time about the perils of objectifying the body.) He was smart, boisterous, and loud in that ingratiating American way, the only person I knew who could read a newspaper to himself loudly. I would soon be madly in love with him and slipping unsigned poetry under his door. He, along with Paul, would soon join me, Ed, and others in communal living. Hugh Brewster, younger than the rest of us, fresh out of the University of Guelph, handsome (albeit of flawed complexion), somehow patrician in both his bearing and his voice (a rich baritone, with more than a hint of mid-Atlantic cadences). John Forbes was almost certainly there since his column, "Twilight Trails," debuted in the next issue. He'd recently moved to Toronto from Vancouver, where he'd helped form a satirical/surrealist/drag parody group called the Ephemerals. He was Twilight Rose, "a hippie Tiresias," the name taken from a shade of lipstick spotted at the makeup counter at the Bay, a man with a face that was all sharp angles and high cheekbones. I can still hear his flat, affectless voice saying, "Catch me, Tarzan." His column, meant "to bring taste to the revolution," was arch, camp, and short-lived. (As he would put it later, "Twilight Rose was only useful in the androgynous period — then rock stars picked up on drag and I knew androgyny had no impact anymore. I didn't have a role anymore.") There would have been a few other men (the collective list in the second issue names three other men besides me, Ed, Herb, Jearld, Hugh, Paul, and John). I no longer remember who those others were, though David Newcome, who appeared on the cover of the first issue, was almost certainly one of them. The name Kathy Picard is on that list, though I can't bring her to mind. I don't think she was one of two women I do remember, "simmering lesbians," as I would later describe them, "who fought violently against the use of a male nude on the back cover of Issue 2" and who wanted the collective list composed of first names only as a way of "fighting the patriarchy." They lost those battles, left, and never returned.

That didn't bother me. I'd found them doctrinaire and shrill. It also didn't bother me that the room was not only male-dominated but entirely white — not a fact I would even have remarked on at the time. There's a tendency these days to look back at early gay organizations with a hint of embarrassment and with an apology at the ready, an apology for the fact that they were composed almost entirely of young, white, middle-class men with university or college degrees. Many, like me, had working-class backgrounds but were eager to leave them behind. None of us was racist, except in a relatively benign way — no distaste, no aversion, but some stereotypes for sure and evincing little interest in the cultures and lives of people who weren't like us. No surprise there — Marathon had been an entirely white town, except for the Indians (which is what we mistakenly called the Indigenous people then) and the family that ran the Chinese restaurant. Toronto was a white city. (According to an analysis of the city's 1971 census data, almost 96 percent of its population was of European descent.) I was only beginning to learn not to refer to Brazil nuts as "n-toes." I had a sense that "negroes" wasn't quite the thing either, but what was one to say? So no apologies: gay liberation in its early years was developed and guided, at least in Toronto, by well-educated, twenty-something white men. I am so very happy it didn't stay that way.

By the end of that meeting, both Ed and I had writing assignments for the upcoming second issue. I can't remember if we volunteered or were asked. Ed was to write a review of *Dancing the Gay Lib Blues*, a book by New York activist Arthur Bell, and I was to report on my experiences as a paid volunteer in a sexual response study underway at the Clarke Institute of Psychiatry. ("Curiosity," I would write, "and the exigencies of penury" were my motivations.) The study involved attaching a device to my penis that could measure very slight changes in tumescence. Then I would be shown slides and video clips: naked men, women, and children, most frequently in non-erotic contexts, interspersed with landscapes and hideous skin cancers. Stiffies and shrinky-dinks would both register. (I don't recall my penis doing much of either, though I was startled when I got a full erection watching a video of a fat prepubescent boy walking stolidly toward the camera. I was not remotely turned on, and yet my cock got hard — a phenomenon that has continued throughout my life. It seemed to cause some consternation in the control booth — the slide show came to a halt until my penis returned to its usual state of indifference. Years later, when I had become a sex worker, I dubbed that useful and happy phenomenon my "courtesy boner.")

I had my assignment. I knew I would have to read it aloud to the collective at the next meeting — that's how content was approved. I did. I was a hit. Ed was, too. People laughed at the funny bits and seemed to take seriously my attempts at a critique of experiments allegedly designed to prove homosexuality was not a neurosis. We were living proof, I thought. Who needed more?

We had content. Layout was next, and not long after we gathered in the CHAT office, upstairs at 6 Charles Street East, and typed and pasted and rearranged and consulted giddily under the direction of David Newcome, who seemed to know what he was doing. My article was called "Porn at the Clarke" and included a drawing of a penis (a generic penis — I didn't pose) strapped into the measuring apparatus. And there, hand-lettered at the bottom of the article, my first-ever byline: Jerry Hannon. (It would be several years before I started to insist on Gerald, a way, I thought, of sounding more grown-up.) I shared the page with an article by Hugh Brewster, "The Non-Urban Gay Ghetto," a look at small-town gay life so evocative that it surprised no one when he surfaced years later as a successful author and publisher.

The rest of that issue bubbled with activist fervour — it's surprising today to look back and see how quickly we'd gone from the love that dare not speak its name to the love that won't shut up, an oft-repeated joke. Page one was devoted to a CBC documentary, *Nothing to Hide* — sympathetic, for the times, to the gay cause, but which still felt it necessary, for "balance," to include Dr. Lawrence Hatterer, a proponent of the sickness theory of homosexuality. He'd written a book called *Changing Homosexuality in the Male.*

It also rankled that this Canadian production had been filmed mostly in the United States. Herb Spiers wrote about the ensuing demonstration outside the CBC building on Jarvis Street, pointing out that there were thirteen of us, but that the count could be conceivably raised to seventeen, given that four regulars were absent. "It was not the greatest of successes," he wrote, "but neither was it a failure." He also recorded that we gave a copy of *The Body Politic* to each of the four police officers who were there to ensure we didn't take up too much of the sidewalk.

That issue may have been dated January/February 1972, but the hippie ethos of the sixties still reigned. We called the editorial the "Headitorial." The letters page was called "Write-ons." It was cool to be opposed to the war in Vietnam, and it was cool to look down on the commercial gay scene as exploitative and run by hostile or indifferent straight men. (As one proprietor famously put it, "You guys are lucky to have any place to go.") Unfortunately, that distaste for the exploiters transferred to some degree to the patrons — for years, some of us activists felt a vestigial disdain for the gay men and women who patronized institutions that treated them badly. We knew there was nowhere else to go. But why, we thought, couldn't they be satisfied (as we pretended to be) with strategy meetings and consciousness-raising sessions? For a time, *The Body Politic* collective was reputed to be a humourless, stringent lot — the Jacobins of the gay movement. One of the articles in that second issue declared that the final aim of gay liberation "must surely be the destruction of the gay ghetto."

But what was to take its place? We had the answer. We had the answers for everything in those days. Community would replace ghetto. The centre spread of the second issue of *TBP* was devoted to the Community Homophile Association of Toronto's imminent move to a large heritage building, a one-time church and then a synagogue at 58 Cecil Street near College and Spadina. "A Great Moment Has Arrived: The Alternative," the headline trumpeted. CHAT would have its office there and offer counselling, a twenty-four-hour distress line, legal assistance, and information on venereal diseases (as they were then called). There were to be dances on the weekends, a coffee house and rap centre, a library, Moldenhauer's fledgling bookstore, and meeting space for *The Body Politic* collective — on alternate Sunday evenings, the radicals in Toronto Gay Action could hold their meetings. "We have a home," the text continued excitedly, "a place run by gay people for gay people. Responsive to our needs. Where gay community is a reality."

6

The Body Politic: Summarized History

· ·

TBP WOULD LAST FOR 135 issues — the first dated November/December 1971, the last February 1987. I was involved with every issue but the first. It was my job and, in every important way, my life. Over those fifteen years, I would write dozens of major features and reviews, including "Men Loving Boys Loving Men," the article that would precipitate a police raid, criminal charges, and a sensational week-long trial. I would also write about the plight of gay youth, about religion, about censorship, about aesthetics, about park sex, about sex toys, about the gay disabled, about anything that grabbed my interest. I profiled other activists. I would take on the roles of news coordinator and features coordinator. (We didn't say "editor" in those days — too hierarchical. And coordinator did make more sense — I coordinated the work of a lot of volunteers.) I was our principal photographer for most of those years (I knew nothing of photography, so I took a course offered by the YMCA, bought a camera, then set up a darkroom in the communal house I lived in). On the administrative side, I tried my best to be what today would be called the organization's chief financial officer, but I had no training and little interest in the subject — not a recipe for success. I also, at various times, handled advertising, promotion, and subscriptions.

The Body Politic lasted for fifteen eventful years. Photo collage: Lucinda Wallace

Unofficially, I was the magazine's version of Miss Lonely Hearts — we frequently received letters from closeted and frightened youth, often in small towns. It was my job to write supportive, encouraging letters, putting them in touch with local gay organizations if any such existed, keeping up the correspondence if, as was usually the case, none did (I'm still in touch with two of them, both successful men now in their fifties). I went, with my camera, to almost every gay rights demonstration. I swept the office floor. One night, after everyone else had gone home, I tried to push a broomstick up my ass. I found lovers, and lost them.

I lived, for a period in the early years, in an apartment at 90 Oxford Street in Kensington Market (the area, with its low rents and ethnic flavour, was a first address for many people). I had a roommate, Art Whitaker, who was a manager at the Library Steam Bath (long gone, but then on Wellesley Street just west of Yonge; he would eventually hire me to run the concession and then fire me not long after — customers allegedly complained about the slow way I filled a Coke glass). For a short period after my return from Europe, I went back to work as a teacher of English as a Second Language, and later I took a position as a subscriptions clerk in Dora Hood's Book Room, an antiquarian bookstore. I took the odd housecleaning job — a way for affluent older friends to funnel money my way. I occasionally worked as a nude model for JAC — a gay art collective made up of John Grube, Alex Liros, and Clarence Barnes. It all meant I could pay the rent each month, putting my financial life together with scraps, the way most of us did at the time. (The modelling gig for JAC led to the most erotic nonsexual experience of my life. When I turned up for the session, I was told there was another model, and the group wanted to us to pose together. We were introduced — his name was Yoshi Oida, a slim, tight-bodied Japanese man, perhaps a decade older than I, slightly reserved but not unfriendly. We chatted a little, and then we were asked to strip. I found him sexy, and we were soon asked for a variety of intimate poses, which we'd then have to hold for minutes at a time, the erotic excitement growing out of a sublimated frustration. Left to our own devices, we would have started having sex. Because we had no other choice, we focused on each other's bodies, the rhythm of each other's hearts, the caress of each bead of sweat as it slid down his chest and then on to mine, the nestling of our penises together, slowly getting hard and then soft again, the gentle rise and fall of our diaphragms as we breathed, belly to belly, lost in each other's eyes for minutes at a time if that's what the pose required. Afterward, we went back to my place and did have sex, and though it was fun, it was, somehow, anticlimactic. I would find out later that he was an actor, and he would become a favourite performer with Peter Brook's company in Paris and a film actor with several artsy movies to his credit.)

What I remember most about that Oxford Street address is that it's the place where I fell in love with Robert Trow. We met in late winter 1972 or early spring 1973 — he was then dating fellow collective member Hugh Brewster, and he and Hugh, Ed Jackson, I, and a few others attended a performance of John Herbert's new play, *Born of Medusa's Blood*. (Herbert was the only well-known Canadian homosexual playwright at the time and is remembered today for his groundbreaking prison drama, *Fortune and Men's Eyes*.) The work featured an all-black cast and was running at Theatre in Camera at Bathurst and Lennox Streets, and it was truly dreadful. We were convulsed with barely suppressed laughter through much of it, and a few of its more egregious lines became catchphrases for our crowd ("On your feet, foreskin" and "Do you fuck, suck, rim or blow?" were two favourites).

Robert was about five years younger than I, was attending library school at the time, was the eldest son of a well-to-do family in Thornhill, and lived with a roommate not far away in an apartment on College Street just east of Spadina. We'd run into each other frequently in the market area. We made each other laugh. He was very teasable, not doctrinaire politically, and, that greatest of virtues, unafraid of being silly. He could make a fine dinner out of leftovers (a friend described his culinary system as "cuisine poubelle") and was the slowest eater any of us had ever met. One might be considering dessert while Robert was working on his appetizer. He was careful with his money but wildly generous — he underwrote several trips to France we took together and was proud of his command of French but joined in the amusement when the yogurt he'd ordered turned out to be cheese dogs. Soon we were sleeping together, and on April 22, 1973, Easter Sunday morning, we awoke, all giggles and caresses, and he said, "I adore you" and giggled again, but I knew he meant it, and I said the same thing, and I meant it too, and we were lovers for the next nine years.

We awoke that morning on a mattress on the floor in my roommate's scuzzy smaller bedroom. We were there because Arthur was at work and we'd surrendered the larger bedroom to Ed Jackson and Merv Walker, who had begun dating around the same time

I fell in love with Robert Trow, who worked at Hassle Free Clinic. Although HIV+, he died suddenly of an unrelated aneurism in 2002. Photo: Gerald Hannon

as Robert and I had. Merv was nineteen, cute, smart, shy, a recent arrival from Saskatchewan (he was saddled with the nickname "the Prairie Chicken" for a period). His name had appeared on *The Body Politic* contributors' list as early as Issue 7 ("Winter, 1973" — we seemed slow to adopt the conventional periodical dating protocol); Robert's had shown up by Issue 9 ("1973" — not even the season is mentioned).

Such bounce and joy in those days. We had boyfriends! They were gay activists too! We weren't going to replicate monogamous heterosexual bonding rituals, and we went so far as to have a one-evening switcheroo: I would have sex with Merv, and Ed with Robert. It was fun, but it also made clear that the original pairings were the right ones. Still, Robert and I were never monogamous — both of us were fairly regular bathhouse patrons, and I was an ardent devotee of park sex.

I was lucky. I may have had a lot of sex, but the worst I had to cope with was hepatitis B and crabs. Robert was not. He was diagnosed with what came to be known as HIV in 1982, the year the first stories about a "gay cancer" began to appear in the press. At first, it seemed a distant but ominous drumbeat, emanating mostly from the States, though Randy Shilts's book, *And the Band Played On*, would wrongfully place a lot of blame for spreading the disease on Gaëtan Dugas, a Canadian flight attendant who became known as Patient Zero.

I WAS IN LOVE, but I was also passionate about journalism, though we never thought of ourselves as journalists. We thought of ourselves as activists who happened to publish — we didn't pretend to be impartial or even balanced. We hoped to be fair and accurate. That's evident in a piece I wrote, "School Is a Drag?" in Issue 3, March/April 1972. It concerned the plight of gay teens in high school, particularly when it came to sex education. The picture wasn't rosy, of course (some resource material described homosexuality as "a pathetic little second-rate substitute for reality, a pitiable flight from life"), but what impresses me now, looking back at it, is that it wasn't just a screed. I actually did some research, calling twenty-two schools in the Toronto area, interviewing teachers, identifying myself as a member of Toronto Gay Action, asking whether homosexuality was part of the sex ed curriculum and, if so, how it was treated. My conclusion: "Of 22 schools, 15 must be considered as inadequate, and that's nearly 70%." (But what really surprised me was that seven schools responded with invitations to speak or requests for more information, and I remember several of us visiting at least one school, speaking and answering students' questions.)

That was the first of my articles to concern itself with young people. Issue 5, July/August 1972, would feature "Of Men and Little

I was also *TBP*'s main photographer. Here getting the best shot of a demo in Saskatoon, 1977, with Halifax activist Robin Metcalfe.
Photo: *The ArQuives*

Boys," an attempt at making sense of pedophilia (I elaborated further in Issue 6 in a verbose piece entitled "Children and Sex"). In Issue 26, September 1976, I wrote "Seven Years to Go" on the plight of gay youth, given the disparity of age of consent laws (sixteen for heterosexual acts, twenty-one for homosexual). Issue 28: "Advice on Consent," advertised as "the second part in a series which aims to keep us all thinking about the sexual rights of young people." Issue 39, December 1977: "Men Loving Boys Loving Men," "the latest in a series on youth sexuality." Issue 84, June 1982: "Letters from High School," letters between me and "Robert," a high school student in Red Deer, Alberta. (An extraordinarily sophisticated, eccentric, and witty young man, he would eventually move to Toronto and get me into bed. I turned out to be low-hanging fruit, though — he would one day add a late-developing, flagrantly heterosexual Canadian literary icon to his list of conquests.)

That's only seven articles out of the more than eighty major pieces I wrote in my fifteen years with *The Body Politic* — less than 10 percent — but the fallout from two of them ("Of Men and Little Boys" and "Men Loving Boys Loving Men") was disproportionately huge. I've often been asked — in fact, have sometimes asked myself — why I should concern myself so ardently with the sexuality of young people, a topic guaranteed to provoke and disturb (even more so today, the era of pedophile panic). It wasn't because I found children or youths sexually attractive. (I've sometimes joked that the only way a prepubescent boy could get me into bed would be to ply me with alcohol. On the other hand, if there were "grass on the playing field," as the crude old saying goes, I'd consider it.) Partly, I think, it was because addressing such a topic made me seem like a radical thinker, someone willing to toss aside all the old bromides about sexuality. I wanted a place in the hierarchy of *The Body Politic*'s intellectual activists, people like Jearld Moldenhauer, Tim McCaskell, or Herb Spiers, men who read deeply in political and social theory and talked and wrote about their ideas. I didn't do the reading. But I saw I could write persuasively. Maybe that would be enough.

There was another reason too — I was in my late twenties when I wrote "Of Men and Little Boys," not that distant from my high school and university years, years of grim torment and sexual ignorance, a condition I could see was still true for most young people. I still remembered a childhood where adults ruled — a life of curfews, beatings, mindless obedience. Though it had been years ago, all of that still resonated, still felt personal, still wounded. Wounded enough that I felt compelled to write about it.

I also felt, naively, that all it would take to change things would be a rational article or two. People would read my work, there'd be some discussion, and then they'd say, "Of course. How silly of us! How prejudiced we've been! Thanks for the enlightenment."

It turns out not to have worked out quite that way. Not surprisingly, given how feeble that first effort was. "Of Men and Little Boys" included no interviews with either men or little boys. Only one book was referenced, turned to for a quote to bolster my assertion that the straight world was right in seeing gay people as "dangerous where children are concerned ... not to the physical well-being of their offspring, but to the family structure that imprisons them, a structure based in part on the concept of possession." Heady intellectual material, or so it seemed to me at the time. Now it's cringe-making — not heady but head-in-the-clouds.

NOTHING WOULD HAVE COME of it (the world didn't eagerly anticipate each new issue of *The Body Politic*), except that the issue was on the stands during the city's first Gay Pride festivities.

That celebration was a wildly ambitious undertaking for a fledgling movement. A single day was deemed to be insufficient — we were to have a whole week of Pride, starting with an opening ceremony at the Cecil Street centre on Saturday, August 19 (although there were letters of support from Ontario NDP leader Stephen Lewis and city alderman William Kilbourne, then mayor William Dennison has the distinction of being the first of many chief magistrates to refuse to declare Pride Week). I remember it well — we hung coloured streamers off the fire escape stairs, tacked up a big Gay Pride sign, and a group of us, wearing Gay Pride T-shirts (featuring a lambda in a maple leaf), trooped down those stairs singing, "Hello, Gay Pride Week" to the tune of "Hello, Dolly!" The recently formed CITY-TV, broadcasting then on channel 79 ("that's

69 hanging ten" one of the cameramen joked), turned up — we'd be on television news! Jearld Moldenhauer's photographs show us all: I'm there, the only one wearing a hat — a hipster *avant la lettre*. Ed Jackson, who claims not to be able to carry a tune, is singing gamely along. Hugh Brewster was there (in recent years, he and I have been asked by interviewers to belt that song out, something we're always happy to do, though I think neither of us is confident about the words). There are two women, Pat Murphy and Linda Jain, both of them associated with the Community Homophile Association of Toronto. I can pick out friends Paul Pearce and Paul Macdonald, all of us members of what we called (for reasons unknown) the Cecil Street Aquarium Choir. There had to be a drag queen, and of course there was, done up as HRH the Queen Mother. She cut a ribbon. Gay Pride Week had begun.

It would end with editorial condemnations in *The Globe and Mail*, the *Toronto Star*, and the *Toronto Sun*, a call for criminal charges against me and *The Body Politic*, and the first significant public fracture in the community we'd been so devoted to building.

"PRIDE AND PREJUDICE!" WAS the headline on the centre spread of Issue 6, Autumn 1972. The "pride" was there in the photographs — an art show inside the CHAT centre, a picnic on Ward's Island, a march of some two hundred to Queen's Park and down University Avenue. The "prejudice"? A selection of quotes from the city's daily papers. "No Open Season on Children," trumpeted the *Toronto Star*. *Globe and Mail* columnist Kenneth Bagnell, in his condemnation of my article, added, "Along with most psychiatrists, I regard homosexuality as at least a handicap." The *Globe*'s editorial, entitled "Within the law?", wondered whether legal action would be taken against the newspaper or the author, and the *Toronto Sun* began its indictment by noting, "Toronto has just endured Gay Pride Week."

It's just as well none of them had attended a seminar on the Open Society, held in the CHAT centre on August 22, the day before the press onslaught began. I was one of five panellists and, as a representative of Toronto Gay Action, was clearly the designated "radical." I fully intended to play that role to the hilt. I began my speech by nattering on about the "need for the organic evolution of social change" (whatever that means) but then segued to the two practical and immediate goals we could set ourselves: close the churches and get the kids. (In my memory, I added, "Burn the schools," but that incendiary recommendation doesn't appear in my typescript. Perhaps it was an impromptu inspiration.) I announced that the Christian religion was "imperialist, intolerant, materialist, anti-sexual, anti-woman, anti-reflective, anti-Semitic ... and rotten to the core." And as for children, "What can we do now?" I asked. The answer: "Talk to them, have sex with them, work with them toward the dissolution of the present school system, be exhilarated if they threaten our most cherished positions."

I wish I could say that it prompted either cheers or jeers, but I think mild consternation and a smattering of applause more or less sums up the response. Within days, though, George Hislop, then the director of CHAT, disassociated the organization from the views expressed in my speech (CHAT was the recipient of a federal grant for its counselling service). But none of that — the threatening media coverage, the internal dissension — got in the way of the thrill of it all, and may in fact have bolstered it. We had become what we thought we wanted to be: a serious threat to the sexual status quo. Why, the daily newspapers said as much! We'd become developed enough politically to have division in the ranks (though a very Canadian, polite division — as I recall, at least in the early years, voices were never raised when differences surfaced, perhaps because at some level we realized how truly small and fragile a group we were). We could pull together some two hundred people for a march to Queen's Park, down University Avenue, and over to City Hall. Who cared if almost no one noticed? I'd wanted the gut-level exhilaration I'd experienced during that Fleet Street march in London, and I got it.

I would get more of it from the way we chose to live, and that was communally. It was very much in the attenuated hippie spirit of the day, but it was also very practical — none of us had much money, and sharing rent and food costs would make a huge difference. There was romance too — Robert Trow and I were in love, as were Ed Jackson and Merv Walker. Herb Spiers, my one-time passion, had become close with the four of us, and he lived with Paul Macdonald, who came with a patina of somewhat knee-jerk left-wing politics ("Scab!" he wrote once on a jar of Kraft peanut butter that we'd bought during one of the many corporate boycotts he endorsed). Surely six people could live more cheaply together than apart? We found a house on Marchmount Road, a curved street running south off Davenport in the west end of the city (memories differ as to whether the address was 34 or 38), then mostly populated by second-generation Italian families. (Artist Charlie Pachter, who lived just down the street and to whom we paid rent, was trying to position it as an artsy enclave. He was, even then, gay as a diamond tiara, but it took years before he felt he could, in his mother's words, "come out of the cupboard.") We opened a bank account under the name "A Half Dozen of the Other." Herb and Paul had separate bedrooms; Robert and I shared, as did Ed and Merv. We volunteered at Karma Co-op and bought groceries there. We shared cooking and cleaning responsibilities. We shoplifted food, but only from large corporate stores (our way of hitting "the man"), and once prepared an entire Christmas dinner with shop-lifted groceries (and that included caviar). I once got into a street fight with a few of the local teens — I was wearing my idea of "radical drag" (a short grey skirt and a purse I'd bought through the mail, called the Lady's Organizer), and they found that outfit, to their credit, worthy of mockery. The fracas was broken up by neighbourhood mothers before any damage was done. But it felt like we were living the revolution (though I think that was the last time I wore the little grey skirt).

That Marchmount house had a grotty basement, low ceilinged and paint splattered, that became for a time the production office of *The Body Politic*. Merv Walker, perhaps the only one of us with skills that might involve hammers and nails, built primitive light boards, and those, in combination with an IBM Selectric typewriter and a waxer, meant we could work from home. Photographs show us, long-haired and skinny, wearing our Gay Pride T-shirts, typing, editing, and proofing, gazing proudly at our handiwork. (Some newspaper, I think the *Sun*, likened us to "mushrooms in a damp basement." It was a more accurate analogy than they knew.)

Those were the years we thought it was wildly funny to feminize everything (it seems a bit puerile now, but back then, as gay men recently out of the closet, we were the equivalent of toddlers). Male names got changed to their female equivalents or "Miss" got affixed to a surname — I was usually "Miss Hannon," Ed Jackson answered to Edwina and Merv to Mervina, while Herb had a range of names, from Herbeen to Herbinity to the Lady Spiers. In the Marchmount house, we sometimes went so far as to address one another in the third person just so we could hear ourselves say, "She!" Some men we knew seemed to be exempt — they were friends who might have a strong feminist bent or whose capacity for silliness was a little parched.

AFTER FOUR OR FIVE years, we moved from Marchmount Road to 48 Simpson Avenue in Riverdale, shedding Paul Macdonald and gaining a larger house with a backyard, home to Robert Trow's long-time obsession with rhubarb. *The Body Politic* had also found new space — first in a storefront office at 193 Carlton Street, from 1974 to 1976, and then in a fifth-floor walk-up loft at 24 Duncan Street. Now part of the trendy "entertainment district," the area was then off the mainstream cultural radar but home to a burgeoning Queen West art and music scene that included General Idea and singer Lorraine Segato.

I'd become a paid staffer in 1976, joining Merv Walker, who had been hired earlier, our pay so minimal that we were always tied for the lowest rent payments in our from-each-according-to-his-ability domestic setup. But it was a thrill that we could actually pay people. That meant we were a success, at least in countercultural

Body Politic communards at our collective house on Simpson Ave., 1975: (from left), me, Robert Trow, Herb Spiers, Merv Walker, Ed Jackson.
Photo: Gerald Hannon

terms, selling enough copies, subscriptions, display advertising, and classifieds each issue to cover not only the rent but subsistence salaries to two people (though only if you lived communally).

I was also a text machine — scarcely an issue went by without at least one article with my byline, and several featured both a lead article and a review of a book or theatre piece. Among the highlights: "… it's more important to be nice," a look at the country's first male beauty pageant. (I adopted a now cringe-inducing Wildean persona, churning out phrases like, "With one's friends one can be an artist. With one's acquaintances merely a connoisseur.") After a trip to Mexico, I wrote about its fledgling gay movement. In a special issue on religion, I penned "Was Christ a Cocksucker?", taking the prize for the year's most jejune headline. "Throatramming" and "Learning to Kill" explored what happened if you held hands in public (you got yelled at or attacked) and the martial arts lessons I took so that I could defend myself. (Not that they would have helped the night I was surrounded, in Riverdale Park, by a half dozen adolescent guys, clearly out for blood. They walked around me in a circle, punching into their fists, calling me a faggot, one of them chanting, "Let's do him now, let's do him now." Somehow I persuaded them that I wasn't gay, that I was just out for a late-night walk — I'd be dead or badly injured if I hadn't. They ran off to continue the hunt, and I, trembling at the sheer level of hate in their eyes, walked home. The irony is that I had just had sex among the trees minutes before they'd met me. Riverdale Park, a magnet for horny immigrants and new Canadians, had become a rich source of sexual satisfaction.)

And then, in the December 1977/January 1978 issue, "Men Loving Boys Loving Men."

I'd worked hard on it. I wanted it to be all that "Of Men and Little Boys" was not: researched, personal, balanced, passionate. I had the good fortune to count two boy-lovers in my circle — the teacher I call "Simon" had been a boyhood chum in Marathon; the affluent "Peter" I'd met through a mutual friend, and that connection led me to "Barry," with whom I went on a camping trip as a way of watching him interact with "Billy," his twelve-year-old friend. The adults all agreed to be interviewed, and I had a short, somewhat awkward talk with Billy. I also interviewed "Don," a heterosexual adult friend of Peter's with whom he'd had sex between the ages of eleven and fifteen. I'd hoped to speak to more boys, but Billy and Don (remembering back to his boyhood years) were the best I could do. Remember, it was hard enough to meet ordinary gay men willing to talk to a journalist about their sex lives. And those lives were technically legal. The men I met were taking chances, and it took a referral from a trusted source to persuade them.

We were apprehensive about publishing it. It had been scheduled for earlier in the year and then withdrawn in the wake of the rape and murder of twelve-year-old Emanuel Jaques. The son of a Portuguese immigrant family, he made a little money working as a shoeshine boy on a section of Yonge Street then known for its seedy massage parlours. On July 28, 1977, he agreed to help three men move some equipment, was lured into an upstairs apartment by the promise of $35, and there was sexually assaulted, strangled, and drowned in a sink. A week earlier, the Ontario Human Rights Commission had recommended the inclusion of sexual orientation in the province's Human Rights Code as a ground on which discrimination be prohibited.

The outrage, often fuelled by homophobia, may have eventually led to the cleanup of that section of Yonge Street, but it also gave strength to those opposed to the OHRC recommendation and led to bomb and death threats against several gay community organizations. The media referred in headlines to "gay sex orgy" and "homosexual murder." A demonstration of some fifteen thousand people, mostly Portuguese Canadians, "clamored for restoration of the death penalty, more power to the police and the eradication of homosexuals," according to coverage in the September 1977 issue of *The Body Politic*.

It didn't seem the time for a dispassionate look at intergenerational sex. We'd decided, though, that one of the editorial themes for the year would be "Children," giving us a chance to report on and critique the "Save Our Children" initiative spearheaded by evangelist and entertainer Anita Bryant. (Her organization had exploited the myth of homosexual seduction of minors to win the repeal of a non-discrimination ordinance in Dade County, Florida. She would bring her campaign to Toronto in January 1978.) The introduction to my article, written by the collective, pointed out, "The real lives of men who love boys and boys who love men are mysterious even for most other gay people." MLBLM, as it came to be known, was to make public a small part of that reality.

What it didn't do was address the thorny issue of consent. Legally, of course, no one under the age of twenty-one could consent to a homosexual act, and many felt that, legal or not, boys couldn't meaningfully do so when their potential partner was significantly older. It wasn't as if the issue hadn't been discussed at the gay organization level — the Third National Gay Rights Conference in Ottawa in 1975 had virtually split on the issue. The "radicals," which included members of *The Body Politic*, advocated the abolition of age of consent, while community service groups and churches argued for a uniform age of consent for straights and gays. Surprisingly, the radicals won two to one in a plenary vote. Not that it made any practical difference — the National Gay Rights Coalition let the issue drop, probably with considerable relief. I was content with that outcome. I supported abolition. Consent there would have to be, of course, but one negotiated by the individuals, not one imposed by the state. It also meant that, when I started preparing to write MLBLM, I didn't have to concern myself with the consent question — that had been settled in Ottawa in 1975 and had the support of collective members I admired, like Ken Popert and Tim McCaskell. Abolition made emotional sense as well. We all lived lives of controlled sexuality — no legal sex at all until you were twenty-one, no sex with more than one person at a time, our lives parched and cheated by artificial age constraints on the discovery and exploration of joy.

There would continue to be exploitation, not always sexual, in schools, churches, families. Perhaps that would be lessened if young people had more agency, felt they had the power to say yes or no and be believed, no matter what their age. As writer Jane Rule wrote in the June 1979 issue of *TBP*, recounting her first sexual experience with a woman ten years her senior, "If I were to improve on that experience now, it would not be to protect children from adult seduction but to make adults easier to seduce, less burdened with fear or guilt, less defended by hypocrisy."

We expected a reaction to the publication of MLBLM — mostly adverse comments in the press. *Toronto Sun* columnist Claire Hoy was reliably homophobic, and he didn't disappoint — vituperative columns appeared over several days between December 22 and 27. That was bad enough. But on December 23, my brother John called me to tell me that our father had died. Fred Hannon had left Marathon by train, heading for Bathurst, New Brunswick, and had been found dead in the bar car. Trois Pistoles, Quebec, was the nearest city, and his corpse had been unloaded there.

I wasn't unhappy that he'd died. I wanted to dance a jig. He'd made four lives hell — mine, my two brothers', and my mother's. *In the bar car!* I thought. *How perfect!* Was there a Red Cap beer on the table beside an ash tray overflowing with the stubs of Player's cigarettes? Did he suddenly slump, but everyone thought he was just falling asleep? Did he have regrets? Was it sudden? Was it slow? There was another reason I couldn't scrape together even the shadow of a hint of grief — I knew why he was heading to New Brunswick. He knew my mother, a runaway, had fled there. He also knew she hadn't run away alone — she had left with a friend, Rita Theriault. What he didn't know but probably guessed was that my mom and Rita had become lovers, the blossoming of a long-time friendship that had taken root in Marathon's hospital, where they both worked, my mother as the cleaning lady and Rita as the laundry lady. He was heading to Bathurst to bring her back, to put an end to their sapphic adventure, to free her from the grip of her lezzie friend, to drag her back to the miseries and beatings of a life with him. And he died. On the train. In the bar car.

I didn't want to leave Toronto — the media storm around my article was building, and I wanted to be in town for whatever might happen — but I knew my mother wanted me with her. She was wracked by guilt and would never quite lose the feeling that she'd caused her husband's death (though the twenty-five mostly happy years with Rita that followed surely took the edge off her pain). So I took the awkward midwinter journey to Bathurst. When I arrived, they asked if I wanted to see my father's body. I did not. I did my best to provide solace and to console, and then I returned to Toronto. I don't know what day I made it back, but I was certainly there on Friday, December 30, 1977.

Late that afternoon, I and a group of fellow *TBP*-ers caught the island ferry to Ward's Island, where we'd been invited to dinner by Michael Riordon, author of the popular column "Flaunting It!" Also on board: Michael Lynch, American by birth, an English prof who was succulent of body and large of cock and probably the first gay academic ever to be a nude centrefold for the American gay skin mags *Honcho* and *Mandate*. He would start or be an active member of a long list of the city's gay organizations. Michael wasn't the only dinner guest with an American connection — Rick Bébout, who would become the most influential and powerful collective member, was a draft resister who grew up in Massachusetts. Jonathan Ned Katz, the author of *Gay American History*, was visiting his Canadian boyfriend, David Gibson, a graphic designer who would eventually help shape the look of the magazine. Winnipeg import Bill Lewis was by then Michael Lynch's lover, though Michael maintained a close connection with his wife, Gail, and his young son, Stefan. Bill was a scientist and could be almost stammeringly shy, but his background in science made him an invaluable asset when the AIDS crisis hit five years later. There were six of us then, full of holiday spirits tinged with a touch of apprehension caused by the headline in that morning's *Toronto Sun*: "Crown to study sex mag."

Our host, Michael Riordon, greeted us as we stepped off the ferry. "Come from the raid?" he asked.

He'd received a phone call from Ed Jackson, who'd stayed behind at the office with collective member Tim McCaskell. At 5:00 p.m., shortly after I and the others had left to catch the ferry, the police arrived. There were five of them, and they had a search warrant allowing them access to corporate records and documents that could afford evidence relevant to charges that might be laid under Section 164 of the Criminal Code of Canada, an obscure and rarely used provision that criminalized "use of the mails for the purpose of transmitting or delivering anything that is obscene, indecent, immoral or scurrilous."

I called Ed as soon as we got to Michael Riordon's cottage. "They're taking everything," he told me. "Everything." Something about his tone suggested that this catastrophe was all my fault. I was in agony because I feared he might be right. He counselled us not to return until the police had left and added that he was frequently on the phone with lawyer Clayton Ruby, who was advising him on how to handle the situation.

The police stayed for three and a half hours and filled twelve shipping cartons with subscription lists, distribution and advertising records, classified ad records and addresses, our chequebook, manuscripts for publication, letters to the editor, corporate documents. They opened mail both personal and business, went through photo files, and seized material from the Canadian Gay Archives, which shared office space with us.

As they were doing that, the six of us dining with Michael Riordon ate nervously, chatted anxiously, waited for the call from Ed that would summon us back to the city. Michael Lynch, ever the academic, said it felt like a dinner scene from a Chekhov play — all the important action was happening offstage. We finally got a phone call from Ed. The police had left. It was safe for us to return.

It would be satisfying to report that the police had trashed the place, but they hadn't. They had worked methodically and neatly, sending out for sandwiches when they got hungry, loading the freight elevator with the shipping cartons of material they'd seized. Ed remembers, when they finally left, watching the elevator, with its burden of boxes and cops, slowly descend and disappear from view. He couldn't help but think that our ability to continue publishing was vanishing with them.

The cops, though, had missed something. Under the shipping table, not immediately visible, were two long cardboard boxes containing the computer cards that generated our subscription list. Rick shouted out in glee when he found them — we had a way of reaching our supporters. Perhaps this wouldn't close us down.

On January 5, 1978, Ed Jackson, Ken Popert, and I, as officers of Pink Triangle Press (the name under which *The Body Politic* had incorporated as a non-profit), were charged with using the mails "for the purpose of transmitting indecent, immoral or scurrilous matter to wit: The December 1977–January 1978 issue of the Body Politic journal, contrary to Section 164 of the Criminal Code of Canada." We were commanded, in Her Majesty's name, to appear at police headquarters at 590 Jarvis Street on January 10 to be photographed and fingerprinted and then to appear in provincial courtroom 21 at Old City Hall on January 20 "to be dealt with according to law."

The Trial

THAT JANUARY 20, 1978, court date was merely a formality, necessary to set the wheels of justice in motion. There were other legal skirmishes — a challenge to the legitimacy of the search warrant went all the way to the Supreme Court and died there — but the actual trial began almost a year later, on January 2, 1979, in a small courtroom in Old City Hall. A week long, it would convulse the city, pinning a harsh spotlight on newly elected mayor John Sewell and providing a feast for the media, who turned up daily and who clamoured on the second day to have the trial moved to a room large enough to accommodate them. The request was granted — a move to courtroom 34 allowed the press to sit in the seats usually reserved for the jury, an irony we appreciated given that many of us believed that the charges had been provoked by articles in the *Toronto Sun*. Ed Jackson, Ken Popert, and I sat on chairs facing Judge Sydney Harris in the small, fenced-off area reserved for the accused. Our lawyer, Clayton Ruby, was at a table nearby. The court clerk read the charges. We stood and were asked, one by one, how we pleaded. I think we were all aware that our voices had to be firm and loud enough to be heard by the judge, the court reporter, Crown Attorney Jerome Wiley, the press, and the many supporters, some wearing Pink Triangle pins, who were sitting behind us in the body of the court. "Not guilty," we each of us said, I think with credible conviction.

Only other members of the collective and a handful of supporters knew that those pleas were not a foregone conclusion. We'd been offered deals. The Crown, it seems, did not want to go to trial and offered, through Ruby, several relatively painless ways of avoiding one: plead guilty, said the Crown, and all will be well. There will be no jail term, no fine, perhaps an admonishment, a suspended sentence at worst. We might be asked to sign a peace bond, a promise to be on good behaviour for a certain period of time — surely the most anodyne of punishments. Those offers prompted vigorous debates, but there seems to be no record of them, no minutes taken of one of the most politically significant decisions we made.

Ed remembers several of us thrashing the issue out at Ruby's home on Bedford Road. He and partner Harriet Sachs had just finished dinner, their infant daughter, Emma, asleep in a baby basket. (All grown up now as Emma Ruby-Sachs, she's a lawyer herself, a lesbian, a published novelist, and involved for years with Avaaz, the international advocacy group.) I recall one of the discussions happening in the front room of our communal house at 48 Simpson Avenue, with Ruby sitting on the floor, offering advice but waiting for us to decide. He recommended that we accept a deal — he recognized that we saw the case as an attack on the freedom of the press, but his job was to mitigate damages and uncertainties. If we chose to go to trial, he would defend us to the best of his ability, and we might win. But we might lose, and if we did, we would have criminal records, and the press might face a crippling fine. Accepting a deal would mean the Body Politic Free the Press Fund could stop raising money to pay Ruby's substantial fees. (The fund was legally and financially independent from the paper. Only five of its ten directors were from the collective, and the money it raised was held in trust by a lawyer, available only to cover legal costs. None of the $100,000 it eventually raised was used for *TBP's* operating expenses.) The purely rational choice, it was tempting. As well, the public hysteria around discussions of intergenerational relationships might weigh heavily on any judge's mind and incline him to be punitive. (We found out much later that, though Judge Sydney Harris tended to favour the accused, he was known as "Syd Vicious" when it came to sentencing. Still, with a background that included support for the Ontario Human Rights Code and the U.S. civil rights movement, he seemed the ideal adjudicator for our case. It was rumoured that he had asked for it.)

I don't recall that any collective member fervently supported a guilty plea, though Ken flirted with the idea for a short time. I do remember that Chris Bearchell, the only woman on the collective at the time, was passionately and articulately opposed, and her fervour may have clinched the decision not to accept any deal. She would summarize her arguments in writing for the December 1978/January 1979 issue, the one immediately before the trial began — "Down to the Wire" was the cover story. I believe the final decision was unanimous, though I have to admit that I participated in bad faith — I had privately decided that I would plead not guilty no matter what decision the collective came to. It chilled my blood to imagine myself whispering a shameful, "Guilty" to a charge of having written an article that was "immoral, indecent and scurrilous." I simply could not have lived with myself if I had. Nor, I felt strongly, could *The Body Politic* continue to be taken seriously as a staunch defender of press freedom.

Chris Bearchell was short, alternating between chubby-cute and obese, physically more limber than one might expect (she could shoot

out a karate kick that stopped mere centimetres from its target),
a devotee of weed, slovenly in her work habits, politically astute and
impassioned; for a period when I knew her at *TBP*, she worked for
the Girl Guides of Canada, an unlikely connection that amused her
as much as the rest of us. She could work with men at a time when
lesbian separatism was a significant force. She liked pornography
when many feminists disdained it, and she went so far as to make
some of her own. I admired her, though her untidy free-for-all of a
desk offended my starchy Euclidean sensibilities. Still, I tried to see
through that purely personal distaste to the long résumé of organizations and causes she bolstered with her energy and smarts. Those
traits found their fiercest expression just a few years later, during
the bathhouse raid riots of February 6, 1981.

IF YOUR CAUSE IS noble and the issue controversial, there's something exhilarating about being on trial. We, the accused, were the
stars in a drama with real-life consequences for us personally, for
the publication we'd helped build, and for society at large. One
couldn't help but feel under a spotlight. Each day's testimony added
to the level of suspense. Each day's "perp walk" down the steps of
Old City Hall made the evening news. As far as drama went, the
cast list couldn't have been better. Clayton Ruby, our lawyer, was
well known for his progressive views and was celebrated as a civil
rights litigator. The Crown, Jerome Wiley, seemed intent on modelling himself on a macho television lawyer, pacing about the court,
occasionally flipping into the air a pen that he hoped to casually
catch. (He often missed, which meant having to bend over and pick
it up off the floor.) He took to leaning on the jury box, addressing
the media seated there as if they were in fact the jury. Judge Harris,
who came across as everyone's favourite uncle, occasionally made
jokes and then castigated courtroom spectators for laughing at

them. ("This is a trial," he said once, "concerned with unlawful use of the mails, and I spell that M-A-I-L-S.") Courtroom artists took our likenesses, as Jane Austen might have said. (My first non-photographic portrait issued forth from courtroom 34.) After a year of anxiety, of deals offered and refused, of the daily pressures associated with continuing to publish a monthly magazine, the trial, which I had been dreading, became a strange holiday, a period of enforced and welcomed passivity. Perhaps not for Ken — a telephone death threat meant that he had a police escort for one of the trial days, with him even for bathroom visits. All the preliminary work had been done by the Free the Press Fund: defence witnesses contacted and secured, money raised, endorsements arranged for and published. Now, we didn't have to do anything but turn up in court each day. Now, we didn't have to be anyone but the accused — vile perverts or freedom fighters, depending on your take, but the choices were clear and, at the time, refreshingly unmodulated.

The prosecution and defence witnesses stood in stark contrast to one another — the famously right-wing versus the equally famous liberal establishment. The Crown proffered Claire Hoy, the vigorously homophobic columnist at the *Toronto Sun*; the defence called on June Callwood, then vice-president of the Canadian Civil Liberties Union and the Writers' Union of Canada. The prosecution trotted out Dr. Allan Long, a clinical psychologist who termed homosexuality a sexual disorder. The defence brought Dr. John Money, an acclaimed sexologist compared at the time to Freud and Kinsey, to the stand; he would much later encounter strong criticism for his views on gender. For the Crown: Reverend Ken Campbell, co-founder of the right-wing religious group Renaissance International, organizer of an anti-gay protest at City Hall on January 7 called a Faith, Freedom and the Family Festival. For the defence: four theologians, including an Anglican minister, a U of T chaplain, a United Church minister, and a professor at the Toronto Graduate School of Theology.

The Crown called seven witnesses to testify. One of my favourite moments in the trial came during Ruby's cross-examination of Campbell, who had a history of pressuring his local school board into banning classic novels like *The Diviners* and *The Catcher in the Rye*. Ruby asked whether Campbell was aware that Socrates was known to have been a pedophile. Campbell hesitated.

Ruby: "If Socrates came to apply for a job with the Halton Board of Education, would he be refused?"

Campbell hesitated again.

Ruby, sharply: "Yes or no?"

Campbell: "Yes."

Ruby: "No further questions."

Another bright moment came when Wiley was cross-examining defence witness Thelma McCormack, a sociology professor at York University. Perhaps thinking he might shock her, he asked her what she thought of the article's use of the term "bum-fucking." Her calm answer: "When I was younger it took me years to figure out what the term 'buggery' meant. I find the term 'bum-fucking' admirably clear."

I also have fond memories of Edgar Friedenberg, the American-born educational theorist who moved to Canada in 1970 because of his opposition to the Vietnam War. The author of several books, including *The Vanishing Adolescent* and *Coming of Age in America*, he was an endearing schlep of a gay man, rumpled, a clumsy eater likely to have food stains on his suit. He agreed to be a witness for the defence, but we never used him — he believed that writing could influence people to act, both for right and for wrong, and Ruby didn't want to put him on the stand to face a Crown attempting to build its case on the notion that my article could persuade men to rape boys. I remember the decisive moment well — each day of the trial, Ed, Ken, I, Ruby, and any defence witnesses scheduled for the afternoon had lunch at a nearby Chinese restaurant where we'd evaluate the morning's testimony and strategize for the afternoon. That particular lunch featured Friedenberg and Dr. John Money, the former tucking heartily and messily into his food and slurpily giving all the "wrong" answers to Ruby's pointed questions, the latter a precise and joyless eater almost quivering with distaste at the spectacle of Friedenberg's animal appetites. By the end of lunch, Friedenberg was off the list of witnesses for the defence. I've no doubt it was a wise decision, strategically at least, but I would have loved to see him on the stand. (A year later, he would publish *Deference to Authority: The Case of Canada*, with a paragraph that virtually predicted the trajectory of our case: "The Crown can appeal against any acquittal if it can find a point of law to hang the appeal on, and there always is one; no judge is a perfect legal technician. If it wins, the defendant will not be summarily convicted — if he was acquitted by a jury rather than a judge — but he is forced to submit to a new trial; if he is again acquitted, the process can continue ad infinitum. The Crown has infinite resources; the defendant is usually poor. The pressure on the defendant to bargain for a lower sentence rather than defend himself in court, which is usually great, becomes insupportable.")

ON THE EVENING OF January 3, 1979, the second day of the trial, the Body Politic Free the Press Fund had organized a support rally in the auditorium of what was then the University of Toronto's Faculty of Education building at Bloor and Spadina. By the next morning, the city was in an uproar. Mayor John Sewell, in office just over a month, had agreed to speak, and his five minutes on stage, spotlit by banks of television lights and flashing cameras, plunged the mayor's office into one of the hottest controversies in years. His appearance and speech received widespread public support, but a religious television program, 100 *Huntley Street*, orchestrated a massive call-in to City Hall. Two weeks later, Sewell would be unable to leave his office, except under police guard — the result of "believable and detailed" threats to his life. Ironically, he'd agreed to appear at the rally partly "to help calm the political atmosphere." His speech, in front of a large stage backdrop of *The Body Politic* logo in handcuffs, remains one of the soaring moments in the history of Toronto, and I remember sitting among the five hundred people in that crammed auditorium, thinking, *I can't believe what I'm hearing. I can't believe that an elected official is saying that the gay community contributes to the vitality of the city, that it's important to ensure the freedom of the alternative press, that it's not illegal to be gay, and that it's time to make it clearly legitimate to be gay.* That last statement in particular prompted a roaring ovation and brought the audience to its feet — an audience well aware that the provincial government was not keen on adding protection for gays to the Ontario Human Rights Code. An audience well aware that the police had raided the Barracks bathhouse less than a month earlier, on December 9, 1978, charging twenty-eight men with offences under archaic bawdy house laws. An audience that just a year before had heard Mel Lastman, mayor of North York, announce plans to award American entertainer Anita Bryant a medal for "her crusade against homosexual activists." An audience that had endured Bryant's Toronto visit as part of her "Save Our Children" campaign. An audience that would read in the February 1979 issue of *The Body Politic* that fourteen gay men had been murdered in Toronto since February 18, 1975. (The piece, by Robin Hardy, was called "Overkill," a police term used when a victim is repeatedly stabbed, bludgeoned, or beaten, even after death. Several of the fourteen murders could be so described, and as of the date of the *TBP* article, eight remained unsolved. Of the six that were settled, each involved a different killer, leading to a widespread belief that a serial murderer was responsible for the remaining eight. They had personality traits in common — shy, new to the gay scene, reclusive, quiet, lived alone. The police, however, believed that the murders were unconnected and random.)

The story had its grim echo in January 2019, even to the number of victims. On January 29, Bruce McArthur, a self-employed landscaper, pleaded guilty to eight counts of murder and was sentenced to life imprisonment. Overkill? The victims were dismembered and buried in planter boxes. Traits in common? Most had facial hair or a beard, and six were from South Asia or the Middle East.

Robin Hardy had an interesting career. He had been one of those golden boys in the early years of *The Body Politic*, tall, lanky, with a wide mouth and an eruption of a laugh, dark hair that tumbled down over his brow, and an endearing clumsiness that meant just about anything in his immediate vicinity was in danger of suddenly being knocked over. (It didn't surprise me, really, when I learned he'd died on October 28, 1995, in a hiking accident in Arizona's Tonto National Forest. He was forty-three.) He was a figure out of romance — had abandoned a career in law to be involved in gay activism in Toronto, joined *The Body Politic* in 1977, and negotiated the publication of "Lust with a Proper Stranger," the second article to get us before the courts. (We were acquitted on obscenity charges.) He was always trying to persuade us to be more accessible, to be more like *The Village Voice*, copies of which he was forever brandishing or slapping down on my desk. He produced radio documentaries for the CBC. He worked as a human rights organizer for the Coalition for Gay Rights in Ontario. He was a lust object for me. Perhaps he figured that out. In July 1979, we both attended a gay conference in Ottawa, and, when it was over, he invited me to join him at his cabin for the day. He'd built it himself. On the drive up, he suddenly turned to me and said, with that explosively goofy laugh of his, "You should know I'm planning to seduce you."

The cabin was a ramshackle affair, and I think it was the sole building on a very remote lake. It could only be reached by boat. It was a glowing summer day, and we swam naked and sunbathed and talked the big, important topics he loved, and we were silly together too, which came easily for both of us, and then, while we were still naked, I took out my camera. I filled a roll of film with photos of Robin, each one an enticing segue into intimacy. When there were no more pictures to take, he beckoned me into the cabin, climbed up into the sleeping loft, and drew me in after him. I still have those photographs, up until the moment I had to put down my camera. That there's one missing doesn't matter — in my mind I can still picture him lying back on a ratty sleeping bag, lifting his legs high so I could fuck him, never losing that crazy, loopy grin.

He moved to New York City in 1984. He built a career there as a writer and editor, churning out novel after novel for the adult, young adult, and juvenile markets. He'd write under several pseudonyms. (You'd know the book was by Robin because the "author" would thank him in the acknowledgements for his assistance.) He was a little defensive about it, but he didn't need to be — I so admired the sheer narrative skill he had in him and the intuitive understanding of the needs of the different audiences who bought his books. He tried very hard to write strong female characters into formula fiction ordinarily obsessed with big boobs — he never lost the politics that had been forged in the gay movement.

"Robin Hardy was a lust object for me." Photo: Gerald Hannon

It was the best of the worst of times, with apologies to Charles Dickens. There's no doubt that there were days, weeks, and months when any sensible person would have felt that the push for gay rights was slowly being garrotted. Young people who hear this history are almost universally appalled by what we endured, and they're eager for war stories, eager for details of atrocities I hope they'll never have to confront. We all have them, and we love telling them, but we all, I think, feel a little guilty because it isn't easy to convey how much fun we were having in the midst of all of it. There was so much laughter, sometimes even at ourselves. Life was gay, in the old sense. Life was vivid and extreme and not careful. We weren't isolated — support and donations poured in both locally and internationally. On top of that, we were hanging with the most arcanely talented people of our generation, as became clear when a community of artists centred around Queen West (blocks away from *The Body Politic* office, and then a much scruffier neighbourhood) took to the stage after Sewell's exit had emptied the auditorium of media, which was momentarily disconcerting — in seconds we'd gone from spotlit newsmakers to nobodies. I was ignorant of performance art at the time, and the work made little impression on me, except for the Clichettes, a four-woman team in beehive wigs and white vinyl miniskirts who strutted their way through a lip-synced version of "You Don't Own Me." It brought down the house. Looking back, I realize what a stellar list of performers were on the stage that night: Lorraine Segato, General Idea, Lisa Steele, Randy and Berneche, Marion Lewis and Andy Patterson, Clive Robertson — all people who were creating what made Queen West, at least for a time, the heart of a vibrant, youthful arts scene.

I spoke that night from the stage, with Ken and Ed on either side of me. (I was briefly cranky at Ken's decision to eschew our jacket-and-tie courtroom drag and opt for something less formal.) I was nervous and too soft-spoken and concerned that the lectern seemed to be sinking under its own weight. It wasn't a long speech — I couldn't comment on the trial, being one of the accused. I could speak to community, though, to the people packed into the auditorium. "Though the arm of authority very often has reached out to stifle the voice of dissent, and has often shamefully succeeded," I said, "it has never stopped its heart. All of us are that heart tonight, and we won't be stopped." I stood there like a deer in the headlights through the roar of applause, until Ken had the presence of mind to grab one of my hands, and that prompted Ed to grab the other, and we stood there, arms raised in the classic victory pose, and knew that we would be back in courtroom 34 the next morning amidst the furor that would be generated by Sewell's speech. And furor there was. The remaining three days of the trial passed in a haze of headlines, television and radio newscasts, and photo ops.

Body Politic defendants at the Free the Press rally, Jan. 3, 1979.

My emotional landscape became a mix of bravado and a growing uncertainty. Had we been fools not to accept a deal?

WE WERE BACK IN court on January 16 for summation arguments by both Ruby and the Crown. It was a long and boring day of competing legal citations. I became dissociated from the proceedings. It's odd how one can be at trial, realize intellectually how important the outcome will be both personally and professionally, and find one's attention wandering. Judge Harris paid attention, though, closely questioning both the defence and Crown. Once Ruby and Wiley had finished, Judge Harris said he would render judgment on February 14, 1979. We would find out our fate on Valentine's Day.

AND WHO WERE THESE two men whose fates were now so inextricably linked to mine? Ed Jackson had been my friend since we were hired on the same day in 1968 to teach ESL. He was now working full-time for *TBP*, but without a salary. He wanted the job that badly, and he managed on savings from a previous job in education. At the time of the trial, we lived communally with two others at 48 Simpson Avenue in the city's Riverdale district. I was still with my lover, Robert Trow, though Ed's relationship with Merv Walker had ended, and student nurse Billy Sutherland (who died in 2019) had moved in. I would write about Ed in more detail in the magazine's tenth anniversary issue (January/February 1982), describing how his insatiable need to know made the news department "the most labour intensive section of the paper. People are called and called again, contacts and sources cultivated and stroked. He *thinks* like a journalist … He is a tireless talker. He smiles — a lot — and pushes people into that conversational corner they feel most comfortable in: talking about themselves…. The magazine's outward thrust into the community has often been his, tilting it away from sounding like the production of a group of academics with time on their hands." He's still a tireless talker. He can also be waspish, with an unerring sense of where to sting. We are still the best of friends.

The cover of the tenth anniversary issue shows a photograph of thirty-nine happy, celebratory men and women, the collective members and volunteers we could pull together for a photo shoot. Ken Popert, mustachioed like most of the men, is so positioned that the handcuffs dangling from his belt are clearly visible. A B&D top, he wanted his tastes public — he said once that he used to let his politics dictate his erotic life but found both were improved when that influence was reversed.

At the time of that anniversary issue, he was a full-time staffer on a half-time salary of $4,500 a year. I wrote about him too in that issue. "He is possessed of the coolest, most clinical intelligence of anyone on the paper. It has its drawbacks. You will sometimes hear from Ken an argument that is utterly clear and irrefutable — but bloodless, and true to everything but the way people operate. He once told me, in jest, that he wanted to become human. By that I think he meant what tantalized many more of us from time to time — a desire to step off the gay lib professional treadmill, to find time … for the bars, baths, brunches and parties that made up the community of options for many urban gay men," I said.

"Ken will never be really popular," I continued. "His sense of humour is such a fine dance on the edge of the abyss that it makes people nervous. At his worst, he can be cruel and mean-spirited. At his best, he can make the whole tragicomic business of being gay in Canada in 1981 mostly comic. ('How's Art,' he asked Ed Jackson, who was just off the phone from a conversation with Toronto's moribund mayor, Art Eggleton, 'still imitating life?')"

He's an acquired taste, and I seem to have acquired it. For years, we dined together once a month after Pink Triangle Press board meetings. He's still the smartest person I know.

KEN HAD A COMPETITOR in the brains department at *The Body Politic*, though he and Rick Bébout differed widely in their social manners. Rick's inclination was to be conciliatory, Ken's to be archly confrontational. They balanced each other, and, though they didn't always agree, they respected each other's choices and strengths.

Rick Bébout had arrived in Toronto in 1969, nineteen years old, a draft resistor who had fled his small hometown of Ayer, Massachusetts. Like so many American draft resistors, he fell in love with this town and this country. He ended up knowing more Canadian history than any Canadian I knew. He even added the acute accent to his surname, changing the pronunciation from *bee-bout* to *bay-boo*.

I can't remember when I first met him. We must have crossed

paths before 1977, when he became involved with *The Body Politic*. He began by editing one news story. He did it well, and it wasn't long before he was doing a good deal more. With the help and guidance of volunteer graphic designers, he took a scrappy counterculture rag and turned it into the best-designed gay publication in North America. On top of that, he wrote. He edited. He wrote promotional copy for ads. He could typeset (a two-finger whiz). He could administer. He seemed to have his hand in everything, and he wasn't technically qualified to do any of it. He didn't have a university degree (before *The Body Politic*, he'd worked in a bookstore, at a library, and — a job he grew to hate — as part owner and full-time slave of a bakery targeting the Rosedale bourgeoisie). "No credentials, no permission" — that phrase became his favourite advice to aspiring activists.

He was a control freak. He prepared for meetings by writing long, articulate, thoughtful, and persuasive memos. As a former lover once told me, his reaction to Rick was always a mixture of awe and irritation. I understood that. You were in awe and you were irritated for the same reasons: because he was smarter than you, better read, more thoughtful, more strategic. It probably made it worse that he didn't flaunt it. He wasn't a snob — he worshipped competence. You could be a dancer at Remington's (a Yonge Street strip bar), a waiter, or a prof, but all that mattered to him was that you did your job well. If you did, he was yours.

He and I were not intimates, though for the decade that began with his arrival at *The Body Politic* in 1977, our lives were entwined in ways that not even lovers could compete with. We worked together every day. Rarely took a day off. We'd pull one all-nighter after another together, be near delirious with exhaustion together, giddy with lack of sleep together, dozily happy together as we'd pile into a cab, often at dawn, clutching the precious box of flats we were

Rick Bébout called his time working at *The Body Politic* "the best years of his life."
Photo: Gerald Hannon

taking to the printer. He often called those the best years of his life. They were mine, too. I think they were for all of us.

FEBRUARY 14, 1979. JUDGMENT day. Courtroom 34 was packed with press and supporters — we knew that, whatever the verdict, we'd be splashed all over the evening news and the next morning's newspapers, a media environment that can generate considerable self-importance if you're at the centre of it. (To my shame, I'd told my partner, Robert Trow, how I'd turn to him, in the event of a guilty verdict, and blow a kiss as I was being led off to jail. Such insouciance, such nobility!)

We stood when Judge Harris entered the courtroom and took his seat. He looked down at us. "The defendants may be seated," he said. "This will take a while." Indeed, it did. It took Harris an hour and a half to read his forty-five-page judgment, and my emotions skittered wildly about, half the time sensing he was going to convict, half the time feeling that he would acquit. He ended with, "Since the word 'immoral' being undefined does not establish an

Defendants with lawyer Clayton Ruby after acquittal, Feb. 14, 1979.
Photo: Bill Loos

acceptable area for lawful action, and that neither indecent nor scurrilous apply to either Exhibit One as a whole or the article therein primarily objected to by the Crown, it follows that each of the accused is Not Guilty of this charge and I so find."

The court exploded into cheers and applause that became a standing ovation as the three of us left the defendants' table and were swept into the arms of jubilant supporters. I was giddy with delight. We'd won, and won decisively. The judge had described *TBP* as a "serious journal of news and opinion." He read long sections of the article into the court record, including the entire preface and conclusion. He declared that "were 'immorality' the only offence alleged here, I would dismiss the charge without hesitation." That was a decision so provocative that Ruby muttered to me, as we crossed Queen Street to the hotel where we'd arranged to hold a press conference, "The Crown is sure to appeal. There's going to be an appeal." He was right, of course; but, for the moment, we revelled in the bliss of it and were a little cocky with the media at the press conference and wildly exuberant with our supporters at a celebratory party that night at the gay bar Buddies, then at Church and Gerrard. The media followed us there, and I was described by them as indulging in "long, smoldering kisses," and indeed I was, as many as I could get.

THOSE CONGRATULATORY KISSES WOULD have to last me many more years spent in litigation. On March 6, 1979, less than a month after our acquittal, the attorney general launched an appeal. On February 6, 1980, we arranged for a full-page ad in *The Globe and Mail*, signed and paid for by eight hundred supporters, headed: "We urge the Attorney-General of Ontario to drop the appeal against *The Body Politic*. Not guilty means not guilty." The next day, County Court Judge George Ferguson heard the appeal, and on February 29, 1980, he ordered the case sent back to trial, citing many errors of law in Judge Harris's acquittal. On March 7, we appealed Ferguson's decision to the Ontario Court of Appeal. That went all the way to the Supreme Court of Canada, who refused to hear our case. In December 1981, the word came down: we would stand trial a second time, on the same charges, on May 31, 1982. On May 7, 1982, two police officers raided our offices, and on May 10, the Crown charged the entire collective with publishing obscene material, in this case a piece by the pseudonymous Angus MacKenzie called "Lust with a Proper Stranger," an article concerning "the etiquette of proper fist-fucking." There were nine of us listed as collective members for the allegedly offensive issue: Roger Spalding, Ed Jackson, Stephen MacDonald, John Allec, Chris Bearchell, Rick Bébout, Tim McCaskell, Ken Popert, and me. The charges felt like a sucker punch, coming just three weeks before the retrial for "Men Loving Boys Loving Men." I'm not a paranoid person, but I couldn't help thinking they were really out to get us. (In the background, as a kind of litigation obbligato, we continued our efforts to have the material seized by the police returned to our office. None of it, save a copy of *TBP*, had been entered as evidence at trial.)

The second trial, in courtroom 503 at College Park before Judge Thomas Mercer, went on for three and a half days, the Crown entering no new evidence and calling no witnesses. We called fifteen. There was no excitement, no spectacle — it felt as if the Crown was more interested in grinding us down and bankrupting us than in seeking an actual conviction. In any case, they didn't get it: Mercer acquitted Ken, Ed, and me on the spot after the Crown's final arguments on June 3. He acquitted Pink Triangle Press, charged separately, on June 15. On July 13, the Crown appealed that acquittal — but not that of the three of us. We, at least, were finally off the hook, except for the obscenity charges related to "Lust with a Proper Stranger." It was now triple jeopardy — Clayton Ruby called our case "the most appealed summary case in the history of mankind," and even *The Globe and Mail* took note. A July 19 editorial asked, "Does the Attorney General's office intend to go on prosecuting until it finds a court that will convict? Does it think that is justice?"

On November 1, 1982, the nine collective members charged with obscenity for publishing "Lust with a Proper Stranger" went on trial, in College Park again, and again before Judge Mercer. In the morning, after asking us to stand, he acquitted us on the spot. After lunch, he acquitted the press, charged separately from the collective. All that was left now was the appeal of the second acquittal of "Men Loving Boys Loving Men." On September 15, 1983, when that case came before the courts, it was rejected. The Crown had thirty days to appeal that decision, but they let the clock run out. We'd won, on every front.

There was a coda — the police still held most of the material seized on December 30, 1977. On April 15, 1985, they brought it back — a mere seven years, three months, and sixteen days later. As we reported in the June 1985 issue: "None of the material was ever introduced as evidence in the long series of trials and appeals which, after six years, resulted in the magazine's full acquittal. Long-time staff member Rick Bébout recalled that on the day the material was taken away he feared we'd never publish again. A few hours after signing the waybill for the cops' final special delivery, he took the 114th issue off to press."

That series of legal victories sparked the creation of a national gay holiday — February 14, the day of our acquittal at the first trial, was to be hereafter known and celebrated as Pink Triangle Day, or so said a resolution adopted July 1, 1979, by the final plenary of the seventh annual Conference for Lesbians and Gay Men, meeting in Ottawa. (Although I received a card and a dozen pink roses on February 14, 2019, the fortieth anniversary, this date remains a holiday for only the activist cognoscenti. Valentine's won out.) I also had to accept the fact that, despite many years of journalism, I would be most remembered as the author of MLBLM. As one friend cleverly put it in a satirical alphabet written for my sixtieth birthday, "M is for Men Loving Boys Loving Men/N is for Nothing of Interest since then."

8

Bathhouse Raids of 1981

· ·

FOR MANY YEARS, I was an ardent bathhouse patron, particularly in winter, when anonymous sex in city parks was not an option. I loved the ease of it all — choose one of the many establishments (based perhaps on propinquity, perhaps on vibe), turn up, choose to rent either a room or a locker, get undressed, wrap a towel around my middle, and start to cruise, either by walking the hallways or reclining languorously in my room. The room's light would be lowered, in the days before dimmer switches were common in bathhouses, by pulling a sock partly over the bulb. A room cost more than a locker but guaranteed a private place to have sex if and when cruising paid off. I most often chose a locker — I was young then, in good shape, so likely enough to be invited to join someone in his room, the invitation extended via a lingering glance as I passed the door or perhaps a subtle rearrangement of his towel, one that provided a glimpse of the delights beneath. There was almost always a dark room or a maze, a space you could use if you had to get it on with someone else who had chosen a locker. It meant sex while standing, which had its own excitements, though it could also mean that third, fourth, and more parties would try to join the fun by caressing my body or imposing their erections without so much as a by-your-leave. I could subtly try to discourage that, but often I had to just put up with it. There are worse fates.

I can't remember my first visit, but it was probably to the Roman Sauna Baths at 740 Bay Street at College. After a renovation in 1978, it became the much grander Romans II Health and Recreation Spa and featured a burly masseur whose attentions I would occasionally pay for. (There was no happy ending, but the rubdown, complete with "accidental" brushings against my penis, put me in the mood to cruise.) I would also patronize Club Toronto, part of an American chain. Located in a Victorian-era townhouse at 231 Mutual Street, it was the scene of one of my more memorable New Year's Eves. I went there with my friend Gerry Oxford, both of us somewhat drunk after a boisterous, champagne-fuelled party, only to discover, not surprisingly, that there weren't many other lads to choose from. I ended up with a cute young man who wanted a scene — we were to be brothers, get down on our knees beside the cot in my room, and, with hands reverentially folded, say our prayers. We were also to be watched by a friend of his, who would stand on the room's only chair. We knelt naked beside each other, he muttering away unintelligibly, I reciting the Hail Mary, his friend standing on the chair and slowly jerking off. Our prayers over, we slipped onto the cot and began having sex, the boy on the chair getting more and more frenetic until he started shouting, "Cunt, cunt, cunt" at the top of his lungs and came, shooting semen across the room. And so I welcomed in the new year.

There have been many bathhouses in Toronto, not all of them explicitly designed for gay men to meet, socialize, and have sex. The Royal Floating Baths, back in the 1830s, seemed to want a posh clientele, offering a drawing room and a reading room. The Oak Leaf Steam Baths, at 216 Bathurst Street, was patronized largely by elderly Eastern European men, though it also attracted curious gay men and hustlers looking for business. (I went once and made the mistake of cruising a young man who turned out to be a hustler. "I'm commercial," he was very quick to say when I hit on him.) Others I patronized: the Back Door Gym, where I had sex with CITY-TV celebrity interviewer Brian Linehan (he was curiously homely but had a very sculpted body), the Barracks, the Hot Tub Club, Library Baths (where I had a brief stint as an employee), the Richmond Street Health Emporium, Spa Excess, and St. Marc's Spa.

It's not surprising that the bathhouses would eventually attract the attention of the police. Bawdy houses were illegal, and though prostitution played a minimal role in bath culture, much common bathhouse activity would be captured by the part of the law that forbade the practice of "acts of indecency," undefined in the Criminal Code.

The police struck for the first time on December 9, 1978, just a few weeks before the *Body Politic* trial began. They chose to hit the Barracks — one of the raunchier establishments, set up to appeal to a leather and S&M clientele — charging twenty-eight men as either "keepers" or "found-ins." This event turned out to be a rehearsal.

The evening of Thursday, February 5, 1981, Ken Popert, Ed Jackson, and I were working late at the office on the fifth floor at 24 Duncan Street. At some point, Ken left to go home; not long after, as Ed and I were preparing to leave, the phone rang. It was an acquaintance, Richard Mehringer, whose then partner had noticed several police cars parked near the Barracks as he left the establishment. Once he got home, he told Richard, and the two of them decided to drive by and check out what was happening. It was clear that a raid was in progress. They raced home and called *TBP*, knowing that we often worked very late and there'd be a good chance of catching someone in. We knew we had to be on the scene, so I grabbed my camera, and Ed and I headed out, though before doing so I called Ken and Tim McCaskell to alert them.

And now begins the *Rashomon* of bathhouse-raid narratives. Each of us has a slightly different memory of what happened.

The "Rage" issue of *TBP* (March 1981) reports that cab driver Adrian Hamel picked me up and drove me from bath to bath, and that someone named Tony did the same for Ed. Adrian says that he didn't pick me up until we met at the Club, and he drove me only from there to the Richmond. Ken remembers being surprised that his partner, Brian Mossop, was not at home when he got there, though he figured out why after I called him. He believes he stayed at home until Brian was released and returned. Brian recalls that Ken wasn't at home when he arrived, figured he'd gone to 52 Division, followed, and did find Ken there, and me as well. I'm convinced I was never at 52 Division. I remember returning to the office once we'd ascertained that most, if not all, of the baths were being raided. Ed is convinced we didn't but went home, knowing we'd have to be up early. What follows is an approximation.

When Ed and I left the office, we must have hailed a cab — it would have taken at least half an hour to walk to Romans II, our first stop, and we didn't want to waste time. When we arrived, we found a police officer standing at the door. (Even given the outrage being perpetrated inside, we remained homosexual enough to register how cute he was.) He wouldn't provide any information, so we went, probably on foot, to the Club at Carlton and Mutual — there the raid was clearly in progress. When I'd phoned Tim McCaskell, I'd told him to go to the Club, so we probably ran into each other. There was a paddy wagon parked on Mutual Street, and men were being led out of the building and told to get in. At that point, a cab pulled up — the driver turned out to be an acquaintance, Adrian Hamel, who figured out what was going on, told his customer to get out, and asked me, "Where do you want to go next?"

"Richmond Street," I told him. I got in. He didn't turn the meter on, and we sped down to the Richmond Street Health Emporium, the city's newest and best-appointed bathhouse, one that featured rooms on several floors and a large pool. Police surrounded the doorway, and there was a waiting paddy wagon. I would find out later, through Norman Hatton's photographs, that the police inside were on a destructive rampage — smashing doors and lockers and terrorizing the patrons. I would also find out later that 150 police officers, part of the code-named Operation Soap, had descended on four bathhouses, arresting 266 men as found-ins in common bawdy houses and twenty men as keepers. And I would find out later that my lover, Robert Trow, was one of them. He was arrested and charged, though he was there in his capacity as an employee of the Hassle Free Clinic, providing free VD checkups. Even ignorant of that, I felt a strange combination of rage and defeat — rage for the obvious reasons, but defeat because this felt like the Big One, the attack that would crush us, that oh yes, we'd be brave and fight back, but we would be smothered by the intractability of the police and the justice system and its political masters.

Then I remembered the plain brown envelope.

Not long before, one had arrived in the mail. There was no return address. I don't think it was addressed to me personally. It contained a handful of papers with no apparent theme, but one sheet stood out: it listed the home telephone numbers of a selection of Ontario cabinet ministers, Attorney General Roy McMurtry's among them. Ed and I returned to the office. There were phone calls to make, even though it was something like 2:30 in the morning. He began by calling other *TBP* collective members; I called Roy McMurtry. The phone rang several times before a woman answered.

"I want to speak to Mr. McMurtry," I said. (We weren't on a first-name basis, and I didn't want to be impertinent.)

There was a silence. Then: "What's this about?"

"It's about the fact that every gay bath in this city has been raided by the police, that I'm assuming the word came down from him, that he should know the rage that's out there, that he should lose a little sleep right now hearing about it from me, that he should —"

"Can you hold?" she said, interrupting me.

"Yes."

She never returned to the phone. Nor did she hang up. Perhaps the call was being traced. In any case, I waited in silent rage for some five minutes and then hung up. I tried the number again a few days later and got the message, "This number is no longer in service."

Years later, when McMurtry had been sanctified as the judge who okayed gay marriage, I asked him in an interview whether he remembered that phone call. He didn't.

ED MADE IT INTO the office first the next morning. He knew the place would be information central, and it was. The phones rang nonstop — found-ins in despair, others wanting to know what they could do to help, media wanting comments, community organizations wanting to know if a response was being planned. To that last question, all we knew was that something had to happen. Had to. But what? Somehow, we managed to organize a meeting (via landlines alone!) with available community representatives for noonish at our office. (George Hislop used to joke that if you wanted to get information out quickly, you could telephone, telegraph, or tell a fag.) I can't remember everyone who turned up. I believe Peter Maloney and Peter Bochove and possibly Jerry Levy were there, representing the bathhouse owners. For sure Brent Hawkes, pastor with the Metropolitan Community Church, was. There was a representative from the Coalition for Gay Rights in

Ontario and the Right to Privacy Committee. Several collective members, including me, Ken, Ed, and Chris Bearchell.

The meeting was tense, with three possible options up for discussion. We could hold a press conference to express our outrage and tour the media through the badly damaged bathhouses. We could organize a demonstration, perhaps for the following weekend. Or we could risk trying to arrange a demo for that very evening, Friday, February 6, 1981. I can't remember if the decision was unanimous, but we chose option three: a demonstration that night. I was asked to typeset the flyer we planned to distribute through the bars: "Enough is enough. Protest. Yonge and Wellesley. Midnight tonight." (I was so consumed by the urgency of it that I didn't think to add the date, and no one else noticed either.) We ordered four thousand copies from our usual Quick Print shop. By 4:00 p.m. the organization was in place — we'd arranged for a sound truck, volunteers were charged with distributing the leaflets throughout all the gay bars, and marshals had been recruited from graduates of the gay self-defence course. We'd done our best, but the same question, unexpressed, troubled everyone's minds: Would anyone turn up? As Rick Bébout wrote later, "It was winter. We were issuing a call to come out into the freezing dark. I wondered if it would work. This was about the baths, after all, about sex, about things that many gay people, even if modestly out, might still want to keep in the closet. Would they come out now, into the cold, for this?"

Famously, they did, though my heart sank when I arrived, just short of midnight, at the corner of Yonge and Wellesley. There were perhaps three hundred people, and though they were fierce and boisterous and shouting, "No more raids" and "Stop the cops," I wanted more. Fresh in many minds, including mine, were the White Night Riots in San Francisco in 1979, the gay community's response to the lenient sentence handed down to former police officer Dan White for the assassinations of Mayor George Moscone and openly gay city supervisor Harvey Milk. It was violent, with extensive property damage, and set a new standard for an activist response that was relentless and passionate and right. The San Francisco riots had drawn thousands, but I didn't expect Toronto to come anywhere near that. We'd managed only about four hundred at a daytime protest about the police raid on the Barracks a few years earlier. Could we do better than that on a freezing February midnight?

I didn't have long to wait. Over the next half hour, that number grew by at least a thousand. I was in the midst of it as it swelled to two thousand and then three, trying to balance my desire to be just a screaming participant with the need to capture it all in photographs for *TBP*. I did take photos, and many of those images have become iconic, reproduced repeatedly whenever there's an anniversary. I knew I'd have to write about it too, and I did, and because the text is so charged with the fervour of the moment, I quote from it here.

It was the night Toronto came closer to a full-scale riot than it has in the last ten years. It was the night when three thousand people came within minutes of breaking down the doors of the Ontario legislature. It was the night the main street of Canada's largest city belonged to us, and nobody — not even the police — seemed to be able to do anything about it.

It was midnight, February 6 — just 24 hours after the largest mass arrest since the 1970 invocation of the War Measures Act.

It was midnight, February 6 — just 24 hours after what George Hislop has called the gay equivalent of "Crystal Night in Nazi Germany — when the Jews found out where they were really at."

Civil disobedience was in the air, people were drunk on the prospect of it, on the prospect of power over turf we've liked to say belongs to us, but realize is really ours only grudgingly, and on loan.

Civil disobedience was in the air, and speaker Brent Hawkes of the MCC said this was the time for it, this was the night when, legal or not, we'd take over the streets. *TBP*'s Chris Bearchell hit the crowd with the slogan that would be taken up over and over again: "No more shit! No more shit!"

The scene is surreal. Yonge Street, usually a river of bumper-to-bumper traffic, is an empty canyon echoing to the shouts, screams and whistles of an advancing crowd the full width of the street. The occasional car the police haven't stopped somehow makes it onto the street, stops, can't turn around, gets swallowed up. A man jumps up onto the roof of one of them and does a disco turn before leaping back into the crowd.

I went on to write about the near fist-fight between cops and demonstrators, the queer-baiting group of straight guys who tried to block the advancing thousands and failed, the astonishing sight of 52 Division, the building itself, completely surrounded by cops, 195 of them, standing shoulder to shoulder. The attack on the Ontario Legislature, a focus of a particular hatred in the previous six weeks since all three political parties had backed away from an opportunity to legislate rights for gay people. We got there before the cops did.

… and for a few thrilling minutes dozens of bodies throw themselves repeatedly against the doors, and even people halfway back in the crowd report seeing the doors vibrating in the probing light of the television cameras, and hearing the hollow booming of bodies thudding against the barriers.

But that sound is the signal for the cops to come down with a viciousness they'd kept in check till then. A wedge of some twenty officers forces its way through the crowd, and punching, kicking and shoving they beat the crowd back. One man's face is bloodied. Another man is shouting that his sister has been hit over and over again by a cop. But somehow the clash has left both sides stunned, and organizers take the opportunity to encourage people to leave — in groups, for their own safety.

The raids and that night's riot brought people into the streets whose only involvement until then might have been the occasional donation to a community charity. Ironically, the police attempt to

Banner leading the bath raid protest, Feb. 20, 1981. One of my photos most often reprinted to illustrate the history of LGBTQ+ community resistance.
Photo: Gerald Hannon

crush our growing movement only made it stronger. We developed organizational muscle prepared to face future raids, should they happen — and they did. We made connections with sympathetic lawyers who tracked and fought the charges in court. We sought out allies in the labour movement, civil rights organizations, and the art world — Margaret Atwood brought the house down during a support rally at the St. Lawrence Market with a faux naïf speech, innocently asking what the police had against cleanliness. And somehow, somehow, we managed to continue publishing *The Body Politic* and *Xtra*, a biweekly tabloid we started in 1984 to sop up advertising revenues and broaden the Toronto readership.

I wrote for both publications, remained principal photographer, handled — or, rather, mishandled — the finances, and wore several other organizational hats. I was in my forties with no money and few prospects. I was getting tired of the constant struggle to keep the two publications, and myself, financially afloat.

My relationship with Robert Trow ended in 1982, and though we would remain best friends until his death in 2002, our breakup was agonizing. I'd never imagined our relationship might end. I'd thought we were perfect for each other. We shared a passion for music, with me introducing him to opera and him me to the piano repertoire (he played) and chamber music. He had the critical job of handling distribution at *TBP*, which meant he played a crucial role there as well. His passion for community development led him to involvement in public health through his job at the Hassle Free Clinic, where he would pioneer agitating for anonymous HIV testing. Perhaps we were too perfect — I've noted that amorous relationships seem to need some built-in abrasion, a hovering dissonance that highlights the general consonance, a reminder that the edge is the more exciting place to dance.

I would get my fill of dancing at the edge soon enough.

My mother Yvonne and
Robert Trow, mid-1970s.
She eventually came out as
a lesbian, fled an abusive
marriage, and found a
female partner.
Photo: Gerald Hannon

Perhaps it isn't just coincidence, but 1982, the year Robert and I broke up, was also the year he discovered he had been infected with what would become known as HIV. He treated it lightly at the time, made it something of an anecdote. That was just possible then. "Gay cancer" was in the news, but mostly out of New York and San Francisco. Toronto's Hassle Free Clinic was being asked for what little info there was and whether there was a test for it. There wasn't, but Robert volunteered to be a demo patient, offering himself up for palpation of his underarm lymph nodes, a standard test for viral infections. He was in fine health the day the test was done. To his surprise, and the doctor's and staff's embarrassment, his lymph nodes were swollen. This meant he probably had it, whatever "it" turned out to be. "It" got an official scientific name that year as well: AIDS. Acquired Immune Deficiency Syndrome.

The story had been breaking its way slowly into *TBP*, mostly on the page or so we devoted to international news. That changed with *TBP*'s November 1982 issue, with articles by Michael Lynch and Bill Lewis setting the tone for Toronto's community response to AIDS.

They were lovers as well as frequent contributors to *TBP* and lived together in a smartly renovated house on Ross Street near College and Spadina, Bill taking the upper floor and Michael converting the ground floor into an elegant living space suitable for musical entertainments (it featured a grand piano). Michael was American by birth; Bill was from Manitoba. Michael was an academic, poet, and activist; Bill was a scientist. They were well paired for the massive undertaking they'd proposed for the November 1982 issue: two articles, one each, the theme summed up by the cover draw — "The Case Against Panic." The ten-thousand-word piece by Michael was called "Living with Kaposi's" (a rare cancer associated with AIDS). Bill's almost seven thousand words was titled "The Real Gay Epidemic: Panic & Paranoia." The size of the articles, and Michael's insistence they be published together, meant that the authors and their supporters had to contribute money to cover the extra printing costs.

It was money well spent. I think of those articles as setting the rational, scientific approach to a mysterious disease — an approach rare at the time, when the media, both gay and straight, often blamed gay men's lifestyles. As Bill put it, "Everything gay men did that straight men didn't was dragged forth as a possible cause. Abundant sex, poppers, fisting, drugs, ingestion of too much sperm, staying up too late — all have been put forward as an explanation." Michael saw the moralizing not very far below the surface: "Gays are once again allowing the medical profession to define, restrict, pathologize us. What used to be a psychiatric pathology is now an infectious one. ... This panic could never have set in so quickly and so deeply if within the hearts of gay men there weren't already a persistent anti-sexual sense of guilt ready to be tapped."

Rick Bébout, who edited the articles and much later wrote about the reaction to them on his online blog, noted, "Panic ensued nonetheless, American panic the most fervid. The next few issues had nearly four pages of letters responding to Michael Lynch and Bill Lewis, only two from Canada and only two (not the same two) supportive, some full of scathing condemnation."

Noted New York AIDS activist Michael Callen set the tone: "I have to point out that all this 'panic' is because gay men are dying! ... By refusing to see that the promiscuous lifestyle is potentially fatal, we may permit the ultimate triumph of the Moral Majority: we will kill ourselves."

We didn't kill ourselves. On the contrary, we cared for each other. As a community. As individuals.

And we didn't deplore the "promiscuous lifestyle." An early piece by Bill Lewis in *TBP* was called "AIDS: Discounting the Promiscuity Theory." We understood that promiscuity was also an epidemiological plus — we could reach gay men because we knew where to find many: bars and bathhouses. We would have much to tell them about what came to be called "safer sex."

We cared for each other as a community. In March 1983, my old friend and *TBP* colleague Ed Jackson pulled together ten activists, including Michael Lynch and Robert Trow, in response to a call from the Canadian Red Cross. The Red Cross wanted to know what message they could provide to people about AIDS and blood donation. Recognizing that much-needed leadership on the issue of AIDS in Ontario would have to come from the community, Ed decided to call a meeting.

At the meeting, this group of ten formulated a public statement about blood donations, but they also began to plan for some kind of entity that would provide ongoing support for people with AIDS.

This meeting became de facto the first meeting of what would become the AIDS Committee of Toronto. It's still in existence.

We cared for each other as individuals. Bill, who had been getting ill in ways by then all too recognizable, went into Toronto General on Thursday, August 28, 1987. Rick Bébout wrote in his blog, *Promiscuous Affections*: "I visited him on Friday ... He was using an oxygen mask intermittently and threw up his meagre supper while I was there. I'm glad I was there: he was hooked up to an IV and couldn't have got out of bed to find anything to puke into.... Michael was due to pick up Bill's parents at the airport, in from Winnipeg. He asked if I could come back at 11:00 and if no one else was there stay the night."

He didn't have to stay; I was there by then. I'd be there the next three nights, all night. In fact, the nurses began to turn people away: there were too many visitors. Rick remembers, "We had to wear gowns; the more insistent nurses pushed masks and gloves on us too. Michael refused to mask while Bill was conscious." Vigils like this would be repeated dozens of times over the next decade — sometimes met with understanding and compassion by hospital staff. Sometimes not.

Michael arranged a ceremonial gathering on the lawn of the hospital, directly below the window of Bill's room. It was an oddly new-age thing to do — gather together friends, make a circle, hold hands, think loving, healing thoughts. We did it. I felt silly and cynical at first, and then I didn't. I'd sat beside his bed in the hospital intensive care, stroking his hand, feeling that was useless and silly too, but doing it because it was the only consolation open to us. It's an age-old consolation, touching, merely touching. Not many years earlier, before it was clear that the virus could only be transmitted through blood and semen, touching, even casually, would have been forbidden, and visitors and staff alike would have been gowned and masked. Those were the days when some frightened workers would leave food trays at the door, afraid to get too close to an AIDS patient.

Bill Lewis died September 17, 1987, aged thirty-seven. To my surprise, he left me a generous bequest, enough to finance a trip to India a year later with my good friend Gerry Oxford. Bill hadn't talked of India, so that wasn't why we went, but I wanted the trip to include a gesture and settled on writing his name in the Himalayan snow. It seems embarrassingly adolescent now, but at the time it seemed to lend his life a kind of grandeur — those mountains! — while acknowledging its brevity. I walked up, alone, to the snowline in the hills above Srinagar in Kashmir, found a welcoming bank of snow, and wrote his name and dates. It still seems romantically adolescent, even as I write about it here, but there are many kinds of caring, not all of them adult.

WE CALLED OURSELVES THE Lynch Mob with a touch of gallows humour, the family, friends, and colleagues of Michael Lynch who organized a team to provide the kind of care that wasn't available in a hospital. Volunteers weren't hard to come by. Michael had organized or backed groups from academic to activist. A short summary: the Gay Alliance Toward Equality (before he'd ever had sex with a man); the Committee to Defend John Damien; Whitman in Ontario Conference, 1980; Wilde '82; Sex and the State, 1985. He was a founder of the AIDS Committee of Toronto (ACTS, 1983); AIDS Action Now! and the Toronto AIDS Memorial (from 1988); the Toronto Centre for Lesbian and Gay Studies (1990); and Gay Fathers Toronto. His collection of poems, *These Waves of Dying Friends*, was published in February 1989. He was highly respected and much loved.

As many as thirty people were involved, starting in December

1990. Michael wasn't desperately ill at that point, but it seemed smart to get ahead of the game, and the group's arch-organizers, Ed Jackson and Rick Bébout, took that in hand, Ed making sure there'd be someone with Michael twenty-four hours a day, Rick pulling together a manual for the Mob. As he wrote to author and friend Jane Rule, "It's well underway: a fat blue binder with lots of sections: a list of the team with phone numbers; a shift schedule; guidelines on food, medical care, cooking, cleaning up, what to do in emergencies. Imagine a manual for how to run your life if you couldn't: where everything is, using the appliances, what you like and don't like to eat — all the things you take for granted and never imagine having to write down." ACT counsellors Yvette Perreault and Andrew Johnston advised on and coordinated the process, and the manual had a life at ACT for some years after Michael's death.

I began keeping a journal in 1991. It continued until 2018 and covers in some detail the period of Michael's illness, death (July 9, 1991), and memorial service. It is a curious blend of the touching and the trivial, the significant and the silly, and records my sexual exploits as a prostitute with the same level of detail as the changes in Michael's health. (More detail about how I got into sex work in a subsequent chapter.) The January 1, 1991, entry begins with a description of a New Year's Eve party that Michael, Ed, I, and other friends attended, but I interrupt that to describe a sex work client I'd had earlier that evening. I include it here, though many may find it jarring and vulgar. It is important to me to show how ordinary life goes on, even when preparing for a death. The client that afternoon was "a very little South Asian man who said on the phone he'd pay me $25 just to talk with maybe a massage on the second visit. Of course, there was boner action after a few moments chat, and he didn't demur when I suggested he undress, though he kept on T-shirt and underwear, complaining that the room was cold, which it is. I got the undies off in no time though — a good average-sized cock, which looked much larger given that he was child size himself," I wrote. "The eyes of a waif too. But bright, wanting to talk about his obsession, which seems to be touched in places that are rather public. Recounted travelling by bus and the man beside him putting his hand on his cock during the night. I could relate to that. He loved my just rubbing my hand gently over his balls and brushing his cock. I described the delights of David Balfour Park for him, and I think it was somewhere in the depths of that story that he came, preparing himself with a strategically placed tissue. I accepted $25, though I should have pressed for more."

I segue back to Michael and the party, not missing a beat. "It was a fundraiser for the AIDS Memorial, so we paid $10 at the door. Michael sat in a chair beside the tree, doing, as he said, his 'Rose Kennedy number' and he even danced, briefly, with Frank Kostin and John Clintworth and of course one felt oh my gawd a danse macabre and of course one felt like kissing him and crying."

There's something theatrical about that scene, and about the remaining months of Michael's life. I kept almost daily notes, and I turn to them here to try to recapture the pain, the exasperation, the tedium, the humour, and, yes, the love, expressed and experienced over seven months by thirty-some community members, not all gay and only two of them family: his wife, Gail, and his teenage son, Stefan. The following excerpts are chronological, but not always dated. They start in January 1991 and end with Michael's death in July.

Michael seemed rather better, if tired. I was to leave him alone while he worked in bed at his book — I stayed in the front room for quite a while, reading the *National Enquirer* — "Natalie Wood is alive and well and living in Mexico with a matador lover" — but when I went back in I think he'd been dozing since nothing seemed to have been touched. We chatted in a desultory way for a while. I finally saw an opportunity to bring the money/power of attorney issue up and did. Michael is convinced that I have a copy of the papers and that we'd even been to the bank together to see his safety deposit box but we haven't. I think he thinks that we have, and that I've just forgotten. He tells me that everyone bursts out laughing when he tells them he's chosen me as attorney, and the person to make binding decisions on his medical care, or cessation thereof, in the event of his not being able to make them himself. I'm surprised too. Why me? I'm hardly as close to him as half a dozen other people, and however much I may be liked, I don't kid myself that I'm valued for my responsible behaviour. I tried to leave him openings to change his mind — but he doesn't seem to want to, though he said I should think about it for a few days and let him know for sure and of course I don't know if that means he thinks my question means I don't want to do it, or whether that's his graceful way of saying he doesn't want me to do it. I'll say I want to. Anyway, I know where the documents are now and he says he'll get me copies of them and we'll start going over his finances.

It's funny how we all begin chatting and joking among ourselves — the gravity of the deathbed can't hold for long and people become themselves and just socialize. Ed and I went upstairs to start going through the mail on the desk and see what was financial and try to figure out how to deal with it. We finally did get stuff sorted out, with a folder of things to ask Michael about though we never got to that part, or at least

I didn't since I had to leave and it wasn't something we could do with a lot of people there. During our work, Michael had come out to the front room to sit and chat with people, and yelled up at me and Ed that we were whispering and trying to keep things from him. We started talking in shouts.

I don't look forward to this but the awful thing is I sort of wish we could shoot him. It would be so fast and he wouldn't feel a thing. Except who of us could do it?

He's still alert, dozy sometimes, certainly still cantankerous. When I said I was off to the bank, he said, "If you fuck up, you're cut off!" And I said, "From what, honey?" And he said something like, "That's right, you're not getting anything anyway." Which leads me to assume I'm not in the will, which in some ways is a relief since I have this horror of getting rich off the deaths of friends, but on the other hand it would be nice right now to get some money to tide me over since there's no work.

All he wanted was broth. He was in the hospital bed, which had been set up, and looking better I thought and he said he was feeling better because he'd made some decisions. He's stopped taking the drugs, except aspirins and a bit of codeine, and has more or less decided to starve himself to death. Needless to say, painful scene. I became quite tearful and really couldn't control myself very well, and I don't even know why, in a way. Of course, I like Michael and I don't want him to die but it seems like I'm overreacting though I'm not forcing anything. Maybe I'm wrong to feel that that kind of grief is reserved only for your closest friends. Maybe I'm just

stupidly sentimental. Too much opera, maybe? I've wept my
heart out for Cio-Cio San. Michael tried to console me by
running his fingers gently through my hair while I sat beside
the bed and cradled my head on his legs though it suddenly
occurred to me that I was probably crushing them and I said
so and he said I was. He spoke about always having seen
suicide as an option, even when he was much younger, but
not because of unhappiness. Only if he saw himself out of
control. Taking these decisions has meant taking control, and
it's made him happier. I asked if he was mad at the world. He
said he has been, but not now.

Getting him ready for bed was difficult because I had to
change the sheets, which meant getting him out of bed
and then back into it and he's pretty weak. We also tried the
catheter and finally got it to work, and I just can't believe
myself but I started getting a boner while fixing the thing to
his cock. To bed around 12:30 maybe a bit later. He woke me
maybe three in the morning, bad cold attack. I went down
and climbed in with him — not so easy anymore because
the bed is much smaller. I held him while he rattled with
cold — he spoke clearly, not at all like raving, about some
high tech device and a bear. I had no idea what it was about
so I just made agreeing noises.

Saturday morn, the core group meeting. It was more
emotional for Michael than it seemed to be for us — he had
trouble controlling his voice, but then all we had to do was
listen and not cry and maybe ask a question. He talked about
taking decisions, taking control. That he wasn't trying to
hasten the end of his life — I countered that I thought he had

by deciding not to eat and he said that he'd changed his mind somewhat and had decided to eat if he felt like it. He told us that none of us was in his will (Alan Miller and I joked about getting up and leaving at that point); that he had agonized about that but couldn't decide how to apportion money among so many people and just decided to leave Stefan his inheritance and the rest to the Centre for Lesbian and Gay Studies so that finally it filters down to the whole community. He did want us to look around the house, though, and pick some item as a souvenir. Alan is eyeing the same thing I want — that sculpture in the niche on the kitchen barrier wall. Overall, we didn't say much during all of this — people are not up to the sublime and I think everyone was relieved to get on to practical matters and have Andrew talk to us. He is, thankfully, informed, brisk and efficient. He showed me and Stef how to put a monster diaper on Michael — must be strange and embarrassing and even heart-rending for Stef to watch his father, nude and mostly helpless, lie there and be treated like a baby. Stefan has hair on his arms! The world's most protracted puberty is over.

Nurse Mary Lou got me up at 5 a.m. because Michael was asking for me — having a chill, so I lay beside him and cuddled him till 7:30 or so when the nurse came back and told us she was getting ready to leave. I did sleep a bit, I think, even though it's not the most comfortable arrangement.

When Stef came back, we actually had quite a long talk, first time, about how he was handling this, about how nervous he is about the prospect of being an heiress, about how crabbiness has always been an aspect of Michael's character and that most of his friends haven't seen it, but how he, Stef, always has and has been afraid of him. Michael could say "Stefan" in a certain way, says Stef, and he'd get goose bumps. I told him how he always used to frighten me, too, with his judgmentally "daddy" character. We talked a bit about securing more info re suicide, since Stef doesn't want Michael to continue living if his mind goes, and he wants to talk about that option again with him.

I noticed one of his comments in the log — all in caps — I HATE IT WHEN HE'S CRABBY. And Michael is. With me a lot too. With me, about others. And now that he's feeling better, he's starting to worry himself about his finances and I'm going to tell him next time: "Michael. You may have only a few months. Don't spend them worrying about stupid details like whether you might have to spend a few bucks on interest if I miss a Visa payment. I'm taking care of things, but I'm not taking care of them in the way you would because I'm not you."

Robert brought up Michael because M had had a talk with him about my alleged inability to deal with M's dying and Robert's HIV status. Now it's probably true but I'm getting positively sick of having to deal with my "inability" to deal with M. There's nothing left to say except that I'm dealing just fine, as fine as anyone could be and that if my emotions are more on the surface than some that's probably better rather than worse.

Mary Lou, the nurse, woke me at 5 a.m. Michael having one of his chills and wanting me. I crawled in with him, held him. He was shivering so violently that the whole bed was shaking, and its clanking drew Mary Lou in to find out what was happening. M threw up. Mostly phlegm and crap. Mary Lou took over at that point, and I went back to bed, though not too much sleep. Stef came in to get a sputum sample to the hospital. Michael's coughing a lot, and we know what that can mean. I came in to find him sitting in the darkened room beside his father -– something about it was immensely tender and I can't quite put my finger on it. Perhaps that he still had his winter coat on. That he had just one hand on M's leg. That neither was saying anything.

A Michael care team meeting at ACT in the afternoon. Promised for 2 to 3 and I left at 3:45 at the break! Way too much check-in poop. I don't care how other people are handling this, and it would be impertinent if they cared how I was handling it. Yvette and Andrew had valuable things to say, and they're smart articulate people who say them well and that was worth it. And Stef was good too — he's someone whose feelings I do care about, and he's analytical as well as emotional.

We let off a lot of steam about Michael and his crabby ways, some of the humour verging on rather dark. Stef talked after he went to bed about how much M is driving him nuts. The rest of us played our long-rehearsed roles: Alan mostly quiet, occasionally obscure, often irreverent; Rog silent; Ed officious, slightly barbed, a control-queen too, as he said; me half silent, genial but not that useful.

April 3 & 4, 1991
Last night at Michael's much the same, except that he was extremely depressed. He'd slept most of the day. The same

old thing — just healthy enough to feel that something like
a normal life is almost within his grasp. Yet not quite. No
strength. He really crabbed on about just about everyone.
Stef had a comical routine about the woman who came by to
do touch therapy, which seemed to consist mostly of rubbing
the air above Michael while talking about how she was
removing the "Saran Wrap of anxiety." Ed got to probe me
about how I was handling Michael's viciousness. I said I had
a doll and some pins.

May 15
Made him dinner, we chatted a lot about the AIDS memorial,
which, as of Saturday, has a winner. A young man gets the
$5,000 prize, and apparently the committee's decision was
unanimous. Michael spent the whole day there on it, and it's
clear he's very proud of himself for having originated this and
seen it through. Let's hope he lives long enough to see it built.

He didn't. The memorial, designed by Patrick Fahn and situ-
ated in Barbara Hall Park, formerly known as Cawthra Square Park,
opened in 1993. It's a semicircle of columns, each bearing a plaque
with the names and dates of the many who died of AIDS-related
illnesses. The poems "Cry" by Michael Lynch and "Circle of Stones"
by Shoshanna J. Addley are engraved on the first pillar of the
memorial. New names are added each year, and it is the site of the
annual AIDS Candlelight Vigil. In the mid 1980s, Michael and a
group of volunteers had proposed constructing a permanent AIDS
memorial and had opened the design to a competition. Until then,
Michael and his team had constructed a temporary memorial every
year on Lesbian and Gay Pride Day.

July 1, 1991 [from a journal entry on Pride]
M in his wheelchair looking perfectly ghastly. They were
waiting for Ger since R had to leave. When Ger arrived
with Kirk, the three of us took M home in a cab. I'd gone
to see him that morning and he really is a skeleton now —
massaging his hip I could see the full outline of the pelvis and
the skull beneath the skin is climbing to the surface. I forgot
there was a meeting at his place today. With me and Ed and
Roger and M and Stef but not much happened and I had to
leave to get back for my 3:30 client. Mostly talking around the
issue that people are getting fed up caring for Michael, and
the team, especially in the summer, is getting very hard to
hold together. I don't think we'll have to do it much longer. I
think he's going to die soon. He's so proud of his success with
the AIDS Memorial. He went on and on about it yesterday.

July 2 & 4, 1991
Wednesday night I left Michael's at midnight when Mary
Lou arrived because I wanted to get back here so I could
get up early and work. M wouldn't have known I was there
anyway; he was almost comatose. When I arrived and
identified myself, he did work up the energy to croak, "I
hear you're leaving at midnight." So something of the old
guilt-inducing Michael survives. Little else. There'd been a
big change since Monday and Jeff Blum, the doc, had been
there just before I arrived. He fears M has pneumonia, but
there's no way of telling short of a hospital visit and M won't
want that. And even if it were diagnosed M would refuse
medication, so what's the point. He's saying now, especially
to Stef though also to Gerry, who I visited Thursday night
(writing this Friday morning) that he's fading and wants

to go. Using euphemisms, though, as Stef pointed out. He's
certainly coughing, and can't even raise his head from the
pillow anymore. I lay with him awhile and cuddled. He
would occasionally make soft and, I hope, pleasurable sighing
noises. Both Rog and Ed came over Wed night and we chatted
till after 11, when they left. I didn't have much time alone
there. Stef left earlier, saying he was going to bed but phoned
to say the nurse should reach him there if she has to.

July 7 & 8, 1991
After the Y, I raced over to Michael's to pay a brief visit
to Gail. Her girlfriend Sandy was there, large and blonde
and rather solid looking. Stef there too. I went in to chat to
Michael, who was mostly out of it, oxygen tubes going to his
nose. He did recognize me, and said something like, "I've
been anticipating this sad hour." I said, "This? Sad hour." And
he said, "I guess you've more to come." I don't even know
what he meant in that exchange. It seemed lucid of Michael,
but it may just have been an accidental lucidity, according
to Gail and Stef. He had the delusion he was a maitre d' this
morning. Rog called me tonight to ask if I'd want to see the
body after Michael dies. I said I didn't know yet. I'd decide
when it happens.

Sunday afternoon was given over to a general meeting of
Michael's caregivers at the ACT office. I arrived late, hoping
to miss check-in, but it had only just started and there were
30-odd people. It took an hour. I passed, when my turn
came. Bun [Robert Trow] said he felt what everyone else
felt. Ed got close to tears. Perhaps even did cry — something
has to explain those dry, scratchy sounds emanating from
him. Berinati, of course, blabbed and choked. The awful

tyranny of feeling, again. Saved by Andrew, again, who has the smarmiest voice and I dare say is given to having feelings but nonetheless works them in discreetly, appropriately, and mixed with a lot of useful information. Ger seemed to think that the check-in was basically OK, and even sort of defended banality. He and I and Bun left at the break. Ger met cute boy-toy Kirk outside. Ger has a new bike. Kirk was riding it.

July 10, 1991

Writing this the morning of my birthday. Michael died yesterday. On the day Stef calls his half-birthday. He died about 10 to 3 in the afternoon. Ed was there, as were Gail and Stef. Rick too, I think, but not in the room. It was Jeff's shift, and he was there. Ed got there just in time, Jeff having called him at ACT and pulled him from a meeting. M had been breathing with difficulty for a few hours and they saw it coming. I kind of wish I'd been there — I think I was just heading out the door to meet Philip McLeod for coffee, as I always do on Tuesdays around three. I guess I got home around 4:30 and there were messages on my machine from Roger, Ed, and Chris Lea all about the death. I headed right over, after picking up Bun.

There were quite a few people there. Gail was heading in the door next door where Stef has been staying and looked as if she'd been crying. She didn't stop, except to say something about eating. Ed was there and Rog and Yves I think and Kate and Natalie and Jeff and maybe Alan and Russell maybe, can't remember. Oh yes, and Regan Morris and Michael Fitzgerald. I spoke with Ed for a while up in Michael's office, hearing about how it ended. No great struggle, it seems, some laboured breathing, and then finally no breathing. Major

embrace from Stef, who, according to Ed, was inconsolable
for a while, in the room alone with Michael, sobbing. Chris
arrived after a while. We sat outside, holding hands and
talking. Bun with us, he and I smoking a cigarette. Michael's
last words may have been, "Where do you live?" This to
Gail, who had come into the room and just identified herself
to him.

People were going in to spend time alone with the body.
Regan came crying. Rog too, I think. I went in alone. I didn't
cry. I felt sad but I couldn't cry. Why? The steps of his dying
were so small that this last one didn't seem so very big after
all? He just wasn't close enough to me? I don't know that I'd
ever seen a dead person before. I couldn't get over the feeling
at first that he was just holding his breath. He didn't look that
much different than he did yesterday, though now the skull
beneath the skin was surfacing in triumph. The nose and the
ears looked too big. The dead are very still. Stupid to say, but
you forget how animated the body is even in sleep. His skin
was cool and waxy. Strips of light moved on his face as the
wind shook the blinds. They'd folded his hands on his chest
and moved the sheet up to cover them. I wanted to pull back
the sheet and yet I couldn't.

Michael died relatively early in the epidemic, before antiretro-
viral therapy was developed to turn HIV/AIDS into a chronic,
manageable illness. Many gay men (and others) died over the next
decades, although increasingly fewer every year, and often suc-
cumbing to conditions not directly related to HIV. One of those was
my former lover Robert Trow.

The red message light on my landline phone was flashing when
I woke up on the morning of October 21, 2002. I ignored it, as I

did every day. I turned off the ringer before I went to bed each night and didn't take voice mail messages until I was fully awake the next day, prepared to handle the hang-ups, insults, and requests for my sexual services that had built up. There were some of those on this day, but Robert's lover at the time, Denis Fontaine, had left a message saying that Robert was in St. Michael's Hospital and that I should come.

I did the stupidest thing. I followed my morning routine, and I showered, though I don't usually shower, repeating a single word, *please*, over and over again. The time I spent in that shower, pleading, might have made the difference, might have allowed us a few minutes to recognize each other for the last time, but when I got to the hospital and joined Robert's parents and Denis, his vital signs were flatlining. Not much later, he died. Ironically, given his years of activism around HIV, that wasn't what killed him. It was an aneurysm.

The others finally left. They'd been there for many hours. I stayed, holding his hand. It had living weight still and was warm. I politely rebuffed the hospital chaplain who offered prayers and consolation, and then I too left.

I had to speak to someone. I biked up Bay Street, heading for the government law office where I hoped to find Scott Feltman. He was one of my closest friends (we are gently estranged now), generous and funny and a brilliant government lawyer, now retired. We shared a love of music (though he outdid me in breadth of interest and knowledge), and we'd been more than friends since the late eighties.

Scott was a good choice for the first to know. He was organized, came home with me, allowed me to moon about, and began making telephone calls to the many friends who would be shocked and surprised at the sudden death of someone who hadn't seemed gravely ill in the usual HIV ways. In fact, just two nights before, Robert had been over to my place for dinner, making time to coach me on my upcoming Toronto Opera Repertoire role.

We shared a meal once a week, and had for years, even though our formal lover relationship had ended in 1982, twenty years earlier. We continued to celebrate our anniversary on Easter Sunday each year, usually with dinner in an expensive restaurant. I called him "Bunny" or "Bun," as did many of his friends. (He had worn a Playboy Bunny outfit at his fortieth birthday party, and the candles on the cake had been shaped like carrots.) He underwrote our trips to France. He contributed several thousand dollars to the down payment on my condo.

I loved and valued our deep connection after the breakup, but I greatly missed sleeping together. "I don't know if you know how important it was that you stayed with me, and that you slept with me, and that you let me hold you and that you held me," I wrote to my friend Gerry Oxford, who stayed with me for several nights in the wake of Robert's death. "That is the way Robert and I slept together for all the years we did, and I remember how often in the early years we would go to bed exhausted. I don't know why, really, but we would hardly be able to keep awake and yet we'd keep talking and laughing though even then I was more of a sleepyhead than he, and sometimes I would realize that he'd said something, something that I should reply to, but I'd be already mostly asleep and not sure whether I'd answered or not and sometimes the last thing I'd hear before I finally slept was him whispering, 'I love you.' We said that to each other before we slept for years."

Robert had worked for years as a paramedic at the Hassle Free Clinic, in operation since 1973; he helped to make it a crucial force in conveying information about HIV/AIDS and, most importantly, successfully persuading the newly elected NDP government in

Friends and lovers who died way too soon: (from left) Michael Lynch, Bill Lewis, Roger Spalding, Robert Trow in New York. Photo: Gerald Hannon

Ontario to legalize anonymous HIV testing. Previously, nominal testing (where a person's name was attached to the test) meant reporting to public health and, if positive, the contact tracing of partners. Many gay men and other marginalized people did not want to risk that, and it often prevented them from getting tested and connected to care. As a city council citation put it, "Robert was a pioneer advocate for legal anonymous HIV testing across Ontario, and with his guidance, the province became one of the first jurisdictions in North America to offer anonymous testing. The current protocols are based on the innovative program developed at the Hassle Free Clinic." A large portrait of Robert by Kirsten Johnson now hangs in the waiting room of Hassle Free's offices on Church Street.

Another *Body Politic* colleague who lived for years following his HIV diagnosis was Rick Bébout. He died in 2009 of complications from a stroke. I was one of the people who helped to close up his apartment.

It's a sad task, clearing out someone's apartment after he dies. Our culture measures a person's worth in stuff, and Rick Bébout didn't leave much for us to pack and give away.

The bedroom, the closet, and the sunroom were lined with banker's boxes, twenty-seven of them. They were meticulously identified and labelled, and they were filled with file folders, also meticulously identified and labelled. They seemed sad at first too — a monument to an obsessive neat freak. Then you opened any one of the twenty that were his.

The contents crackled and hummed and yearned and sighed and wept; they protested and acclaimed; they laughed and agonized. They shouted. They fell in love. They plotted. They thought: so much energy spent on thinking and debating and analyzing, but allowing time, always making time, to lick some cute dancer boy's belly at Remington's or revel in being called an amazing cocksucker by some blissed-out, lucky neighbour. Those boxes were the gift of a life, Rick Bébout's life, recorded in journals, letters, memoirs, e-mail exchanges, and photographs.

It was a rich bequest. At least two of the twenty boxes were filled with his decades-long correspondence with novelist and essayist Jane Rule, a gift to literary scholars and the record of the kind of friendship that seems almost archaic these days: a friendship initiated, elaborated, and maintained almost entirely on paper (they rarely spoke and met only a few times). Rule's death in 2007 hit him very hard. Those letters helped him to analyze and make sense of his life, he told me. Long after she died, he'd catch himself formulating, analyzing, and structuring the record of his life for that week's letter. Ten years of that exchange have now been captured in *A Queer Love Story: The Letters of Jane Rule and Rick Bébout*, meticulously edited by Marilyn Shuster (UBC Press, 2017).

Rick cherished gift culture, a way of life in which a person's worth is measured not by how much he keeps but by how much he gives away. Rick did more than gift his life on paper, destined for the queer ArQuives. He launched his own website (www.rbebout. com) on January 11, 2000, his fiftieth birthday, setting the tone for a memoir he called *Promiscuous Affections* with these words: "What I hope to make happen, or at least encourage, is a fresh look at who we are and have been as gay people. Whatever 'gay' may mean … In the mad rush to 'equality' with everyone else we have leaned on claims that we are 'just like everyone else.' … But many of us, thankfully, are not. We are truly queer — our lives and our values distinct, not 'normal.' Maybe even (though we rarely dare say it these days) better than normal: more open, generous, and humane."

For those of you not lucky enough to have known him, the hundreds of thousands of his words you'll find online are a virtual hand reaching out to you and to the world, offering a gift. If I were you, I'd take it.

9

Making Ends Meet

· ·

THE BODY POLITIC CEASED publication in 1987, the February issue
its last. I was still on the collective and on staff — I didn't give notice
until June 30 — but the last months of 1986 had made it clear that
accumulated debt and an exhausted staff meant that something
had to change, that we couldn't continue publishing both *TBP* and
Xtra. Although we held several meetings to discuss options — we
remained relentlessly democratic — one fact was brutally clear:
Xtra made money; *The Body Politic* lost it. On December 16, 1986,
the collective voted to suspend publication of *TBP* indefinitely. We
couldn't bring ourselves to say we were killing it, but we were.

The Body Politic was unique: a publication that explored and
celebrated gay culture without ever becoming a slick promotional
rag, a news medium that decried objectivity and encouraged street-
level dissent, a Canadian magazine respected internationally and
particularly in the U.S., a kind of institution fearless in dealing
with that third rail of gay activism — youth. Any young man or
woman who came upon a copy of *TBP* would soon have no doubt
that their gay identity was good, would learn that there were
organizations committed to changing discriminatory laws and that
they'd be welcome to join and help. They'd also gain glimpses of a

future when social acceptance might extend as far as marriage.

TBP didn't initiate all those changes, but it kept track of them, supported them, celebrated them — and it did so for fifteen years.

I have few memories of the closing days and weeks — I seemed to be going through the motions, dully aware I had to build a new life, find work, make money, find a new place to live. Our communal house had splintered — without rancour, but with the same world-weariness that half-explained the death of the paper. I knew that *Xtra* would continue, but the collective would not; it would be replaced by a conventional hierarchy under the direction of Ken Popert. I had no problems with that; I admired Ken's willingness to take on what seemed at the time to be a futile, hopeless exercise. At a personal level, I was alone — though I'd made new friends, my relationship with Chris Lea had ended. He was an architecture student when we'd met in the wake of my breakup with Robert. He was fourteen years younger than I. We had sex for the first time on the eve of his twenty-fourth birthday, with me having turned thirty-eight less than a week earlier. He crackled with a kind of goofy energy and was full of high-minded theories of the role of architecture in the modern world, taking bad buildings as almost a personal insult. He was unrepentantly sexual, cruising other men in my presence, aware and grateful that I didn't believe in monogamy and always strove to suppress any nascent jealousy. We had sex in his parents' bed once, when they were away, and he got his pet dog to lick the come off our hands. He introduced me to the first microwave oven I'd ever seen. On a beatifically mild Christmas Eve in 1982, we played naked on the roof of *The Body Politic* building at 24 Duncan Street, "bodies just singing with the nonsense of it, with that much freedom and that much silliness on Christmas Eve." I'm quoting myself there, from the last page of the last issue of *TBP*, number 135, February 1987. It was a valedictory column, citing images and memories from the previous fifteen years and worrying that "nothing again will ever be so new and fresh and young and eager, so pig-headed, so infuriating, so clumsy and so young."

Raptures aside, I wasn't so young anymore myself. I was soon to be forty-four, and I needed a job. Writing was all I knew how to do. I had, through the fifteen-year life of *TBP*, become a skilled journalist with a distinctive style. I figured I could, at the age of forty-three, start a freelance career. My reputation had been tainted by the "Men Loving Boys Loving Men" scandal and trial, but I hoped that journalists' short memories might mean few awkward questions. Of course, one doesn't just *become* a freelancer — one needs to secure assignments, do the research, write well, meet dead-lines, and be likeable enough that editors are willing to assign a second project. That takes time, which I didn't have. I was near broke, and though I had managed to get a contract job editing a newsletter for the television producers' union at the CBC, it didn't pay enough. My rent, not shared anymore with several roommates, was $500 a month. I was scraping by.

In an unlikely sort of way, *The Body Politic* came to my rescue.

The paper's advertising manager had quit, and since *Xtra* was to continue and depended entirely on advertising, we had to hire. There were two applicants. One was a young man with a long connection to *TBP*. He was the obvious choice. The other was Colin Brownlee — twenty-six years old, cute enough to be easily dismissed as a pretty boy but fascinated, since coming out at seventeen, by the development of a gay press and the role he might play in it. After Rick Bébout and I had a short interview with him, we hired him. It felt like a gamble, but he'd managed to sell himself to a couple of staunch old liberationists, and, more importantly, he turned out to have a passion for entrepreneurship. He hadn't finished high school, but he would eventually put *Xtra* on firm financial ground, first through ad sales and then through the development of dating/hookup applications, first via telephone and subsequently over the Internet. The latter, Squirt, continues to fund activism and the digital version that eventually replaced the print edition of *Xtra*.

We became friends, Colin and I, and I worried to him about my finances, about my ability to keep my head above water until I managed to build a successful writing career. I had no doubt I could, if I managed to survive in the interim. To my surprise, he suggested one day that I hustle and added that he had, and still did occasionally, and that it was the easiest way to make quick cash. Now, it didn't surprise me that men would be willing to pay Colin for sex — he was a very cute young guy, personable, in good shape with a certain lush voluptuousness. But me? I was in my early forties, trim but not muscular — at least not to the degree I imagined would be required. I wasn't well hung. Sell what you do have, he told me. Stretch the truth. Take a few years off your age, but sell your age, not everyone's attracted to young guys. Advertise yourself as a masseur.

I got the same message from Danny Cockerline (his real name), an activist and friend who made of his sex work a political act and who was eventually a poster boy for safe sex when the AIDS crisis hit. He told me to take out an ad in *NOW Magazine*, that the sex trade was a dizzying array of niche markets, and if I thought there wouldn't be a demand for daddy types wearing bifocals, I was very, very wrong. He was very, very right. His advice made it possible for me to take the time to build a career as a writer; money from sex work was easy, fast, and didn't use up a lot of brain cells. On the downside, one did spend a lot of time doing laundry.

We'd met when Danny came to volunteer at *The Body Politic*. He was twenty-one, fresh out of North Bay, eager to learn whatever we could teach him. He was on the contributors' list by April 1982, writing news stories, and had joined the collective by September 1983. As Rick Bébout would later write in a short eulogy, "He was already too queer for the conventional gay-male world (then late-clone: 'Everybody looked right off the rack,' he said; only after AIDS made facial hair an unfashionable mark of Seventies sleaze did Danny, in solidarity, grow a moustache). When cops busted a 1984 *TBP* party as a booze can, Danny mouthed off enough to get arrested, dragged out into the cold in nothing but a little blue dress." He could be a handful; many a regular patron of Woody's (a Church Street gay bar) would have seen Danny tossed out for deciding to party naked. Partying naked was something he did very well — he made two porn films, *Midnight Sun* and *In the Grip of Passion*, and appeared in photo spreads in both *Honcho* and *Mandate*, classic skin mags of the day. When the AIDS Committee of Toronto decided to make a safer sex video targeting the deaf community, and they needed a hot, shameless guy, they turned to Danny.

He was a founding member of Maggie's (the prostitutes' rights organization), the Sex Workers' Alliance of Toronto, and the Prostitutes' Safe Sex Project. He was an outrageous presence at sex workers' conferences and AIDS conferences the world over. He was hard to resist.

He took his own life on December 11, 1995. He'd spent the early part of the evening at a bar with friends, paying for everyone's drinks with his credit card. He was thirty-five years old. He was boyishly handsome, but he was also a drama queen with a femmy, nasal voice, a prostitute, a drug user, a porn star, a young man who partied too loudly, too often, and too hard. He left a note. Danny was HIV-positive, and he wrote that he did not want to put his family and friends through a lingering AIDS death, though he was in fine health and nowhere near getting sick. He also referred to that

"Nazi, Harris." He meant then-premier Mike Harris. Danny had become increasingly depressed and frightened in recent months, worried that Ontario's newly elected Tory government would cut off the funding for the medicines he needed and could never have paid for on his own.

He had a right to be worried. Harris did make massive cuts in social services and health care funding, but the Trillium catastrophic drug plan survived. It seemed that the son of a key Harris adviser had died of AIDS, and the word came down: AIDS funding was to be untouchable.

Still, his death struck me as excessively drama-queen, and I was too angry with him to grieve when first I heard the news. I did grieve later, easing my way to it through the hastily arranged service held in the chapel at Rosar-Morrison Funeral Home on Sherbourne Street. Well-known social activist and journalist June Callwood was there. So was then city councillor Jack Layton, who would have the city pass a resolution honouring Danny's life and work. The music was a tape by the Pet Shop Boys, and the service, as Rick Bébout noted, attracted "more hookers and hustlers than, I'm sure, have ever gathered under that fake-church roof. One of them, young, tattooed, wearing a 'Safe Sex Professionals' T-shirt Danny had given him off his own back, said in tears: 'Without him, I wouldn't have survived.'"

I wrote Danny's obit for *NOW Magazine*. I would memorialize another whore the same month. *The Globe and Mail* had asked me to write about Elizabeth Spedding, Toronto's oldest madam, also known as the Contessa, for its end-of-year roundup of significant deaths. (In July, I had visited her at Mount Sinai Hospital on the occasion of her eightieth birthday. She died soon after.) I'd taken notes on that occasion but needed more background, and I heard, through the grapevine, that there was a box of material stored in a bordello out in the west end at Bloor Street and Kipling Avenue. My friend Mike Kibbee was chronically ill but felt well enough that week to offer his motorbike to get the two of us out there. It seemed the fastest way to get there, and it was an adventure too, Mike being well suited for that. For a while, as we hurtled down Lake Shore Boulevard, he put one hand on my leg to help warm it, and I found that unbearably sweet even though it was probably perfectly reckless.

The whorehouse, a seedy little apartment above a porn video outlet in a strip mall, was probably (at least I hope) on the low end of the scale. A woman named Lee let us in. We'd had to spend some time in a pizza parlour after we got out there as she'd had a date when we called, and then she was reluctant to let us in because another was allegedly coming. I wondered if that wasn't a ruse because when we finally got into the apartment and she saw we were just a couple of harmless fags, she warmed right up and got very chatty. Half Chinese, half French. A lot of cats. A black-and-white television, of all things, gave the place a retro feel. I spent my time going through a box of stuff that had belonged to the Contessa. There were photos of other girls I thought were in the biz too. I found a newspaper story from the *Toronto Star* that gave me the details I needed for my piece. I also found two impossibly glamorous photos of her, taken in Mexico City; she was young and gorgeous.

I tried, in that obit, to capture the spirit of the gathering in July when I'd found her in Mount Sinai Hospital, wearing a paper crown, attended by a family of whores. There were girls in tight skirts and heels, girls in sweaters with plunging necklines, a girl in a black sheath dress that winked out just a hint of tattoo. One of the whores brought her kids along. Another brought her hubby. It felt very family. Everyone addressed her as "Contessa."

Elizabeth Spedding was probably Canada's oldest whore and undoubtedly the country's most famous madam. She'd achieved a certain notoriety in Toronto in the late seventies, when police busted her call girl service and the story played out in the papers. But Toronto was just the last chapter in a story that had begun in Regina when she was seventeen, with modelling gigs that brought extra cash for doing, as she put it, "personal favours."

She didn't stay in Canada for long. She was very beautiful. She was poised, aristocratic, and ambitious, and soon there was an apartment on New York's Fifth Avenue, champagne parties, and trysts with the likes of Miguel Alemán Valdés, president of Mexico. She said American president Harry Truman wanted in her bed, and she said she turned him down. She received postcards from Elizabeth Taylor. Cherished an autographed photograph from Richard Burton. She made a lot of money. In 1951, she married a Romanian count, and, though the marriage ended only a few years later, "the Contessa" she remained until the day she died.

She also spent time in American jails — once for two years, on what were then called "white slavery transportation" charges. After she was released, she returned to Canada, headed for Toronto — "it was a good choice," she wrote later, "it's a wealthy city" — and started right back into the business. She would eventually remarry (her husband predeceased her), and though she was busted, convicted, and fined in 1979, she continued to work and madam well into her seventies.

For most people, it's the tales of presidents and movie stars that enthrall. The family of whores knows all the glamorous stories, but there are others they cherish more. They talk of the Elizabeth Spedding who always had room for a girl in trouble. Who helped out with money. Who kept a smaller percentage of the take than any other madam. Who was proud of her profession, and who taught her girls to take the same pride in their work as she did.

Some of them made it to that hospital room for the birthday party. They brought champagne, balloons, and streamers, and the hospital looked the other way. The girls teased her, and she teased right back. She told anyone who came in, including the doctor (very cute and young), that all the girls were available, though perhaps she didn't mean to include June Callwood, who was also there. I remember Doug, that strange, crazy boy, in white pantyhose and a fur-trimmed gauze thing, the Contessa writing something racy across his butt with a marker. An old friend with a strong British accent, though everyone called him Roy Rogers, told me he'd met her in a laundromat on Avenue Road. People kept snapping Polaroids. And up on the wall, there was a black-and-white photo of an oil painting of the Contessa when she was in her twenties, I would guess, looking terribly glam. She took a particular shine to me that afternoon and wouldn't let me leave until I'd signed her guest book and given her my phone number. Some people thought she was a little gaga by then, but I like to think she could still spot raw talent.

I'd never had any ethical or political objections to prostitution. I had no fears that friends or close acquaintances would be scandalized, though I did put up with a lot of teasing when I announced my decision. A friend pretended to drive me off his front porch when I arrived, as invited, for dinner. I didn't open the subject with family members; none lived in Toronto or followed the media, and it would have required a major re-education in sexual politics. (I would one day regret not having made the effort.)

I put an ad in *NOW Magazine*, a free weekly. I put an ad in *Xtra*. "Massage Plus," it read. "Trust your body to this muscular, hairy guy. Relaxation and sensual pleasure."

I sold my body for the first time at five o'clock in the afternoon on August 29, 1987. I was nervous but not squeamish. Years of anonymous sex in parks and bathhouses had made me open to a range of body types and sexual idiosyncrasies. I spent half an hour massaging a quite presentable gentleman, happy ending included, and made fifty bucks. The joyful ease of it put me in a laughing, dancing mood after I'd closed the door on him, and I threw the money into the air as I spun about gleefully in my kitchen. I sensed I could make a go of it, sensed that I could survive until I'd made it as a journalist.

And I did. Even just one client a day meant an extra $1,500 a month, and I sometimes had two or three, and some would tip. I never worried about my safety, and I got ripped off only a few times. I never asked for the money in advance, comparing my service to that of a fine restaurant. I had a thirty-dollar student/senior rate, and though many students took advantage, I don't think any seniors did. Some men became regulars. Some were obnoxious. Some fell in love with me. I never reciprocated; I tried to handle those situations delicately and adroitly, but, love being love, I wasn't always successful. I infused this new career with the politics I'd developed over fifteen years with *The Body Politic*, joining the board of Maggie's and the Toronto Sex Workers Action Project, which advocates on behalf of prostitutes of all genders.

I tried to take sex work seriously and do a good job, even developing the philosophical position that "the proper business of any prostitute is to become a saint." I'm quoting myself here, from an article on sex work that I wrote for *This Magazine*, and here's more, somewhat revised and updated:

I don't mean piety here. I mean that I'm working, in my professional life at least, to obliterate, or at least subjugate, my own needs.

The thing that struck me about saints when I was growing up a devout Catholic boy was not so much that they did good things. Some of them, in fact, did very weird things indeed. No, what impressed me was that they had their needs and desires so carefully tamed, so managed — though they usually chose a life of denial as a way of making this happen. I've found that a life of excess works equally well.

I noticed it the first time I saw hustlers at work in groups. The boys often worked the baths, and what struck me most as they sat and smoked and talked and laughed together was that they didn't look. Everyone else was acutely aware of every finely calibrated change in body language; the bathhouse clientele were looking. But these boys, these talking, laughing, smoking boys, floated above desire, empty of need, loose and clumsy and drunk sometimes, but promising to be anything I or anyone else could want. I don't think I'm romanticizing them. Because I know now how they got that way.

Something changes when you've had sex with hundreds of men — I suppose, in my case, it's now thousands — particularly when you do not choose your partner. You discover, eventually, that there isn't much difference between having sex with someone you find very attractive and someone you think is ugly, though I should add that it remains difficult to have sex with someone I don't like. This was a revelation, particularly in a culture as looks- and image-obsessed as ours. When it starts to happen, it means you are witnessing the beginnings of the slow erosion of the power of need.

Need is always an engagement with the particular — a certain body type, the way hair falls across the forehead, the fullness or thinness of lips. When you discover that particulars are losing their power, when one set of particulars might just as well substitute for any other, you have taken the first steps toward a version of sainthood that only prostitutes can know. And you will be a better whore. Freed from the demands of your own needs, you will do a much better job catering to the needs of others.

I am in awe before the extent, the power, the range of human need. Need is a seething presence beneath the polite fictions of our everyday lives. If need were a force field, the city would glow at night. You could hover above it and see the lines of light reaching out and crossing and missing and connecting, everyone pretending there is no light at all, people making dinners, reading books, watching televisions. But I see it. I feel, on some nights, when I am doing an out-call and sweeping across the city on my bicycle, that I am tracking the current of human need, a current visible only to me and to other whores, a current that will draw me to the grown man who wants to be treated like a two-year-old and have his diaper changed, to the seventeen-year-old high school student who hasn't figured out any other way of meeting people, to the Italian grandfather who's finally getting the fuck he's always wanted, or to the man who does nothing but tickle my feet and tape-record my laughter. There can be needs so sudden, so urgent, that I am called from shopping malls, from bars, from the lobbies of cinemas. There are needs so ordinary they can be satisfied simply by an orgasm in the presence of another warm, receptive body. And needs of quite byzantine complexity. I have given philosophy lectures in the nude. Had sex with someone who could be excited only by touching the fillings in my teeth. Been videotaped in a wrestling scene by a gentleman who brought along both the wrestling outfits and my opponent. I even had a brush with Hollywood celebrity — albeit at one remove. I met a client at the Four Seasons Hotel in Yorkville during the 1987 Festival of Festivals. He was a Los Angeles businessman with a big, confident face and a greying ponytail — very central casting. He wouldn't let sex get in the way of business. He answered the telephone twice while I was sucking his cock, the first time from Faye Dunaway, who called to complain about the hairdresser she was assigned. The second from Jackie Collins. The reason for her call escapes me, but on his side of the call it inspired some unctuous flattery. He tipped generously and offered me a glass of Chivas before and after his happy ending; I accepted both.

For contrast, on one unpleasantly memorable New Year's Day, I agreed to defecate on someone.

It was gross. I did it, and didn't charge extra, because I felt sorry for someone whose erotic life depended on finding a partner happy, or at least willing, to do something most people would find disgusting. I think I did a good job (I leave the details to your imagination), but I made it clear that it wouldn't happen again. Of course, I turned the occasion into an anecdote. The punchline? That it was my one Close Encounter of the Turd Kind.

There are the occasional calls from women — the most intriguing being from women who wanted to watch their boyfriends having gay sex. The guys seemed not exactly thrilled, but willing. I remember one woman in particular, sitting on a kitchen chair I'd brought into the bedroom, her hands primly in her lap as her boyfriend increasingly got into it. The saddest? A woman who did not want sex but needed a presentable escort for a holiday office party. Single and plain, she'd told her coworkers she'd started dating, but she hadn't. She picked me up, and we drove to a restaurant in a suburban mall, where we joined her crew for drinks and dinner. I tried my best to be a charmer. She drove me home and gave me a hefty tip.

Then there are the endless needs of married men — gay men who married back when they felt they had to, who love their children, who want the marriage to continue. Straight men who just seem to want to be on the bottom once in their lives.

I realize I can be accused of special pleading. Yes, I needed money, but no, I wasn't destitute or in danger of living on the streets. I was a cis male, mature, middle-class, white, and well educated. After my income stabilized, I saw the whole adventure as a bit of a lark and frequently dined out on the stories. Dined in as well — one client, who went by the name Brent, loved to have people admire his penis and masturbate him, an entertainment provided at several of my dinner parties, the most notorious featuring a guest list that included a lesbian couple and a straight man. The lesbians were unfailingly polite but kept their physical distance. The straight man, willing to try his first hemi-semi-demi homosexual experience, jerked Brent off, noting that his many years of practice hadn't prepared him for the awkwardness of doing it from the front.

The sex work continued long after I had an established career as a journalist, but I understood how unsettling it would be if it were my only source of income. Too much need can be aggravating as well as exhilarating. There was the perennial smelly bum problem. There were the no-shows. There was the laundry. There was a deeply buried worry: what if this more or less open secret should become public in a way that torpedoed my writing career?

This fear didn't keep me awake nights, as it seemed so unlikely. Friends knew, of course, and a few trustworthy colleagues like

David Hayes, Lynn Cunningham, and Don Obe, but that's as far as it went. I was a little apprehensive at first about being dismissed as the "gay writer," but I decided that being openly gay gave me a leg up in the competitive world of journalism. If you wanted an article about the gay community, who better than me? Mainstream magazines were beginning to take notice of the AIDS crisis, and early in 1988 I had an assignment: Lynn Cunningham, then an editor at *Toronto Life*, asked me to write a major feature with the title "Gay After AIDS." It appeared in the November 1988 issue.

I'm still proud of it. The blurb on the opening page described the piece as "A personal celebration of the culture of promiscuity," and it was. It began with a description of that year's Pride celebration, opening with the public reading of the names of those who had died since 1981, but the text moved from grief to erotic celebration. There was a full paragraph describing a park sex scene. Here's just one sentence: "Or over there, where that tall guy is on his knees blowing the cute blond kid and there are three other guys just standing around playing with themselves." I'm still surprised at what *Toronto Life* let me get away with. I argued that being detailed and specific about sex acts helped men make informed choices about what was safe and what wasn't. One has to remember that, according to an Ontario Ministry of Health brochure, the number-one piece of advice for staying safe then was "abstain from sex."

"Gay men have a language for talking about sex," I wrote. "It's what is obscene about the way we talk that will save our lives."

The piece was a splashy debut in the glossy mainstream Canadian press. My few published articles before then had appeared in either jerk-off magazines or the *Advocate*, a gay American newsmagazine. I'd be back in *Toronto Life* a year later. Lynn Cunningham assigned me a profile of then *Globe and Mail* art critic John Bentley

Mays. The article appeared in the December 1989 issue under the title "John Prickly Mays." It would win me my first National Magazine Award.

"John Bentley Mays is not a drag queen," it began. "He is the art critic for *The Globe and Mail* and arguably the most ostentatiously cerebral critic in Canada writing for the daily press. But I can tell you what he looks like in a dress." That was a playful attention-getter. (He had been in an art world performance piece and was said to look "exactly like Gertrude Stein.") But it also touched on a theme — his obsession with the body in art and his discomfort with his own. I famously described it in almost clinical detail, culminating in a sentence I was often teased for: "I didn't run my hands over his skin, but I imagine it would be cool and coarsely textured, dry." I intimated he might be gay. He was married. He hated the piece, as I would find out when he contacted me in August 1994, almost five years later. This also taught me that picking away at the edges of people's private lives can have unpredictable results.

I kept an account of his visit in my journal:

> Mays came over Thursday at 11. He stayed for two hours, and I was an agitated, exhausted mess by the end of it and could not stop pacing around the apartment. Part of me feels that the whole scene between John and me was a carefully orchestrated drama, that there was not a shred of real feeling in it (even at those moments when I think he was close to tears), and that he got what he wanted and left when he got it. And part of me feels that it was orchestrated, but that it was real too. Those strange dead eyes. They're what throw me.
>
> It became clear as the talk continued that the memory of me and what I did has tormented him over those years, and deeply, and plunged him into some of those famous

depressions. "I wanted to kill you," he told me. "And if I couldn't kill you, I wanted to destroy you." He then went on to a rather movie-of-the-week line about really hating himself and it was things in him that he wanted to kill. But he felt compelled, he said, to ask my forgiveness.

He questioned me closely on my pursuit of his sexuality in the piece. I seemed to want to establish him as gay. Then he said, "I'm not gay. I'm omnivorous." Which struck me as a rather ghastly way of putting it. And he had an anecdote about picking up a woman at an art party in New York years ago, and I guess that was supposed to prove omnivorousness. I wonder where the bones are. Somehow this developed into an admission that he didn't know what his sexuality was because his psychiatrist, whom he's been seeing for twenty years I think, wouldn't tell him. I had to jump in then with more than sympathetic noises. The nonsense of it. From a smart man. Waiting to know what you are until your psychiatrist tells you! As if he'd risk losing a profit centre like John Bentley Mays. Who does he look at, I asked? Men. Who does he fantasize about? Men. Who does he jerk off too? Men. You're a fag, John Bentley Mays. And I don't care if you have a wife and a marvelous relationship with her that you don't want to ruin — you're a fag who's married his best girlfriend, and that's not exactly writing a new chapter in the history of sexuality.

He finally said it. "I'm a gay man." Then I think we got a long meditation on shame and guilt, and how guilt does not bother him at all, but seems to consume everyone up here, whereas shame, or its avoidance, was the principal motivator in the South. I tried to suggest that shame, as an inhibitor, might have made some sense in a rural, agrarian society but hardly made any at all in downtown Toronto but he didn't pursue that. I did get to hear about two homo relationships he'd had. One with someone he'd met in Vancouver, I guess on a business trip, and how it was fun. They listened to music together, and laughed and had sex and it was fun. But that was Vancouver. And he's lost touch. But he did meet someone here — he referred to him as the "monster" throughout — who turned out, J said, to be a star-fucker. Wanted JBM as a trophy, and hurt him a lot in the process of bagging him, it seems. Probably some little art-world bitch, some next-to-no-talent who wanted the *Globe*'s art critic in his back pocket.

He wants sex with men. That came up next, I think. And I tried to say that's not really how the homo world works, or at least that there's lots of sex, but it makes more sense in context and that really a circle of friends is what's important. But he was very clear. That's not what he wants. He's got his wife. He has a few friends, none of them gay. He wants sex. I was to tell him how to get it. He made it clear that he would not go to bars — not that I would have suggested he go in any case. So I said, "Pay for it." And that finally led to, as he put it, "the next inevitable question." Could he pay me for it? All he wants (at least right now) is a blow job. No lovemaking, no sucking my cock. Just a blow job.

I have to say that, even though I began to see it coming, I was still struck dumb by it. I felt I was about to become another chapter in the grotesque southern melodrama of his life — he was going to make the man who plunged him into years of depression kneel down and suck his cock and take money for it. I babbled a bit around the issue. It wasn't like that, I said. You find people you're attracted to, you don't just ask whoever is sitting across from you. "Your face is fine," is what I think he said. Finally, I said no. I couldn't do it, at least not now. Maybe, should he call back. And if he wanted, I could find someone else who didn't have our history together and wouldn't steal his wallet. This brought out a comment on the problems of being rich. "Are you rich," I asked him. "Yes," he said. Maybe he would call. And that's more or less how we left it. We switched instantly into proper parting behaviour. And I don't know if I'll ever hear from him again.

I don't believe I did. He died of a sudden heart attack on September 16, 2016. He was seventy-five years old.

I would go on to write more than two hundred articles for all the leading Canadian magazines and newspapers. Very rarely did I pitch. Editors wanted me and, when told — only half jokingly — that I had no ideas of my own, were happy to assign. I became the go-to guy for profiles. In fact, "Tomson and the Trickster" (March 1991, on Cree writer Tomson Highway), my next for *Toronto Life*, not only won gold at the National Magazine Awards that year, it was selected in 2001 by the National Magazine Awards Foundation for inclusion in a twenty-fifth anniversary compilation of the best work over that quarter-century. The editorial intro for the reprint noted that I was "the best profile writer we have."

Profiles weren't my only beat. I wrote book reviews, opinion pieces, essays, art criticism, even the occasional business article. I'm proud of a well-received, mostly humorous piece on a Toronto dog show. In 1994, my fiftieth year, I wrote about returning to Marathon, my hometown, for its fiftieth anniversary celebrations.

I WAS A REASONABLY successful freelance journalist, but it's a financially perilous career. The best glossies might pay a dollar a word, but I could spend months researching, interviewing, and writing and end up with only $5,000 to show for all that time. And there was a lot of competition for the magazines — *Toronto Life, Saturday Night, Chatelaine* — that paid those rates. I began to fantasize about getting a regular paycheque, having some sort of part-time job, making ends meet with less stress. I started teaching at what was then Ryerson Polytechnic Institute in 1992. I can't remember how I heard of an opening in the night school's continuing education program for a teacher of magazine journalism — it might be that friends who worked there, like Don Obe or Lynn Cunningham, knew the position was available and suggested I apply. The interview process was very informal. I recall meeting Paul Nowack at a neighbour-hood coffee shop. We talked of matters journalistic for a short while, and then he offered me the job. There seemed to be no real academic requirements in those days. One had merely to be a successful practitioner of the skill one was to teach, and that I certainly was. I even had the experience, though by now it had been decades, of teaching English as a Second Language, which turned out to be not a bad background for some of the students I was to encounter.

I knew my way around a classroom. The only problem was that, though I was very good at writing magazine articles, I had no idea how to teach the craft or how one would structure a series of lesson plans that might, at least in theory, achieve that goal. Lynn Cunningham suggested I get in touch with David Hayes, a journalist who had taught the course before and who might be generous with advice.

We met for drinks at a bar on the Danforth. A relentless conversationalist (I've often described him as the blabbiest straight guy I've ever met), a handsome man with a shaved head, a fine journalist with a real passion for his craft, he was more than generous. He gave me his lesson plans, showed me how to structure classes, provided photocopies of articles he'd found useful to put before students, suggested guest speakers I might want to contact, and generally behaved like the good friend he'd very soon become. (He would be an invaluable ally during the scandal that would break in 1995.) Without his help, I would have blundered about for a very long time.

With David's aid, I became a good teacher, though not a great one. To be great at something, you have to believe in it, and I didn't. I couldn't quite believe that all the lectures and readings and assignments and illustrious guest speakers I dragged in from the world of journalism could turn a mediocre writer into a good one. A competent one, maybe. One who knew the outlines of the craft and the demands of the business, sure. But I could always pick out, after just the first assignment, those who really didn't need me because they were already on their way to a career and those who might get only marginally better no matter how hard I worked with them. (In the former group, I remember columnist-and-author-to-be Rebecca Eckler, whose snap, smarts, and ambition were evident from day one, and later Michael Grange, not only disconcertingly sexy but so clearly in command of sports writing that it was no surprise when his byline began to appear regularly in *The Globe and Mail*.) Still, I tried with everyone, and I really admired the fervour of most of my night school students. Many had jobs during the day and arrived in my classroom tired but eager. Some already worked in journalism but wanted a more creative role. Others just liked to write and hoped that their passion could lead to a lucrative new career. I tried to let them down gently.

The job also meant I had a reliable source of income, something of a holy grail for freelancers, even though I was doing reasonably well as a journalist. There was also my prostitution income. I was averaging about $650 a month from sex work in 1992 (about fifteen guys a month). Though that was cash, I kept careful financial records and was devoted to being a good citizen and paying my share of taxes.

No encounter took more than an hour; much of it was fun, some of it distasteful, and all of it a valuable glimpse into the hidden world of men's lusts. That revenue stream came close to paying my monthly rent.

I am not sure what I would have done if one of my students had appeared at the door. It would have been awkward, but I would probably have invited him in, sat him down, and talked. I'd have let him know that I would have no objections to this incident becoming public, but that if it did, it would have to come from him. I would say nothing to anyone. I would also have said that, given that I'd have to mark his work, we shouldn't have sex. Had a student of mine appeared, though, it would have been satisfying if it had turned out to be the one virulently homophobic man I encountered among my night school students. He was a combative troublemaker in class, which didn't necessarily mean a distaste for gay people, but another student took the time to write to both me and the administration, saying that he bad-mouthed me regularly as a fag, that it poisoned the atmosphere, and that she feared for my safety. I took consolation in the fact that he was a terrible writer and had no future in journalism. However, I would soon change my mind about terrible writers having no future in journalism.

He knew I was gay because I always came out to my students, usually during their first class. Ryerson encouraged its instructors to begin the term by describing their qualifications, and mine rested mainly on my fifteen years with *The Body Politic*. My sexuality was unavoidable as a topic. Sometimes, instead of simply reciting the facts of my life, I would get them to interview me during class, knowing they should have as much practice in that difficult art as they could get and hoping they would ask the personal questions about which nascent journalists often feel shy. I'd then hand out a sheet, "Facts You Should Have Discovered about Gerald Hannon," so they could see whether, through some misplaced delicacy, they had avoided relevant topics and issues. I always mentioned that I'd been tried and acquitted more than once on charges of obscenity, immorality, scurrility, and indecency. I wanted to make the point that, if they aspired to be a crusading journalist or favoured provocative topics, there were dangers. Those infrequent references to "Men Loving Boys Loving Men" turned out to be a trap I was setting for myself, a trap another crusading journalist at the *Toronto Sun* would be happy to spring.

I think, too, I was a good teacher because I liked young people — liked looking at them, listening to them, arguing with them, going out for a beer with them, and watching them calibrate the level of impudence they might get away with. They seemed so young, fragile, and hopeful; they seemed ignorant of the difficulties that lay before them, yet they dazzled me with their confidence and their schemes, amused me with their belief in the power of journalism, and humbled me with their sophisticated analysis of how fatuous it could be.

The classroom is an erotic petri dish, as any teacher of young people knows, and I liked that too; I liked trying to figure out who was dating whom and who might be gay, liked imagining the guys naked, liked having to try to avoid paying too much attention to the men I found particularly hot — not a huge struggle, as it turned out, since I adored many of my female students. It didn't occur to me (though it should have) that some students might have erotic fantasies about their teachers. At the Spa Excess, the local bathhouse I patronized, I was accosted one evening by a young man who seemed miffed that I didn't remember him from the previous year, while he tried to refresh my memory by reaching up under my towel. "I never missed a class," he told me as he caressed my penis, "and I used to sit there and imagine you naked." And now I was, and he had me.

I left the bath early that evening. His doting persistence was a turnoff to the point that I couldn't bring myself to have sex with him. I got dressed and biked home. There would be other guys, other opportunities.

IN SHORT, I LIKED teaching, and, a few weaknesses aside, I was good at it. When the opportunity arose, late in 1994, to "graduate" from the school of continuing education and take a contract position with the journalism department, I decided to go for it. I had the good fortune to be recommended by Don Obe, then the magazine-stream director. It would mean more work — two three-hour classes a week and considerably more time spent in preparation and marking — but it would also mean more money while still leaving me time to freelance. I sent a letter of application to John Miller, then chair of the School of Journalism at what had become in 1993 Ryerson Polytechnic University. My application was accepted, and in January 1995, I became an instructor at what was then reputed to be the best journalism school in the country. I should add that I was never a professor, though even I find "prof-titute," the label I would eventually be saddled with, irresistible.

10

The Sex Ring that Wasn't

I WAS A TEACHER and a prostitute and, in many ways, a standard-issue, albeit talented, journalist. But I'd never really lost the sense, honed at *The Body Politic*, that writing could make a difference, could spark social change, could afflict the comfortable. I longed to recapture that sensation, but those heady days seemed over. I seemed to have become a good writer but one who wrote about mostly unimportant things. Joseph Couture helped me change that.

He was twenty-four years old when we met. He had severe problems that manifested in physical pain, and he took a strong, debilitating drug daily. He wasn't mortally ill, but life for him was a trial in ways it wasn't for me, and he would eventually abandon a promising journalistic career.

I wrote about him for *The Globe and Mail* shortly after we met, describing him as "slight, boyish, blond-haired and blue-eyed, with the bee-stung lips of a twenties movie vamp." I noted that he survived on junk food and lived with his mother in London, Ontario. He was smart, politicized, not over-educated, and — by his own admission — an ardent fellationist. I often provided bed and board, and we slept together fairly often, but always as chastely as sisters. He was extraordinary — a working-class boy with neither pretensions nor journalistic training who doggedly pursued what turned out to be the biggest story ever to come out of his hometown — police chief Julian Fantino's staged-for-the-media investigation into a charade the police were calling a kiddie porn ring. Couture had begun by writing stories on the subject for *Xtra*, the successor to *TBP*. Max Allen, then a producer for the CBC radio program *Ideas*, took an interest in what Couture was revealing and hired him to research the story, resulting in a four-part series, debuting in October 1994, called "The Trials of London." I'd become aware of the whole juicy mess some months earlier, in June, when I'd met with a handful of gay activists and street hustlers in Max Allen's office. The object of the meeting seemed to be to engage my interest in writing a major investigative piece for a mainstream media outlet. It worked. Couture also contacted me, offering to turn over his research and be my guide through London's community of work-ing boys. I arranged to interview Chief Fantino — he was happy to speak to a reporter from the nation's most prestigious newspaper. *The Globe and Mail* published my article on March 11, 1995, flag-ging it on the top of the front page with a photo of four young male bodies in silhouette. The story, categorized as "Analysis," led off the paper's Focus Section and was called "The kiddie porn ring that wasn't." It did not please Chief Fantino. I, and my editors, would be hauled before the Ontario Press Council to answer his complaints. The piece was surprisingly anti-establishment for a newspaper with a conservative bent, but it happened for two rea-sons — I was already a frequent contributor whose articles provoked the heated discussion that newspapers love, and my assigning editor was Sarah Murdoch.

Sarah and I shared a sensibility — offbeat, ironic, intolerant of mushy earnestness, suspicious of the official line on almost any-thing — and on top of that we made each other laugh. We loved

working together — no small advantage in an editor/writer relationship. Most of my articles for her prompted a deluge of letters to
the editor, both pro and con. I was a hot property. In 1992, then
editor in chief William Thorsell sent me a handwritten note com-
mending one of my articles as "excellent" and another as "brilliant"
and expressing the hope that I would continue to write for his newspaper. Between 1992 and 1995, I delivered several major features.

I remember the anxieties attendant on writing the London
story, which would turn out to be the most significant article I
would write for Sarah Murdoch. Joseph Couture was an invaluable
source and guide, but I was haunted by the suspicion that he
might also be a paranoid fantasist. I felt slightly guilty that I hadn't
jumped on the story sooner. It was crusading journalism — the
kind of exposé that legitimized my craft — and I'd had to be dragged into it. In truth, I was also a little paranoid myself: I was about
to take on the London police force. (Shortly before the piece was
published, I awoke screaming from a nightmare in which I'd been
asked to write a profile of the devil, who, suddenly aware of what I
was doing, clawed his way through the floor to get me.) Once the
research and interviews were over — I spent several days in London,
staying with Couture at his mother's house — I turned out a 4,300-
word piece in two days. Sarah Murdoch loved it. She told me she'd
only meant to glance at it when I faxed it to her, but she couldn't
put it down. I submitted it in mid-February, but I was heading to
Mexico with my friend Gerry Oxford, and coincidentally, she was
going on vacation as well. I had hoped it would be published while
we were away, but, unlike me, she said she wanted to be around for
the consequences. The publication date was set for March 11, 1995.

It appeared at a time that was charged with hysteria about the
sexual abuse of children, real or imagined. In August 1993, Parliament had passed what came to be known as the "kiddie porn law."

Section 163.1 made it illegal to depict, in text or images, sexual scenes involving anyone who is or appears to be eighteen years or younger. The age of consent for most sexual activity was fourteen, which meant the new law made it a crime to depict activity that in itself would be quite legal. Police Chief Julian Fantino had actively lobbied for it. Just four months after its passage, Toronto police raided the Mercer Union Gallery, charging artist Eli Langer and the gallery director under the obscenity and child pornography provisions of the Criminal Code. The Crown eventually dropped the charges against Langer and the director. Instead, the paintings themselves would go on trial. If found guilty, they would be forfeit to the Crown and destroyed.

The paintings were undoubtedly disturbing. This is how an Ontario Supreme Court judge described them: "Exhibit 50 shows a naked child with her head near the genital area of a naked elderly man. Exhibit 51 depicts a naked young girl defecating. Exhibit 52 depicts a young person and an adult under the covers of a bed. It is apparent that the adult is engaged in some sort of sexual activity with the child, who has a look of anguish on his/her face. Exhibit 53 depicts a naked young girl standing over an elderly man lying in bed. A drop of liquid is drooling from her mouth, and she has a look of sorrow on her face. Exhibit 54 depicts a naked man, apparently with an erection, lying on his back on a bed. Straddling his chest is a young girl, whose labia are clearly visible just inches from his face, which is turned to the side. A barely visible masked figure is entering through the window."

Disturbing, yes. But so was Goya's print series The Disasters of War or any painting, from quite a different perspective, by American artist Thomas Kinkade. More disturbing was the fact that paintings, rather than people, could be put on trial. It reminded me of a time in the Middle Ages when animals could be tried on capital charges. Some were found guilty. Some were executed.

The arts community rallied. There were demonstrations outside the courtroom, which I joined. I appeared on a panel at the Art Gallery of Ontario, along with video artist Lisa Steele, Opera Atelier artistic director Marshall Pynkoski, and several others. Eli Langer was there, but the event wasn't well attended. I noted that only half the seats were filled. Defending what might be kiddie porn was not a popular cause. Once the trial began, the scene in court was devastating. The horrible reality of what it meant to put paintings on trial had to be faced. It felt medieval. It felt Third Reich. The cops — I called them thugs in suits — brought in Langer's paintings, wrapped in brown paper, and then proceeded to tear the wrappings off. The sound of paper ripping is not in itself offensive, but there was something truly monstrous about the violence of that sound. Those men were gangsters at their squalid, noisy work. They propped up the paintings — two of them actually leaned against the prisoner dock — and left them to the mercies of the court.

The case was known as *Regina v. Paintings, Drawings and Photographic Slides of Paintings*. It ended with an acquittal (if that's the word to use when it comes to artwork) and featured something of a glory moment for Ronald Bloore, a respected artist called by the Crown to testify against the paintings. Everyone was surprised he'd agreed. (His wife, gallery owner Dorothy Cameron, had been tried and convicted in 1965 on charges of obscenity for a show called Eros '65.) Not even Langer knew that Bloore was a Trojan horse witness — when he took the stand, he denounced the prosecution and praised Langer's paintings, telling the artist later that he'd "waited twenty-seven years to get these bastards for what they did to my wife!"

The Langer case was more or less contemporaneous with the events that were spiralling out of control in London. The first two paragraphs of my article summed it up. "This is the story of an Ontario city in the grip of a police-constructed moral panic. It is the story of Project Guardian, a province-wide investigation authorized by the Solicitor General that is based on a lie," I wrote. "It is the story of a gay community under siege. Of street kids who sell their bodies because they need the money — and want to make their money that way. Of others who sell themselves for money and hate what they're doing. It is also the story of a story — the sex-and-kids-and-money-drenched headlines and the real lives behind them. It is the story of what has come to be known as the 'London kiddie-porn ring.' And it is the story of Joseph Couture."

The *London Free Press*, beginning in November 1993, had printed dozens of articles, based primarily on police press releases, trumpeting the discovery of a kiddie porn ring and detailing the many arrests that followed. At the time of my article, the police had laid 371 criminal charges against forty-five men, most of them involving sex with "children." I put that word in quotes in my story because I thought its uncritical use by the police and press suggested the alleged victims were much younger than in fact they were. The law would see you as a child in both prostitution and pornography cases even if you were fully eighteen years old. The law prohibited sex with anyone under eighteen if payment or "other consideration" was involved. That other consideration could be gifts of cigarettes, drugs, shelter, clothes, or money. Even at that, by the time my article was published, the police had laid only one charge of making child pornography and only twenty for possession. Almost half of the charges involved obtaining the sexual services of a person under the age of eighteen — teen prostitution, in other words. When the story first broke in the local press, though, the headline read "Child porn bust in London may be largest in Ontario." Couture, like almost everyone else, was horrified and at first fell for the official line. However, he had what no one else in the media had — direct connections to what might be called the underworld of London. He'd hustled briefly himself (at the time, he wouldn't let me reveal that fact, but he has since been open about it). Word soon began circulating in that world that there was quite a different story behind the headlines. Couture began his research, examining court records, contacting the accused, interviewing the "child victims." I interviewed several of them as well. They talked of being intimidated and threatened by the police, cajoled into naming men who had paid for their sexual services, men who had sometimes videotaped them during sex. As I noted in the piece, "The police concede the resulting tapes were never meant for commercial distribution. A good eighty-five percent of the more than sixty young men the police finally got their hands on were fourteen or older — legally able, in most circumstances, to have sex."

London didn't have a kiddie porn ring. It had a problem with street youth, young men who sold themselves and were sometimes treated well and sometimes treated badly by the men who bought their services and occasionally videotaped them having sex. On the other hand, they were almost always shamelessly manipulated by the police. As one young man told me, "I was told to live up to it after giving them some names by giving even more, or I'd be charged with prostitution. The police got us to do their dirty work for them." Another said, "They bribe you. 'The more names you give us,' they tell you, 'we'll help you out in court,' but they just got a lot of hustlers in trouble. They told my parents.... My mom didn't know I was gay. If I'd been smart I wouldn't have told them shit. But they have ways of tricking you."

I took care not to suggest that teen hustling was an abuse-free zone:

Do I think there was abuse here, in any of these situations? Yes, I do. And I think it was happening to most of these boys and young men in their families long before they took to the streets in desperation. That it also sometimes happened in the homes of the older men they met seems inevitable. Perhaps as inevitable as the kindness they sometimes found there too.

I do not mean to suggest that all of the men charged were selfless social workers manqué, interested only in helping youth. Some, I'm sure, just wanted sex. Some, I'm sure, were manipulative. At the same time, I know from experience that most young men who hustle are wise in the ways of the world. They often form loose networks, alerting one another to dangerous (and generous) johns, supporting one another, sometimes bringing new blood into the business. It's a complicated, messy world, with its own rules and rituals, with its good times and its catastrophes. It is not the simple, black-and-white picture painted by the London police — that of an organized ring of older men preying on innocent children.

The London police were not happy that the real story was beginning to emerge through Couture's investigations and the CBC radio documentary for which he'd done the research. In the wake of its broadcast in October, police began warning the young men Couture had been interviewing not to talk to him, adding that Couture himself would soon be in trouble. There were other worrying incidents that suggested the police knew what he was up to and might have been trying to implicate him as well. (A caller phoned to ask him to sign for a prepaid video he'd never ordered. He refused, then discovered when he tried to have it delivered to his lawyer that the phone number was no longer in service. Even paranoids are sometimes right.) The Canadian Committee to Protect Journalists took up his case, writing a letter to Fantino citing such incidents and asking for an explanation. Fantino responded: "Mr. Couture quite properly should be concerned about his relationship with and involvement in the Project Guardian investigation; involvement which, in due course, will be officially and appropriately addressed." As the CCPJ spokesperson noted, she'd written to ask for comments on allegations that Couture had been threatened, and Fantino had responded with yet another threat. "I'd never seen anything like that before," she said. "He actually wrote it down."

The man was almost breathtakingly shameless, which gave me the very special pleasure of catching him out in one of the many lies associated with Project Guardian and making his mendacity public. On May 27, 1994, police had raided the home of one Buryl Wilson, then a fifty-year-old high school teacher, and seized more than eight hundred videotapes. On May 31, Fantino held a press conference calling for more resources to handle the insidious evil of child exploitation. Centre stage at that presser were stacks and stacks of the videotapes seized from Mr. Wilson. Fantino was quoted as saying, "We had plans in place to wind this down, but with this latest arrest any plans for quick resolution have been destroyed." A week later, Ontario's solicitor general announced that a meeting would be held involving ministry officials, the London police force, and the OPP, saying, "This is without question a priority for this government, as it should be."

What Fantino and Superintendent Jim Balmain didn't know during my interview with them was that I had a list of the videotapes they'd seized from Buryl Wilson. It had been provided, thanks to Couture's diligence, by Wilson's brother. I began by asking Balmain what percentage of the seized tapes were pornographic. Most of them, I was told. I then handed over the list. It was some thirty-five single-spaced pages long, and the titles were in alphabetical order. The first was *Abbott and Costello Go to Mars*. The last, *Zorro, The Gay Blade*. Every title was a mainstream American or European film. There was a separate list of adult videos, all cleared for sale in Canada. Balmain blustered. Fantino threatened. "I do caution you now," Fantino said, "that you may be influencing the due process that Mr. Wilson is entitled to receive. Nothing should go out of this material. I want to be on the record, and caution you."

Realizing that the interview was essentially off the rails, I figured nothing would be lost by bringing up Couture and "The Trials of London," the CBC program he'd helped produce. Fantino went back into threat mode. "There may be civil litigation," he said. "There may be a number of options. I'm keeping my options open." He did nothing. There was nothing he could do. He didn't have the facts on his side.

The rest of my article was devoted to analyzing what we were to make of this great and tangled mess. I graphed the meaning of Project Guardian on the x and y axes of all politics: money and power — more money from several levels of government to fund this high-profile case and the creation of a power base for a police chief who had initially lost a bid for the top job in Toronto but had no intention of continuing to languish in a small city. My article ended with a prediction — not mine, but that of a well-known London lawyer who wanted to remain anonymous. If Project Guardian continued to unravel the way it was doing, he said, "Fantino would crash and burn within the year." (Few predictions have been so off base. Despite involvement over the years in more false child pornography busts, harassment of the gay community in Toronto, illegal wiretapping, and several corruption scandals, Fantino would go on to run for Parliament, win a seat, and accept several Cabinet posts in Stephen Harper's Conservative government.)

It had not occurred to me that the person who would bear the brunt of the negative public reaction to my article was Sarah Murdoch. Most of my friends were sex-positive activists well acquainted with police malfeasance. They had no problem believing the police might behave badly. Sarah, on the other hand, had to face a newsroom indignant not only that she had made a claim on their turf but that the resulting article was both irresponsible special pleading and pro-pedophile. Many of her colleagues stopped talking to her. "I was really frozen out," she says. "Not confronted. Just ignored. Right up to the time I left the *Globe* in 1999, there were people who wouldn't talk to me." Judy Steed, a journalist preoccupied with the sexual abuse of children whether there was evidence or not, wrote *The Globe and Mail*'s publisher to ask for Sarah's dismissal. (Judy would also enter my life not many months later.) Sarah would receive a visit from that publisher, who asked if she knew what kind of man I was. She was consoled somewhat by the fact that William Thorsell, the editor in chief, had liked the piece. He also reminded her that she was being victimized by a suburban mentality — when the news group goes home, he said, most of them return to Etobicoke. I knew what he meant, but I'd often joked that, given the nature of my sex work clientele, I'd always felt the suburbs would be behind me — to a husband. Thorsell was at a convention of editors in Florida the day the story came out. Every participating city's newspapers were on display. An American editor who'd picked up a copy of *The Globe and Mail* came up to congratulate him, saying the story should have consumed page one — while admitting ruefully that no American newspaper would have dared to publish it. (Though Thorsell was not publicly gay at the time, the chattering classes knew. A friend who had called the *London Free Press* to ask why my article had appeared in the *Globe* and not in the *Free Press* was told that he had to understand that the *Globe*'s editorial board was full of homosexuals.)

The *Globe*'s editorial board was most certainly not full of homosexuals, though the arts and review departments were at one time dismissed as "the pansy patch" by the more red-blooded gentlemen of news and sports. Opposition to Project Guardian, however, was certainly a gay ghetto: Max Allen, Couture, me, many activists in London, and, entering the fray at about this time, filmmaker John Greyson. He was preparing a documentary called *After the Bath*, a reference to the famous painting by London native Paul Peel that shows two naked children warming themselves before an open fireplace. Greyson asked me to participate, and I agreed. (One always says yes to John.) I knew from his other work that this would by no means be a standard documentary. I knew his politics too, and I trusted him. He told me there'd be nudity involved, which didn't bother me and seemed appropriate, given that Project Guardian was all about child pornography and he was riffing on a painting that could easily be read as a lip-smacking nineteenth-century version of same, though it tends to be interpreted as an icon of prepubertal innocence. As if it couldn't be both.

The body of the documentary masterfully dissected the sham that was Project Guardian, a police-constructed moral panic aided and abetted by the supine *London Free Press*. (The interviews with its then editor, Philip McLeod, are particularly revealing of the way the newspaper simply regurgitated police press releases.) There are typical Greysonian touches — the performers, all male and a range of ages, take turns bathing naked in a tub. I was the oldest, a boy of ten or so the youngest. John brings in his own experiences as a teenager, having sex with an older man in the basement of a London library. (The intercut scenes of a 1950s promo film for "fun at the library" add considerable levity.) Perhaps my favourite moment occurs when Fantino, in voice-over, is referring to "mature predators" while the onscreen image is of me, washing myself in the tub. John builds his case incident by incident and fact by fact, bringing in material not available to me when I wrote the *Globe* piece, material that bolstered our accusations of police mendacity, incompetence, gender hypocrisy, and bias. He interviews York University sociology professor Thelma McCormack (she had also been a witness for the defence in the first *Body Politic* trial in 1979), who characterizes the crackdown on this imaginary crime wave as "the new Red scare." Lawyer and activist Brenda Cossman testifies to the fact that there is simply no such thing as commercial child pornography in Canada. The hysteria whipped up by the mainstream media over these largely imaginary cases of child exploitation is starkly in evidence when the film plays, in voice-over, some of the hate-filled calls to a local phone-in show (the image on screen is of me washing the back of one of the other actors). Greyson, in one of the final voice-overs in the forty-five-minute documentary, sums up its thesis rather neatly — the police, the media, and social service agencies couldn't (or wouldn't) distinguish between consensual sex and abuse. The resulting arrests, charges, and predation by social agencies ruined the lives of many men and youngsters. The closing image on screen showed two of the younger actors, cozily naked in front of the fireplace.

MARCH AND APRIL 1995 had been tumultuous months for me, what with the publication of the Fantino piece and the sense that I had endangered Sarah Murdoch's position at *The Globe and Mail*. (Guilt could make me snappish. She told me around this time that something I'd written was too provocative, and I, self-importantly, came back with, "You mean too provocative in the way Socrates was too provocative?" She accused me of being glib. She was right.)

On top of that, the Ontario Press Council had announced their decision to adjudicate Chief Fantino's complaint about my article.

I was also, during April, becoming increasingly agitated about the upcoming premiere, at the Inside Out Film Festival, of scenes from *Symposium*, the Nik Sheehan film in which I had a role. It didn't bother me that I was enacting a scene from my life as a prostitute or that I was nude and sucking off some young guy — I was distressed because I didn't think the scene was very good and thought that the defects were due partly to my inept script and partly to Nik's editing.

Nik Sheehan was trying to create a modern-day version of the famous Platonic dialogue and had engaged a number of prominent homos of the day to provide their take on love "in the age of AIDS." (Among the many others who agreed to participate were Brad Fraser, Sky Gilbert, Scott Symons, Tomson Highway, Daniel MacIvor, and Patricia Rozema.) Nik is a friend. Friends then, as now, helped each other when it came to projects that would be prohibitively expensive if you employed real actors and real writers. I liked what he was doing and wanted to be involved. I wrote a scene for him about the delusions of love, about how having good sex with someone might make you think you were in love, about how desperate for love the young can be and how easy it is to get it wrong. In my life as a prostitute, I'd often run into situations where men, especially young men, saw our good time in bed together as a prelude to something grander or as an overture to romance. Those ambiguities and uncertainties and frailties were what I wanted to explore. It was my first attempt at a screenplay, and I wasn't very good at it. It was based on an actual event involving — too good to be true — a Ryerson student, and it went like this: Young man, having answered my "massage" ad in *NOW Magazine*, appears at my door. He's a little startled that I'm older, but he comes in. He strips, lies on the bed, I strip too, sit astride him and massage him until he gets a boner, and then I suck him off. Or so said the script. In the event, the young man, intimidated by a roomful of cameras, sound people, and perhaps my hovering, yeti-like presence, couldn't get hard and had to go into the bathroom alone to pump it up enough for me to suck. I'm guessing the film's budget didn't extend to hiring a fluffer. I then try to kiss him, but he objects, saying, "I want to save that. It's not for you ... it's for a lover ... it's for when it means something ...," and he pushes my head down to his dick. True to the spirit of the absurdist school of script-writing to which I seemingly subscribed, my head suddenly reappears, and I begin to lecture him on love, which doesn't go very far at all because we cut to post-coital bliss over muffins; the young man asks, half jokingly, if he can move in with me, and I reply, not at all jokingly, "No." As I recall, the scene was one of the few that had any explicit sexual content, which may explain why Nik was using it as a promotional tool.

The Inside Out showing for Friday, May 19, opened with Nik's film, the working title being *Three from Symposium*. The full film was still in edit. I squirmed through my scene and tried to disappear into the upholstery, but it seemed better on the big screen, which puzzled me. I thought its faults would be magnified, but its virtues seemed enlarged. Nik introduced it, and us, and there was some cheering when my name was mentioned. At the end of the showing, a voice called out from the back, "I love you, Gerald!" People were very kind afterward, and I think I got some small sense of how appearing in a film, bad or not, enlarges and sanctifies you. I ran into a group I knew only slightly on the street outside the theatre, and their interactions with me were subtly different, I'm sure, than they'd have been if they hadn't just seen me on screen. I think I recognize it partly because I've felt it myself, on occasions when I've met people who are, even in small ways, famous. (Or famous in big ways — many years later, while doing research for a magazine article, I would meet and chat with both Bill Clinton and Matt Damon at the same Toronto party.) There's a slightly forced cheeriness, a desire to be clever, and a strange cherishing of even the banal things they say. The next night, in the queue for another film, Gerry Oxford said he overheard some people behind us saying, "Isn't that the star from one of the movies last night?" (Curiously, just six months down the road, my role in *Symposium* would bring me face to face with real notoriety.)

I turned fifty-one on July 10. "In good shape, physically," my journal records, "and just about broke. I'm down to $500.00." Luckily, before the month was out, I'd entertain five clients, including Nick, the aged Italian grandfather who came to me to get fucked, and Mike, the devotee of nude philosophy lectures followed by a bout of frottage. I was holding my head above water, but barely.

I needed an assignment and had an idea to propose to Sarah Murdoch at *The Globe and Mail*, but when we finally spoke, it was clear she'd been avoiding my calls. She was worried that the Ontario Press Council was dignifying Fantino's complaint with a full hearing, though she didn't yet have a date for it, and wondered if it would be better if I didn't attend with her, fearing, as she put it, that I might launch into one of my hamburger-flipping analogies, by which she meant some glib comment I'd made about rather having a child of mine work as a prostitute than at McDonald's. She also told me that I always underestimate the fervour of people who are so opposed to the ideas I raise that they'd stamp out free speech in order not to hear them. In spite of those reservations and her uncertainty about publishing anything more from me in the short term, I did sell her on the idea of a piece on Elizabeth

Spedding, the Contessa, initiating the hospital visit, her room crowded with sex workers.

I met several times in mid-September with Sarah and Colin McKenzie, the Globe's managing editor. The Press Council hearing had been set for September 28, and we wanted to devise a strategy. Sarah seemed quite agitated about it all, which made me unsettled. Colin seemed calm and confident.

Chief Fantino was there, as were Superintendent Balmain and several social worker acolytes. They spoke for a good hour, and the loathing they felt for both me and Couture was almost palpable. They accused me of tricking them into believing I was a staff reporter. (I hadn't, but that led to my favourite quote of the day: "As far as this hearing is concerned, Gerald Hannon *is The Globe and Mail*.") They accused me of selling part of the interview to the CBC even though they said they'd granted me an exclusive interview. Indeed, I had sold certain clips to a gleeful Max Allen, though there had never been any mention of exclusivity, and certainly there was no signed agreement to that effect. They said I'd lied when I wrote that the budget of Project Guardian was a secret because I could probably have got the information under the Access to Information Act. And on it went, for an hour. Max Allen, who knew the full story as well as anyone, was astonished that I managed to keep my countenance during this tirade. Significantly, though, the police didn't challenge any of the facts in my article, which I think became the burden of Colin McKenzie's laconic ten-minute response. I felt, when he finished his measly riposte, that I had to say something. I wasn't supposed to, I had nothing prepared, and I kept no notes of what I said, but I believe I commended Fantino and Balmain on the quality of their police work when they stuck to the facts of a case, but when it became a crusade based on mere fancy and ideology, I thought it the responsibility of the press to hold them to account.

The Press Council released its decision in early November. They gave the *Globe* a slap on the wrist. The article had been mislabelled, was the judgment. It had been flagged as "Analysis." It should have been labelled "Opinion." I could live with that, and the *Globe*, when it printed their decision, stressed that none of the facts in my article had been challenged.

11

Queer in the Headlights

· ·

HE DIDN'T LOOK AT me when he spoke. We were strangers approaching each other on the street. I was heading home on a wintry evening in March 1996. When we came abreast, he continued to look straight ahead, but as we passed, he whispered, "You're famous." He was right. Every good self-mocking Canadian will demur and say, "Well, I was world famous — in Toronto," but by that time there had been headlines in newspapers across the country, many appearances on radio and on television, stories in the American press, headlines in a Moscow newspaper, a cover story in *The Guardian*, an invitation to appear on *The Jerry Springer Show*, an attempt to buy the television rights to my life story, and a request from a young choreographer to turn that story into a ballet. I had been compared, not unfavourably, to Socrates. I had been compared, not at all favourably, to Jane Austen. If not famous in the pristine sense, I could at least make a decent claim to infamy.

I keep few secrets, but only my friends and some Ryerson colleagues knew I was a prostitute. Only archivists would have been aware of my fifteen-year history as a gay activist, even though that history had involved several brushes with the law. And only other writers and colleagues in the magazine and newspaper business knew my work as a journalist. All those histories were seemingly in balance, and of no interest to anyone else, until mid-November 1995.

I WAS IN NEW York the weekend of November 10, 1995, attending the fiftieth birthday party of Herb Spiers, my old friend from the days of communal living in Toronto and a one-time object of love and lust. I returned on November 12. The day before, November 11, a conference had taken place in Toronto. The theme was Women in the Media, and it had been organized by the Canadian Association of Journalists. I knew nothing of the event, but within days the fallout from it would begin to consume my life. The resulting tabloid-fuelled scandal would finally bring an end to my career as a teacher.

Judy Steed, at the time a *Toronto Star* journalist and author of a book published in 1994 called *Our Little Secret: Confronting Child Sexual Abuse in Canada*, was a panel member at the conference. Heather Bird, a columnist at the *Toronto Sun*, was in the audience. I'd never had any interactions with Bird — it's unlikely we even knew the other existed. I'd never actually met Judy Steed, though we'd had one telephone conversation some time before, and the previous summer I had been assigned by *Xtra* to review her book (the review appeared in the July 8/94 issue). The phone call from Steed constituted part of her research for *Our Little Secret* — she was aware of, and disapproved of, my 1977 *Body Politic* article "Men Loving Boys Loving Men," and, scrupulous to a fault, she wanted to know whether my views had changed in the ensuing years. I don't remember the exchange very well — it seemed of little significance at the time. I do remember that she became both incredulous and hostile when I said that my views were essentially the same. I found her vehemence somewhat unsettling, but I'd been tried and acquitted in the criminal courts more than once for that piece of writing, and I'd learned never to be surprised when it provoked strong reactions.

My review of Steed's book tried to do justice to legitimate concerns for the welfare of children in contexts ranging from the domestic to the religious to the sexual while arguing that "our reaction must be both reasoned and principled, virtues which have mostly eluded Ms. Steed in *Our Little Secret*. She has let pity and outrage run away with her senses, and has produced a book that takes as its premise the notion that sexual contacts between children and adults can never be ethical. I find that position intellectually unsatisfying. Sex, after all, is among the more ordinary human activities. It is not difficult to do. People are almost unanimous in finding it pleasurable. Many children experiment with sex on their own (mostly, though not exclusively, with each other). Children and adults interact — in fact, must interact — in many, many areas: sports, education, religion, culture. Why is sex exempt?"

I did not hear from Steed in the wake of that review, though I can assume it didn't please her. It may also have had a serious impact on both her revenues and her reputation, especially among feminists. In January of that year, Steed and Random House, her book's publisher, had negotiated a deal with the National Action Committee on the Status of Women to sell copies to the organization's members as a fundraiser. NAC was apparently in financial difficulties, and Random House was willing to sell them five thousand copies on terms that would make resale to their members a profitable enterprise. The deal foundered when opposition within the national executive, led most forcefully by vice-president Shelagh Day, vetoed the project. The decision exposed deep divisions within the organization and led to several resignations in protest. Author and media personality Michael Coren wrote about the affair in

Books in Canada, having hosted a radio show on CFRB that brought together representatives from both sides of the issue. Coren, who used to flavour his distaste for homosexuals with a whiff of Roman Catholic ardour, quotes Steed and others claiming that NAC's executive objected to the book's alleged homophobia and that they were prompted to do so by my review in *Xtra*, "the homosexual newspaper with the largest circulation and the most influence in all of Canada." I wish I could claim to have had that kind of impact on tough-minded, independent individuals like Day — her objection to the deal seemed mostly to rest on the feeling that it would be a money loser. I should add that I did not think Steed's book homophobic and that the word never appeared in my review.

Steed had ample reason to dislike me — she might have believed that my review had sabotaged a lucrative book deal and tainted her reputation. More important, though, was her sense that I was dangerous, a man who gave a patina of respectability to ideas and behaviours that would, in her mind, inflict horrible damage on children. She had only to discover that I worked with young people. That was all she needed.

Sometime earlier that fall, Ryerson students preparing a class project on child abuse had decided to interview Steed. She was, after all, thought to be an expert on the subject. Some of the students who'd read her book would have picked up on its references to me — the journalism department at Ryerson wasn't large, and I would have been a known face — and apparently mentioned in passing, during their sessions with her, that I taught there. On Thursday, November 9, she telephoned the school and spoke with John Miller, the head of the journalism department — she wanted to know if it was true that I was employed there as a teacher. Miller must have been a little puzzled by the query, but said that yes, I was an instructor in the magazine stream. She told him she was shocked, that I was a well-known advocate of pedophilia and that hiring me to teach journalism was the equivalent of hiring a white supremacist like Ernst Zundel for the job. (This would not be the last time that analogy was made.) Miller said that he knew about my views on intergenerational sex but that those views didn't enter the classroom, that I'd been hired to teach journalism and did so, that there'd been no complaints about my work from either students or staff, and that was that.

That wasn't that for Judy Steed. Saturday, November 11, the day of the Women in the Media conference, would provide her with the perfect venue for continuing that conversation, in public. She took some of her time on a panel devoted to the subject of dealing with negative male attitudes to denounce Ryerson for having hired me to teach, claiming as well that she'd felt bullied in her telephone exchange with Miller, who happened to be in the audience. He was shocked that she would move their earlier discussion into the public sphere and argued vehemently that she had no right to accuse someone of wrongdoing if she had no evidence. The exchange piqued the interest of *Toronto Sun* columnist Heather Bird.

I came home from that New York visit to find a voice mail message from Bird. I had no idea what it might be about, so I called her back. As a journalist who relies on people returning my calls, I'm inclined to do likewise, even when the call comes from the *Sun*, a paper whose editorializing almost twenty years earlier had undoubtedly sparked the police raid on *The Body Politic*. Of course, I didn't know then about the conference or the exchange between Steed and Miller, and I can't remember whether Bird put her questions in context for me. Alarm bells should probably have gone off — she seemed most interested in whether my views on intergenerational sex ever entered the classroom. I was honest — I told her that "Men Loving Boys Loving Men" and the subsequent

Body Politic trials came up when I introduced myself to a class and that I sometimes used those trials to illustrate the dangers journalists face if they investigate unpopular topics. I told her I had recently talked to my students about being taken to the Ontario Press Council by Police Chief Julian Fantino, the result of a critical article I'd written for *The Globe and Mail* on a so-called kiddie porn ring in London, Ontario.

Alarm bells didn't go off. They almost never do for me. I have this much-cherished fantasy that, when I go to bed at night, at the very moment my eyes close in sleep, friends, strangers, the whole world really, somehow get together, link up through some vast, cosmic internet, and spend my sleeping hours planning ways to make me happy the following day. Mostly, that's what seems to happen. I'm crazy happy most of the time.

Perhaps something went amiss when I fell asleep on the night of November 13, 1995. In any case, the November 14 issue of the *Sun* featured a column by Heather Bird titled "The professor of desire."

It was a cleverly constructed piece. She quoted extensively from my review of Steed's book, selecting sections that, out of context, would read as inflammatory. She conceded that I taught young adults, not children. She conceded that I could hold any opinions I wanted. But, she wrote, as a teacher I should check my beliefs at the door, and I did not: "By his own admission, he's raised the issues of child pornography and 'intergenerational sex' — a code word for paedophilia — in his classroom." It was at that point that she transitioned me from harmless eccentric to positive danger who had had a profoundly unsettling impact on the "young people" in my class, partly because it was difficult to resist my "charismatic personality." (Anyone who knows me well might find that gigglemaking.) She quotes one dismayed student, without naming him or her. Two paragraphs later, that "one" has multiplied: "students" are now revolted by my views. Only two of my students admitted to having spoken with her, and both said positive things. Bird claimed she reached five — three who were pro and two who were not. A teacher I'd never met and who was on sabbatical at the time (she would apologize to me later for being taken unawares) was quoted as saying, "I don't think academic freedom gives you the right to spout off about anything," which prompted Bird to speculate that there would be those who "cite academic freedom to defend Hannon's right to proselytize." Smart word choice. Readers were left with the impression that I was on a crusade and that Ryerson had granted me, in Bird's words, "the power and the platform to influence young minds."

Young minds had their own views. The front-page November 15 headline on the student newspaper the *Ryersonian* read "Students support Rye prof," and indeed they did. Several from my class were quoted. "As a teacher, he's great — it's not an issue," said Carolyn Gleeson. Stacey Langbein, who would remain a fervent supporter in the difficult weeks to come, was quoted as saying, "He's an excellent teacher and an amazing writer. His beliefs don't impinge on the way he teaches journalism." The *Ryersonian* would later contact twenty-three of my twenty-six students, guarantee them anonymity, and ask them if they had problems with me but were afraid to go public. One admitted to feeling occasionally uncomfortable with my sexual references and to my being openly gay. That was it. Department chair John Miller chimed in, "Our position is that he's teaching journalism here, nothing else. No students have expressed upset to me — rather, just the opposite. They're upset by this [Bird's] column." That same day, he sent out a memo addressed to all faculty: "I have talked with the students and with Gerald Hannon and am satisfied that Heather Bird's column is inaccurate. If any of you plans to talk publicly about this issue, please avail yourself of the facts. Don Obe, the acting chair of the journalism department, will be glad to provide background to anyone who wants it."

The *Ryersonian* story ended with a reference to Miller having received two hate calls the previous day. I am quoted as saying I might receive a few as well, but I am sanguine about the outcome. "I think it will all blow over soon."

The next day, November 16, I received a letter from Michael Dewson, Vice-President, Faculty & Staff Affairs. He began by summarizing the allegations in Bird's column and then went on to say, "It is my obligation to investigate those allegations to determine in more detail what did or did not go on in your classes. To that end, I wish to interview you on Monday, November 27, 1995, in my offices at A1224 Jorgenson Hall at 11:00 a.m. I would ask you to bring a representative of CUPE 3904 with you or be prepared to sign a waiver in respect thereof at the time of the meeting. At this time, I will also indicate that we will be interviewing students in your courses to determine what did or did not go on in the classroom as regards the topic of intergenerational sex."

It was, on the face of it, a very odd decision. Dewson was about to begin an investigation solely on the basis of one columnist's allegations in a famously shabby publication. There had been no complaints from students, from faculty, or from the union. In fact, as Miller had pointed out, most students were upset by Bird's attack, not by anything I'd done. We weren't taking into consideration, however, what a delicate period this was for the institution.

The Ryerson Institute of Technology, as it was known at its founding in 1948, had long been the poor cousin of other institutions of higher learning like the University of Toronto. It was frequently dismissed as "Rye High," the school you went to if you didn't make it into anything better, the school for students who wanted to learn a trade and get a job — an admirable goal, but one often sneered at by academics. Where a university might have a strong English literature faculty, Ryerson had a strong journalism school, devoted to preparing students for careers in both the print and electronic media. The *Ryerson Review of Journalism*, founded by Don Obe in 1984, is regularly cited as the best such publication in North America and has been the recipient of a long list of awards, including several National Magazine Awards.

Ryerson had grown, both in size and in reputation, over the years. It wanted recognition, and it got it when, in 1993, a bill was passed in the Ontario Legislature granting the school university status. It could now institute graduate programs and qualify for funded research. It could now hold up its head in the world of academe and would have been desperate to avoid anything that might sully its hard-won reputation as a newly minted university with serious academic credentials. Ironically, its own behaviour over the coming months would do exactly that. Professional contacts at the University of Toronto were unanimous in assuring me that U of T would not have dignified Bird's column and allegations with a response. Ryerson University would, in its desperate attempts to claim what it imagined to be the high ground, revert to being Rye High.

On the day I told the *Ryersonian* that I thought everything would blow over soon, I accepted an invitation to appear on the Horsman-Lederman show on AM640, a talk radio station. I have never owned a television and, at the time, had not had a radio for many years, so I had no idea of the station's profile. Perhaps that was not the best idea, but I seem unable to resist the impulse to justify myself, to explain what I really mean, to show that I'm not a provocateur but a reasonable guy whose ideas, if you take the time to consider them, will possibly change the way you think about a good many matters related to sex and sexual mores. (I should say that my own ideas have sometimes appalled me, but I try not to let that get in the way of exploring them.) I don't remember much about the interview, but the *Toronto Sun* took note of it, headlining its story "Prof backs adult-kid sex" and quoting me saying things like, "I don't think such relationships are automatically bad" and "I don't see why sex is different from sports, education, religion." The article also records that I admitted to discussing sex often in the classroom, but that's wrong. I did not discuss sex often in the classroom.

The story began to grow. The *Sun* published two pieces on November 17. One, featuring a photo of me in my office at the school, was headlined "Prof defends kid-sex views." The second was headlined "Nobody is going to fire this guy," which was a quote from Don Obe, the acting chair of the School of Journalism. In it, I expressed incredulity that a subject that I wasn't to discuss in the classroom should have become the talk of the town and said that the process was beginning to look like a witch hunt and smacked of McCarthyism. The next day, Heather Bird's column bore the title "Prof pushes a perverse idea" and began with the sentence, "Sex before eight, or it's too late." She claimed — wrongly — that it was the motto of the North American Man/Boy Love Association and went on to say, "Its views on adult-child sex coincide with those of Gerald Hannon, the Ryerson journalism professor under fire this week." The "sex before eight" canard would be repeated by Judy Steed in a letter to the editor of *The Globe and Mail*. I responded, correcting her error of attribution and stating that it was a sentiment with which I thoroughly disagreed. I don't think that made much difference. Nothing I said seemed to make much difference; the story was beginning to take on a life of its own. In her column, Bird reported that she had been deluged with phone calls from outraged "students, teachers, alumni, hockey coaches, a

Crown Attorney, feminists, REAL women and victims, especially victims" — all people "revolted" by my views.

The deluge started for me as well, particularly after November 19, when I appeared on CBC-TV's *On the Line* to debate Heather Bird. I believe this was the occasion when she almost ran me over with her car. We were both racing toward the CBC building, she in her automobile and I on my bike. Rounding a corner, she caught sight of my front wheel, swerved just in time, and missed me by six inches. She was mortified. I was oblivious. I found out only when she mentioned it, in a state of panic, at the studio. I've often thought a collision would have been the perfect ending to our relationship. During the show, she questioned me about an incident I described in MLBLM, one in which, as part of my research, I shared a tent with a man and a twelve-year-old boy who were probably, but not certainly, having sex. (It was too dark to see, but I could hear giggling.) At the end of the show, a gentleman I'd never met came up to tell me that he understood the police would be investigating me for complicity in a sexual assault. I almost crumpled then — the spectre of another trial, in the midst of this trial by newspaper, was more than I thought I could bear. It felt like a kick to the stomach. Two days later, on November 21, the *Sun* headline read "Police sex squad probes professor." Heather Bird's column that day was titled "A question of morality" and contained the sentence, "By his own admission, Hannon was present while a sexual assault took place." It then went on to list the different sections of the Criminal Code under which I might be charged. A few days later, the police would abandon the investigation, claiming that too much time had passed since the alleged infraction for there to be any likelihood of success.

Over the next few weeks, my telephone became an instrument of torture. People called to insult me. People called to support me.

People called just so they could hang up, and they would do it over and over again. That was probably when I got my first call from the man I would dub "My Tormentor." He would call dozens of times a day, always talking in a child's voice, calling me daddy, telling me there was blood in his poo-poo or asking me to kiss his pee-pee. The calls would continue for a very long time, and he would soon start calling Ryerson, asking to speak to "Daddy." The secretary in the journalism department had to put up with a lot. We would eventually trace the calls to the offices of the downtown law firm Borden and Elliot, who were tepidly cooperative in trying to catch him, suspecting he worked not for B&E but for Olympia and York, the building's managers. They came close once, narrowing the calls down to a service area, but he always managed to elude them. People still wrote letters on paper and posted them back in 1995, and my mailbox would often be crammed with support, with threats, with insults. The media were always calling, wanting yet one more interview, extending one more invitation to appear on television or radio. When I left the house, my voice mailbox would fill before I got home, and though I turned the ringer off before I went to bed, I would find my voice mailbox full in the morning. I began each day by listening to hate messages. I decided not to change my telephone number. Whatever happened, I wanted that small victory.

I wasn't facing any of this alone. I had strong support within the journalism department — Lynn Cunningham, Don Obe, and David Hayes disagreed with much of what I had to say about inter-generational relationships but never wavered in their defence of my right to hold those views and teach at Ryerson. On Novem-ber 21, Obe would go so far as to debate Steed on TVO's *Studio 2*, doing his best to keep the issue positioned as one of academic free-dom while she portrayed me, as one friend put it, as "a dangerously charming member of the pro-pedophile lobby" and then read a graphic description (not by me) of an eight-year-old being brutally fucked face down on a carpet. Tim Falconer, then a fellow part-time instructor with whom I shared cubicle space and many hours of conversation, would write a touching essay titled "Loyalty and Controversy." If I'd judged by stereotypes, he would not have been someone I would have expected to come to my defence. Pudgy-cute (I always wanted to pinch his bum), he was what I used to think of as the ur-straight boy: boisterous, hockey loving, beer drinking. Despite our differences, despite his conviction that some of my ideas were "ludicrous and wrong," he came down on the side of loyalty to a friend and cited, as an example to follow, an instance in which ice hockey commentator Don Cherry had done a similarly unpopular thing. (I'm sure, to the relief of both Cherry and me, that will be the only time our names will ever be linked in the press.) Many students supported me — in interviews, in person, and in articles they wrote for the student press. Four women in my class, none of whom I thought particularly liked me, arranged for a cake to be delivered to my door during one of the darker moments in the weeks that followed. Adam Hunt stands out, and not just because he would come out as gay several years later. At the time, he had a shock of multicoloured hair and a passion for social justice, writing a supportive piece for the *Ryersonian* and taking the stage with me and others when a press conference was held the following week. (He would go on to work for various NGOs in Burma and Thailand, write acerbic, witty letters back to his friends in Canada, and invite me for coffee whenever his travels brought him to Toronto. We're still in touch.)

Personal friends were hugely important in keeping me sane, and most would be involved in organizing the press conferences that became our principal way of responding to the media firestorm that was soon to erupt even more violently. It was a measure of my increasing paranoia, though, that my journal began to note and disparage friends who did not call me *enough*, who didn't invite me over for a drink, who offered some slight critique of my behaviour or the way I was handling the media. That paranoia flowered when *NOW*, the city's alternative weekly, published a story on November 23 headlined "Gay journalists desert Hannon." The previous Sunday, I'd been on a panel organized by the National Lesbian and Gay Journalists Association, of which I was a member. The topic was "covering ourselves." As *NOW* writer (and my then editor) Glenn Wheeler wryly noted, "This event had been arranged weeks ago, long before Heather Bird turned Hannon into national news with her *Toronto Sun* columns accusing him of promoting intergenerational sex to impressionable twenty-four-year-old students in class." He went on to say, "The journalists' association has been noticeably silent on the Hannon matter, unlike his Ryerson colleagues and students, who have been outspoken in his defence.... Board members had talked privately about issuing a statement, but decided not to, co-chair Jessica Pegis says. There's a 'fear of the [pedophile] label,' she says. 'It's not necessarily rational — it's a panic reaction.'" Wheeler ended his article by asking, "And what good is a gay journalists' group whose members are so paranoically career-ist that they're afraid to speak up for a colleague who's the victim of a witch hunt?" The NLGJA would later rethink its position and issue a support statement. In a subsequent issue of the organiza-tion's newsletter, writer and friend Rachel Giese wrote, "Our media are not equipped for frank and complicated discussions of sexu-ality and so, for the most part, we didn't have one.... By not taking up the issues that got Hannon in so much hot water, we missed the boat. We also gave up the chance to open up our media to more complicated discussions about sexuality. As gay journalists, we will continue to face the charges of 'homosexual perverts,' 'child molesters,' and 'criminal prostitutes.' By not shying away from these issues and masking them in arguments about freedom of the press, we may help our audience understand them better."

The day after Glenn Wheeler's column about my having been abandoned by the NLGJA appeared, I took a phone call from the *Toronto Sun*. It would end with my being caught out in a truth.

ON THE EVENING OF November 24, 1995, I received a call from Thane Burnett, a journalist with the *Toronto Sun*. I had grown accustomed to speaking with the media — my life had become a blur of radio, television, and print interviews over the previous ten days. I have often been thought naive at best, or a media whore at worst, for acquiescing to nearly every interview request that came my way, but it was the express wish of Don Obe, my boss, that we not avoid the media and that we tell the truth. We had nothing to hide, he said. He was a long-time journalist with an illustrious history, and I admired him immensely. I was happy with his strategy. I don't like lying, except on social occasions. As well, hearing "no comment" repeatedly from a source is a journalist's nightmare, and I did not want to visit that on any of my colleagues, no matter what they thought of me. I had nothing to hide. I would tell the truth.

A very few minutes after I began talking with Burnett, I began to agonize about whether I would indeed tell the truth this time. I could see where he was going. He had in his possession a photograph showing me and a much younger man naked together in bed. It was flattering to neither of us — I looked like a predatory yeti and he like a lamb in the headlights. The photograph was a still from Nik Sheehan's film *Symposium*, the one I'd appeared in and which he was promoting at the time with images and press releases. The reporter had found the photo in *Fuse*, a Toronto arts magazine.

Burnett began questioning me about the script and why I had chosen to play a hustler, and wasn't the film supposed to be based on people's actual experiences? I was evasive, and no doubt sounded so. I could sense he was soon going to pose The Question. I was getting panicky. My life had been in constant turmoil for two weeks. I'd continued to accept almost every interview request that came my way — they were stressful occasions, often with interviewers who were as near to hostile as journalistic propriety would permit. I wasn't sleeping well. I needed pills. I was plagued by abusive phone calls. It was almost impossible to continue to teach. On November 23, the day before Burnett's call, the school had received a serious threat to my life. A few days later, on November 28, police arrested a forty-year-old man and charged him. I never learned how that played out. If students wanted to meet with me, the administration had dictated that they had to be brought, one by one, to the office in which I was locked. When it came time to teach a class, I was escorted to the room by security personnel who remained outside the door, allowing students in one at a time. The classroom curtains had been drawn tight for fear that a nearby rooftop might harbour a sniper. When it was time for the class to begin, the security officers locked the door from the outside and remained, one on each side, keeping guard. I stood inside, at the front of the class, before a room of anxious faces. And then I was supposed to teach a class on magazine journalism. I'm a pretty good teacher, but I did a terrible job. The students were kind and said I did just fine, though they would comment later, to me and to the press, that I looked an exhausted wreck, and they were right.

That had been my life for nearly two weeks. And now I was about to face The Question, the answer to which could determine my future as a teacher and my career at Ryerson.

I can't remember how he phrased it, but it was direct. Was I a prostitute? I believe I dithered incoherently for a few moments, and then I said that yes, I was. I wish I could say that my devotion to truth was my only consideration, but I feared no reporter would ask that question of a not particularly gorgeous fifty-one-year-old man if he didn't already have some solid evidence in his hands. My fear of being deemed a liar — the disreputable obverse of putting one's faith in truth — was also a motivator.

And then I talked. Burnett described our conversation as "lengthy and startlingly frank." I wanted, as best I could in the confines of a media interview, to stress that my sex work was not something I was ashamed of, that I was high-spirited about it, that it was a smart choice for a freelance writer and part-time instructor. I joked that a lot of people have to get grants to make a go of a life in the arts, that I'd been hustling off and on since 1987, and that everyone I was close to, personally or professionally, knew the score. (At Ryerson, Don Obe knew, as did fellow instructors and good friends Lynn Cunningham and David Hayes.) I stressed that prostitution was not illegal in Canada. I told him that I had not discussed it with my students. I think the last thing I said to him was, "I hope you're not going to make too much of this." Despite my conviction that the world is organized to make me happy, I did have the feeling that the paper might run with the story. Before I went to bed, I called Ed Jackson and told him what had happened. I discovered later that he, similarly worried, had called Rick Bébout after speaking with me.

The front-page headline on the *Toronto Sun* the next day, Saturday, November 25, 1995, read, in three-inch block letters: "Ryerson Prof: I'm a hooker." The subhead below read "Gerald Hannon says he supplements his teaching income with prostitution." The article

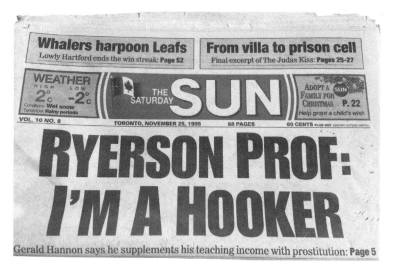

Toronto Sun headline that set off my nightmare year at Ryerson.
Photo: Ed Jackson

was accurate and quoted me extensively. Even some of my supporters would soon begin to feel that my commitment to full disclosure was not always in my best interests.

Heather Bird's column that same day was headed "Ryerson silence is telling." It began with a note of almost grudging admiration: "You've got to hand it to him. That Gerald Hannon is one provocative old bugger. Once again, the libidinous adventures of Mr. Hannon, Esq., are making front-page news." I have to hand it to Bird as well. At the time, I was too distraught to appreciate how cleverly structured the piece was, how it built to a rhetorical frenzy that Ryerson felt it could not ignore. She was very persuasive. "Can you be a neurosurgeon by day and a prostitute by night?" she wrote. "Yes. Does that make you a bad neurosurgeon? No, of course not. Would you, as head of a hospital, hire a neurosurgeon who moonlights on his back? Not likely. Why? You don't have to answer that. When it comes to hiring, you don't have to justify. It's a judgment call." She conceded that Ryerson had exercised good judgment when they first hired me to teach, presumably because of my reputation as a writer. But. Did the school know I was "a part-time whore?" Did they not care? She moved on to suggest that I was the chief architect of my own misfortune, that I could have shut down the controversy "quickly and quietly by refusing to give interviews.... Instead, Hannon was cooperative when asked to expand on his world view, up to and including an hour-long debate on national television." She added a touch of sympathy. Was I ill? she wondered. "Is this a hangover from being physically abused as a child? Is he manipulative? Or merely naive? ... And while we fiddle," she wrote, "Ryerson burns."

She declared that Ryerson's national reputation was on trial, that I had become a "flashpoint for an institution under siege." She added, "There is a clear leadership vacuum at the top levels of the university." She called for someone "somewhere in the ivory tower [who] thinks it's wrong for adults to have sexual congress with children. That there is nothing noble about the sale of human flesh. That those views aren't representative of the school or its values. Or should we simply let the silence speak for itself?"

The silence was broken early the next morning, Sunday, November 26. There was a knock on my door. It was a courier, hand-delivering a letter.

The letter, my third from VP Michael Dewson, announced, "We are investigating whether your alleged conduct is unbefitting the status of a member of the teaching community at Ryerson." I was told to attend a meeting in his office at 9:30 a.m. the following day. I was also told that I was suspended with pay, that I was to have no contact with my students, that I was not to be permitted on campus, and that I was to turn over all classroom materials and student evaluations to John Miller, chair of the School of Journalism.

I don't remember much about that meeting with Dewson. I do remember that I was bolstered by the presence of CUPE representative Angela Ross; her warm, level-headed, almost maternal charm and fierce sense of justice would make her an important ally in the months to come. She could laugh at the more absurd elements of the situation, and I sometimes needed help seeing the funny side to what I was going through.

I also remember that I lied — or was guilty, at least, of *suppressio veri*. Dewson, frigid with distaste at having to deal with matters so indelicate, asked, through pursed lips, if I'd ever had sex with a Ryerson student. I said I'd never had sex with any student in my classes but that I didn't ask for student ID so couldn't say for certain whether I'd had that particular pleasure with someone not in my class. That statement was true, as far as it went. I had certainly never had sex with any of my students, as clients or otherwise, and I didn't ask for student ID. But several young men wanting my $30 student rate had self-identified as Ryersonians, and I'd based my scene in *Symposium* on one such encounter. (When we were filming, the director and I had debated having the client arrive wearing a Ryerson jacket. Perhaps it's just as well we decided against it.)

My life re-entered headline mode: "Ryerson suspends its prostitute prof"; "Embattled professor suspended by Ryerson"; "Hooker-prof flouting law: Minister"; "Ryerson suspends teacher in prostitution disclosure." This last story, from *The Globe and Mail*, was the most accurate and balanced; it recognized that I was a teacher, for starters, never a professor. (Full disclosure, it was written by Michael Grange, a former night school student of mine.) My current students were learning first-hand what it was like to be involved in what often gets called a "media firestorm" — the press, both print and electronic, was constantly tracking them down for interviews and quotes, and some students, on their own initiative, offered themselves up or wrote letters to the editor. Adam Hunt, in a *Toronto Sun* interview, said Ryerson just wasn't ready for a teacher like me and wondered, "How many old white men with two kids and a mortgage do we have to be taught by?" (I may have been old, white, male, and mortgaged, but at least I was kid-free.) Stacey Langbein, who wanted me back on the job and clearly understood how the media was shaping public opinion, told *The Eyeopener*, Ryerson's alternative student paper, that she was going to get in the media as much as possible: "That's where the battles are fought." Carolyn Gleeson, in a *Toronto Sun* letter of the day, wrote that I was "the type of professor that journalism students desire — a teacher who is open-minded, actively involved in the writing community and not afraid to experiment with the conventions of traditional journalism. I hope he continues to teach students at Ryerson. Most of all, I hope he shares with them what he shared with my class — that writers who break the rules of journalism are often those who write the most compelling pieces of work."

I might have added that writers who break too many rules had better be prepared to deal with the dark side of celebrity that we call infamy. Whenever I left my apartment, there were looks, nudges, and whispers as I walked down the street. Cab drivers wondered if I was the guy they'd seen on TV. Young men working on the elevators in my building broke into winks and grimaces as I passed, one of them saying, "I'm going to hurl." Movers in the hall outside my apartment apologized for banging something against my door, and then one of them suddenly said, with what I thought was a threatening voice, "Aren't you Professor Hannon?" When I rather timidly acquiesced, he said, "Could I shake your hand, sir?" adding that he didn't agree with everything I said but admired my courage. One day, near Bloor and Avenue Road, someone suddenly clutched me forcefully from behind, and I thought, *This is where I die. This is where the knife enters my back*. I turned in terror to face a laughing woman, a stranger, who just wanted to say she had really enjoyed my appearance on television the previous night. I found my stress level higher than I'd ever thought possible. The endless harassing phone calls — they increased to fever pitch after the prostitution revelation. Being "up" and prepared and articulate and, if possible, funny and quotable for every media appearance. There were times, sitting in studios waiting for yet another hairdo to interview me, that I would begin to panic. I wanted to run away, give up on attempts to explain myself, slam the door behind me, get my life back. I felt I might be going a little crazy.

According to the *Toronto Sun*, I also appear to have made a hemi-semi-demi sensible decision: "Hannon didn't answer calls last night," read their November 27 story. "His answering machine indicates he's 'taking the weekend off' from speaking with media."

I hadn't stopped speaking with supporters, though. As a long-time gay activist, I'd made a lot of activist friends with a gift for organizing, and they rallied. We met at noon. CBC producer and long-time censorship foe Max Allen was there. There were friends and colleagues from my *Body Politic* days: Ed Jackson, Rick Bébout, Robert Trow, Ken Popert, Mariana Valverde, Gerry Oxford — who said he was there as a foot soldier. And I, never one to resist a quip, said, "And I am the foot. In my mouth, I guess." There were others more closely associated with *Xtra*: David Walberg, Rachel Giese, Gillian Morton. There were friends from academe: Ian Lumsden, Nancy Nichol, and Maureen Fitzgerald. Friends from the arts community: Lisa Steele, Kim Tomczak, and Richard Fung, who chaired the meeting. We created the Committee to Defend Gerald Hannon and decided to hold a press conference the next day. Ed Jackson, who was then on the board at Buddies in Bad Times Theatre, arranged to have it there, in the cabaret known as Tallulah's.

It's an awkward space, bisected by a staircase that leads to a group of small rooms on an upper floor. The ground level features a bar, a dance floor, and a small stage. I arrived early, with friends, and we immediately went to an upper room to discuss strategy. I was surrounded by people I loved and trusted, but I was more or less a mess. I knew I had to be smart. I knew I had to be honest. I knew I had to be funny, thinking it important to undercut the ponderous moral certainties that fuelled my accusers. I wasn't sure I could be any of those. I became even less sure when it came time to leave the upper room, descend the stairs, and face the press. Tallulah's was packed. There were not enough chairs. Some journalists, the *Toronto Sun*'s Christie Blatchford among them, sat on the floor. Heather Bird wrote next day that "a scrum larger than most which greet prime ministers" had assembled, and that I "descended the staircase, à la Norma Desmond, slowing slightly to nod to supporters to the left and right." The table on Tallulah's small stage bristled with microphones; the open space directly in front was a field of cameras.

There was an equally impressive gathering around the table on stage. Lisa Steele moderated for a group that included Don Obe (saying he was ashamed now to be teaching at Ryerson); Jackie Manthorne of the Writers Union of Canada; Professor David Rayside (a former *Body Politic* collective member), representing the University of Toronto; Angela Ross, from CUPE, who announced the union was filing a grievance; lawyer Frank Addario, who was providing legal advice; Thelma McCormack, retired head of the Centre for Feminist Studies at York; and two students, Adam Hunt and Stacey Langbein. (Lisa Steele, tongue in cheek, assured the audience that I would respect the terms of Ryerson's suspension order and have no contact with them on stage.) Writer Nino Ricci, who had organized a support letter from PEN Canada, was in the audience, as were writer Morris Wolfe and at least a dozen of my students.

I was some of the things I wanted to be. I was honest. I was funny. Christie Blatchford began her column the next day with my response to a question on how I could, at fifty-one, still have paying customers: "Now ... that *is* the astonishing thing, isn't it?" It got a laugh. As did this: "I give good classroom. I give good prose. I give good head. Why is that a problem for an institution allegedly concerned with excellence?" Sentiments like that seemed to have won Blatchford over. She described me as an "ironic, provocative showman with a big mouth and brass balls ... a tweedy, rumpled and engaging man with outlandish opinions and a steadfast insistence on expressing them." Her column was headlined "Ryerson gutless in handling of Hannon." Bird's read "Hannon not the real victim." The real victim was Ryerson, of course. "The school is in deeper trouble than ever," she wrote, "judging by the turnout and tone of yesterday's presser. They dramatically upped the ante over the weekend only to find themselves matched and raised by a cool opponent.... They are running the risk now of creating a martyr."

Was I smart? Perhaps not so much. By then, I knew, or should have known, that a press conference was not the place to talk about what I was calling intergenerational relationships. It's not a topic for sound bites. Still, I couldn't stop myself. I had to make people believe me, believe I was a reasonable man. I had to tell them about the fifty-four-year-old man who'd called me to say he'd had sex with an adult male when he was nine, and he'd loved it. That drew an enraged response from a journalist who happened to be the mother of a nine-year-old boy. I can still feel the loathing sweeping up from the floor. Rick Bébout, describing the event in a letter to writer Jane Rule, wrote, "TV crews looking for juicy and damaging sound bites got their fill and some bites ended up on the news tonight, though in general the coverage was pretty good. And this does set the tone this time around: there's no point trying to force Gerald into mealy-mouthed dissembling. All will out, and we'll have to deal." In retrospect, the "giving good head" comment was funny but probably a mistake. I lost my cool with one reporter, snapping back at him that "a university is not a European health spa. Students don't come here to bask and bathe in handed-down ideas. They come to debate issues." Certainly true, but my vehemence meant I was exasperated and close to losing it.

The *Toronto Sun* had more or less owned the story when it came to editorializing, but the *Toronto Star* and *The Globe and Mail* belatedly entered the fray with commentary of their own. The *Star*'s editorial described my views as "repugnant," adding that "it would satisfy our moral outrage to dismiss Hannon for holding them. But for a university — a sanctuary of free speech — to take such action would be to set a very dangerous precedent." *Globe* columnist Michael Valpy began his piece by alluding to Socrates, condemned to death for corrupting the youth of Athens. He didn't feel it necessary to explain why. "You know what this column is about," he wrote. He added, "One wishes nothing more than that Mr. Hannon would shut up and thus not require defending. However …" He went on to point out that the university had violated its collective agreement by publicizing a disciplinary action and by suspending me prior to an inquiry being held. He concluded his column with two questions: "Does freedom to philosophize, however unpopular, necessarily undermine society and conventional morality? Or is a good society impossible without freedom to philosophize?" That same day, the *Globe*, in its editorial "A Private Life," most likely written by editor in chief William Thorsell, argued that calls for my dismissal were based on the "same reasoning used by Canadian school boards, as recently as a decade ago, to justify the firing of teachers who were (or who had married) divorcees. One's private life becomes the gauge of one's public accomplishments. If this is our standard, then perhaps we ought to seek out those academics who have purchased the services of Mr. Hannon and his escort-service peers — a far larger group to hound out of the classroom." He added, "Mr. Hannon is a man of ethics — not everybody's ethics, but consistent ethics nonetheless — and sees no reason to hide his private identity. If his detractors are successful, hiding will be the only option left for those with controversial views."

Curiously, as the big editorial guns of the city's respected news-papers came out with at least grudging endorsements, I also had to face the fact that support from students and staff at Ryerson was beginning to erode. I'd met with some fifteen journalism faculty members the morning before the press conference. (Banned from campus, I'd received special permission from Dewson to attend the staff meeting.) Most didn't know me; there wasn't much interac-tion between the lifers and the contract teachers. All they knew of me was what they had read in the press or seen on television over the previous ten days. They gave me a very chilly reception. Department chair John Miller, who'd defended me from the begin-ning, was thrown by the prostitution revelation, felt I should have told him about it, and was upset that, in his mind, I was using the journalism department as a soapbox to expound my views.

Some students began to waver. Dan Brown, smart, sassy, talented, a man I liked a lot and with whom I'd gone drinking, told the *Globe* that the prostitution disclosure had thrown him for a loop, that "a professor who's a prostitute doesn't fit my ideal of what a professor should be." Six months later, in June 1996, he wrote an article for the *Globe*. Headlined "Gerald Hannon deserved to lose his job," it celebrated my qualities as a teacher, slammed my abhorrent views, and ended with the following: "Gerald Hannon was an effective teacher. He did change my way of thinking. And I hope he never teaches again." I was pleased that the piece was so well written and structured, but I have to admit I was hurt. Perhaps it's egotism, but I couldn't quite believe it, either — it felt more like an exercise in rhetoric than a heartfelt repudiation. A student I'd never met wrote an opinion piece in *The Eyeopener* that called for the "delousing" of the journalism department. Some of my students were annoyed that the affair had screwed up end of term; they had papers due for me, and I was forbidden from meeting them or setting foot on campus. Though I was supposed to hand over to the department all the student material I already had, John Miller, to his credit, overrode that directive. (I can only appreciate now how much of a risk he was taking — he was publicly disobeying his bosses.) He said I was to remain their teacher, grade their papers, and submit marks. He was also gallant enough to stand before my class and read a statement I had prepared for them, assuring them that I would have grades assigned by the deadline Ryerson had set and thanking them for their backing. "I want you to know," I wrote, "that of all the support I've received, both professional and personal, yours has been the most important to me."

The simple, sensible decision to let me mark my students' papers led to absurd and near-comical complications. I wasn't to set foot on Ryerson property, so I couldn't pick them up. I wasn't to meet with students, so they couldn't bring their papers to me. Finally, we settled on a plan: the long-suffering department secretary would call me when she had papers for me to mark. I would walk south on Church Street to the northeast corner of Gerrard Street — which we decided, rightly or wrongly, was not Ryerson property. She would walk north from the journalism school, a block to the south. When she saw me, she would cross the street, hand me a plain brown envelope, turn around, and go back. On return visits,

I would hand her a plain brown envelope of the papers I'd marked. It was giggle-making — it felt as if we were consummating a drug deal or participating in a very low-budget espionage flick — but I wanted to adhere to the letter of the law when it came to Ryerson's strictures. If there were to be problems, I wanted them to be on issues, not on technicalities.

I was no longer on campus or in the classroom, but the issue continued to bubble and simmer. It had taken on a life of its own. Debate still raged in the student newspapers. My favourite headline was "Hannon: More fun than asbestos" in the November 29 *Eyeopener*; it was a supportive and amusing editorial, claiming, "Gerald Hannon is the most fun this school has had since they found asbestos in the Hub [a student bar]," but it went on to deplore the administration's decision to remove me from my teaching responsibilities "one class before the end of semester … the administration has shafted Hannon's charges in a desperate grab for damage control." One of my students, Shane Schick, saw what most of my colleagues on faculty were missing. "I can't help thinking that this has been one of the best learning experiences Ryerson has ever handed us journalism students," he wrote to *The Eyeopener*. "Never before had we appreciated the horror of a Slow News Week as we do now. Never had we guessed at the discomfort we create with the endless phone interviews, the sound-bite camera clips, at having our words taken out of context by another reporter. I've seen the other end of the microphone now and I know the damage it can do.… All the questions and the ghoulish haste to suck this story dry has left me feeling lost, frustrated, like the more that's been written, the less truth has been told."

Among the faculty, debate crackled, but mostly out of my ken. Years later, I would gain access to email exchanges among profs not in the journalism department. I wish I'd known at the time that, though there were those who had no problem with the way the university was treating me, the majority, which included author Margaret MacMillan (who would go on to write the celebrated *Paris 1919*), expressed outrage and endorsed an email signed by John Cook, a professor in the Department of English, and Dorothy Buchanan, Learning and Teaching Coordinator, to Michael Dewson and Ryerson's president, Claude Lajeunesse. It read, in part, "We strongly object to the University's response to allegations, made by the media and not by our students or colleagues, that removes a lecturer not only from a class but from the university as a whole. The *Sun* indulges in demonizing. We shouldn't. The *Sun* indulges in the infantilizing of our students. We shouldn't.... Hannon's activities outside the campus may indeed require legal investigations and a response by Ryerson to those findings. However, in the meantime we would have hoped that this university might have responded with the instincts of scholars, not those of the *Sun*." (Many years later, I would profile Margaret MacMillan for *Toronto Life* magazine. I didn't know, then, of her support. I wish I had. She had a certain formality about her, but she didn't look like someone who would be averse to a hug.)

Normalcy was still a long way off back in November 1995. It receded even further with the publication on November 30 of an opinion piece in *The Globe and Mail* written by Bronwyn Drainie, an instructor in media ethics at Ryerson, headlined "Sometimes, defending freedom of speech stinks." The gap in the journalism department between those who supported me and those who did not became a chasm.

I'd never met or spoken with Drainie. I would undoubtedly have assumed she'd be a supporter: she was both a well-known liberal media voice and the scion of a famously liberal family. (Her father, John Drainie, was a celebrated radio and television performer who had co-hosted the groundbreaking investigative television show *This Hour Has Seven Days*.) As a result, no other piece written about me had a more devastating effect. Heather Bird's columns in the *Toronto Sun* hadn't upset me particularly; she clearly took her job as journalist seriously, interviewing me, attending press conferences, and debating me on television. Though it was very clear she didn't agree with my views, she quoted me copiously in her articles, and, tendentious as they were, she left something for the reader to decide. Drainie (who became known as "Brain Drainie" among my supporters) relied entirely on media reports for her opinion of me. I clearly wasn't worth a phone call. The column was charged with a visceral revulsion that was hard to countenance from someone I'd never met. She wrote that my life as a prostitute, revealed in a "copious, salacious interview" in the *Sun*, "turned a serious issue of free speech into a farce, rubbed Ryerson's face into the juiciest pile of ordure he could amass, and demonstrated utter contempt for those who had gone to bat for him ..." She thanked me for forcing her to think through her own limits of tolerance. She wrote that I'd taught my students that it was all right to lie. She claimed I'd "played us all for suckers, feeding off our worried, Canadian desire to do the right thing, and is probably at this moment sketching out the oh-so-witty article or book he plans to write ('I'm an excellent writer, you know') about his Wildean adventures among the Philistines."

She ended with, "The decent thing would be for him to leave quietly at the end of this term and make a monetary settlement with Ryerson. But somehow I don't think decency is in Hannon's bag of tricks."

It was brutal, and her Wilde comment made me realize the dangers of being flip and nonchalant when it came to issues that many see as ponderously grave.

David Hayes wrote a long letter to Drainie and posted it on a listserv for journalists. He commended her for a thoughtful and honest piece of writing and acknowledged that he and many other supporters "find Gerald's thesis on adult-child sex wrong-headed." He then went on to say:

> *Your portrayal of him as "probably at this moment sketching out the oh-so-witty article or book he plans to write … about his Wildean adventures among the Philistines" struck me as a cheap shot. First, it was pure speculation, quite unlike the tone & substance of the rest of your column. Secondly, those who know Gerald well know how patently false that picture is. You're entitled to your opinion, Bronwyn, but I trust you contacted Hannon to speak to the man himself & gauge your reaction to him. Surely you didn't base that character-damning passage on media reports & second-hand opinions from those who barely know him.*
>
> *I also take serious issue with another statement. The assumption that before the "Prof-as-hooker" revelation it looked as though the whole thing was going to die down and "Hannon would work out his contract and then never be rehired." Excuse me? If the administration had established that he had done nothing wrong in his classroom, you're arguing that an excellent teacher and writer supported by his students who holds highly unorthodox, to some troubling, views would "never be rehired?" On what grounds? Is this part of the "worried Canadian" way? He holds controversial, troubling views but he's done nothing wrong. So rather than take a stand on principle, rightly or wrongly, & fire him, we'll let it quietly die down & then never rehire him. Good Lord, Bronwyn, surely this part of your column was written under deadline pressures. I can't believe you believe that.*

What troubles me about some of the reaction to the "Prof-as-hooker" revelation is the implicit double standard: it might have been palatable if Gerald had been properly contrite, rather than frank & unapologetic. Just as a segment of the heterosexual community has come around to supporting gays, so long as they're in conventional, monogamous relationships, like same-sex copies of the Brady Bunch ideal. That support diminishes when confronted with the unrepentant, randy reality of a large, vocal core of the gay community.

Hayes remembers, "It was a rough period. The faculty split into pro/anti camps, and things were kind of ultra-sensitive after that." Lynn Cunningham recalls, "I didn't spend a lot of time sounding out faculty about where they stood, in good part because I was afraid to learn they were anti — then I would have had to hate them." Don Obe had similar memories. "We tried to keep it civilized," he said, "but the two sides just hated each other and it filled the room during faculty meetings."

November tipped into December, with very little diminution in the media's obsession with the story. *The Globe and Mail*, on December 2, featured eleven letters to the editor under the heading "The much-examined life of Gerald Hannon." Columnist Susan Kastner in the *Toronto Star* the next day was up to not much more than insult: "Look at the guy, I say, face like a spaniel on acid, and, he claims, he still gets paid for it." Of course, Heather Bird had her say that day. Headlined "The last word on Hannon" (it wasn't), the column began with some tepid humour — "This will be the final word (one hopes) from this space on Ryerson's philosophical pederast (or, if you prefer, peddle-your-ass) professor" — and went on to make a case for the danger I posed even to mature students because of my alleged charisma. She quoted extensively from an article by my student Adam Hunt in the November 29 *Ryersonian*, citing his willingness to consider that some relationships between youths and adults might not be damaging as proof that I had corrupted him. Well, pass the hemlock. That same day, the *Star* featured a piece by then columnist Naomi Klein, who tore into the media for their hypocrisy, noting, "Many journalists have unwittingly shown themselves to be identical to the 'special interest groups' they have repeatedly charged with sacrificing academic freedom at the altar of offended sensibilities. What, after all, is the difference between the position taken by Hannon's detractors and the actions of some much-maligned student activists who lobby for 'zero tolerance' speech codes at their universities?"

It was a heartening read, particularly since it came just days after Drainie's vicious attack. Klein went on to say, "Of much greater concern for morally outraged parents/journalists should be all the university professors who receive research funds from private corporations — that's a real threat to academic freedom. ... But perhaps that's just the point. Only someone who is already an outcast from society's sexual norms could have been discarded with such head-spinning speed and with such a chilling display of institutional force."

Klein's point about research funds would get fuller treatment a week later, in the December 7 issue of *NOW*. Writer Scott Anderson (who went on to become editor of *University of Toronto Magazine*) addressed the matter of Ryerson president Claude Lajeunesse's professional background. Lajeunesse had accepted the Ryerson position only a few months earlier, in September, but "he has spent much of his career arranging government-industry sponsorships for university research and lobbying for university funding. ... In his former job as director of targeted research with the Natural Sciences and Engineering Research Council of Canada, Lajeunesse was directly responsible for setting up partnerships with industry." Anderson noted, "University officials will not comment on whether the university has been pressured by financial donors to make Hannon go away," then went on to say that it probably didn't matter because Ryerson's credibility as a university might already have been seriously damaged. He quoted a letter Ryerson's Faculty Association had sent to Lajeunesse, calling on the university's senior administration to "demonstrate moral courage and integrity by admitting to an error in judgment, reinstating Gerald Hannon immediately, and adhering in the future to the demands of due process." The article contained a final kick at Ryerson's pretensions to serious university status — Anderson quoted Suzie Scott, executive director of the U of T Faculty Association: "At U of T absolutely nothing would have happened to Gerald Hannon as a result of what the *Sun* did. There would have been a lot of talk. There would have been people having debates about it, but our administration would not have raised one single finger."

Ryerson's administration, on the other hand, was interviewing my students, privately and one by one. Because an announcement was expected before the end of December, the story still had legs. I continued to talk, often in ways that dismayed some of my supporters. I wanted to be frank on sexual matters, particularly when I spoke with student journalists, and there's no doubt that a long feature by Chris Purdy in the *Ryersonian* on December 6 would have exasperated anyone who wished me well. Even Adam Hunt thought I'd gone too far with explicit sexual detail. Don Obe, in later years, would tell me the same thing. Purdy quoted me saying, "The wonderful thing about whoring — it spins your life out into a whole new world and its people. It's the same with teaching — meeting people you wouldn't ordinarily meet in your social group."

I think Purdy was startled by my frankness and a little

unprepared for it. "The only thing I know for sure about Gerald Hannon is his candour," she wrote. "He's the most straightforward and outspoken man I've ever met." That this was not necessarily a good thing in the minds of many students was brought home by a page of letters in the same issue. As an article in the December 11 Maclean's noted, the Ryerson community was deeply divided. Journalism chair John Miller was quoted as saying, "I told students and faculty to figure out the issue that's most important to you, and make your decision on that basis. But I also told them whatever you decide, it's going to be messy. There are parts of your decision that you're going to hate."

My life clearly needed a boost. I decided I had to have a party. Many friends and colleagues had pulled together quickly and selflessly to support me — arranging press conferences, sending letters and faxes to the Ryerson administration, offering advice, making me meals, doing everything they could to keep me sane in the face of this onslaught. I wanted to thank them, and on Sunday, December 17, I hosted a party in my apartment. It was a packed, jubilant evening that somehow released the pressure that had been building for weeks in everyone, not just me. Gay and straight, friends and colleagues: most everyone who could make it did make it, and it was loud and laugh-filled, consoling and energizing. It had an air of celebration about it. Sarah Murdoch brought along Sandra Martin, who'd been assigned to profile me for Toronto Life magazine. My first impression wasn't positive. I noted in my journal, "I don't think I like Ms. Martin. She's sneering and disdainful, and that's the pose sophisticated people adopt when they are either frightened or closet moralizers." I was wrong about her. She was a sympathetic interviewer and a dogged researcher. Her article, in the July 1996 issue of the magazine, would win her gold at the National Magazine Awards the following year.

I needed the energy that party supplied. The following day, December 18, Barbara Amiel's column in *Maclean's* was headed, "Firing 'a hooker' is an employer's right." It was an odd article in that it never referred to me by name — apparently, I was famous enough by that point that "hooker" could refer only to me. It was vintage contrarian Amiel, who claimed she'd have no problem with a teacher who "held a well-argued class on why, under certain circumstances, sexual contacts between men and boys should be legalized." On the other hand, if she ran Ryerson and discovered one of her teachers was a hooker, she'd fire him.

I was soon to learn whether Ryerson shared that view. The next morning, I received yet another hand-delivered letter from Michael Dewson. It read, "This letter is to inform you that I have concluded the two investigations with respect to your conduct and behaviour and I am now in a position to advise you of the University's decisions in respect of those investigations. You are hereby instructed to attend a meeting in my office on Wednesday, December 20, 1995 at 9:30 a.m." Ed Jackson and Lisa Steele, with the help of U of T professor David Rayside, arranged for a press conference at 1:00 p.m. the next day in Croft Chapter House, an attractive period building and one-time chemistry laboratory affixed to University College. No one seemed to have any idea what Ryerson might have decided. Richard Blair, CUPE's lawyer, said he often had a sense of how a case might turn out, but this was a complete mystery. John Miller had come by the day before to pick up student papers and said he'd been cut right out of the loop, even though the administration was supposed to consult with him. Says so right in the collective agreement. As a friend said in the gym that day, they were making damn sure I got one more sleepless night out of this.

I can't remember if it was a sleepless night. I'd had so many of them. I also can't remember if Michael Dewson read aloud the letter he handed to me the next morning or whether he simply proffered it, sat back, and let me read it. It was just over a page long and very formal. He began by saying that the investigation into my classroom behaviour showed that I did not "expressly endorse paedophilia nor advocate [my] personal views on the subject matter with [my] students.... The University has concluded that there has been no breach with respect to the Collective Agreement provision on Academic Freedom, and, as a result, no disciplinary action will be taken." In other words, my students, interviewed one by one, had told the truth about what went on in my classroom.

That was the good news. Dewson then went on to point number two. "We find that your conduct in openly engaging in discourse and interviews in the media with respect to your sexual activities as a prostitute, including the *Ryersonian* article of December 6, 1995, is conduct unbefitting the status of a member of the teaching community of an academic institution. Such conduct has had a detrimental effect on Ryerson's reputation within the community and, in our opinion, you have exercised extremely poor judgment in your handling of this matter," he wrote. "The University, therefore, will be placing a copy of this written reprimand in your Performance and Conduct File. I trust you will govern yourself accordingly in the future, failing which you may be subject to further disciplinary sanctions, up to and including discharge. We will therefore require you to commence your full teaching duties effective January 8, 1996."

So, I was to remain a teacher. I was exhilarated that the whole edifice built on Heather Bird's misleading columns had collapsed. I was not a pedophile apologist in the classroom, and my students had said so. I thought I could live with a written reprimand in my file, and "conduct unbefitting" had a kind of antique charm about it, as if I were an officer in the British Raj who'd been caught *in flagrante* with a servant.

The press conference that afternoon at Croft Chapter House was the usual beehive and featured many of the supporters who had backed me at the Buddies in Bad Times presser: Lisa Steele, Stacey Langbein, David Rayside, Don Obe, Thelma McCormack, CUPE rep Angela Ross (announcing that the union would file another grievance because of the gag order), and lawyer Frank Addario. The *Toronto Sun's* banner front-page headline on December 21 read "Hannon fights Ryerson gag ruling: Prostitute professor can return to the classroom but sex talk is banned." (I shared that front page with this story: "Queen tells Di, Charles: Get a divorce." Me and the royals — a natural fit.) *The Globe and Mail* that day ran a weirdly convoluted column by Martin Levin entitled "Gerald and Jane," which wiggled down to the perhaps not astonishing conclusion that "Jane Austen would not have approved." It also, along with the *Toronto Star*, ran news stories, all of them noting that I was back on the condition that I not discuss my sexual activities as a prostitute. Columnist Rosie Dimanno had a more insulting take: "In essence, the yakety-yakety Hannon has been gagged by the school, gag also being a synonym for retch, which is what most of us want to do whenever Hannon opens that orifice just beneath his nose." I announced I'd comply, but, lippy and unrepentant, I couldn't resist quipping that "as a good prostitute, I'd probably charge for those details anyway."

I also made a comment I regret. "It's hard, in some ways, to blame the *Sun*," I said. "You know, it's a tabloid and it's doing a tabloid's job. It's a dirty little job and if you hire the right dirty little people to do it ..." Heather Bird, in her column two days later, picked up on that reference. I was clearly alluding to her, and I'm sorry I'd sunk down to that level of personal invective. I'd tried hard until then to restrict my comments to the issues in play, and though I might offend people by being frank and explicit to an uncommon degree, I had no desire to insult anyone. I did, though. Bird, I have to say, got in the last, best dig. "After all, when it comes to dirt," she wrote, "Mr. Hannon would know."

The local media had more or less exhausted the story's potential for the moment. There would be a few quiet weeks, but in that interim the international media began to pick up on it. *The Washington Post* section of *The Guardian Weekly* ran a piece on Christmas Eve. A friend then living in Russia sent me a photocopy of an article in *Sevodnya*, a Moscow daily, which appeared there on December 30. He translated the headline for me: "By day, at the faculty — by night, on the streets." Its last sentence expressed surprise that someone who had "entered his sixth decade" could "enjoy commercial success" as a prostitute. Another friend reported seeing a story in an Indonesian newspaper. All this foreign interest reached its comic apotheosis in January when I received a call from Paul de Souza, a producer with Parkwood Pictures, with offices at 2121 Avenue of the Stars, Los Angeles. He wanted to buy the television treatment option rights to *Gerald Hannon, The Life Story*. He was glib and breathless and eager and flattering, suggesting that he saw Richard Gere playing me. A friend said that if any actor whose initials were R.G. actually qualified, it was Ruth Gordon (an elderly actress who played a loquacious Satan worshipper in the film *Rosemary's Baby*), and I began to joke with friends that I would hold out until they got Roseanne. He also mentioned money, US$35,000 at first, which shocked me into silence. He then added $15,000 more, for "consulting fees." The shocked silence continued. Thinking, I guess, that I found the offer too small, he said, "You're not Amy Fisher, you know. There's not going to be a bidding war on this one." (Fisher had been much in the news a few years earlier. Aged

seventeen — and dubbed the "Long Island Lolita" by the press —
she'd shot and badly wounded the wife of her lover, the incom-
parably named Joey Buttafuoco. Fisher served six years in prison
and eventually went on to become an actress in pornographic films.
Easy to see why it was thought her story had more legs than mine.)
I actually contacted a local entertainment agent to represent me,
but it was clear within a few days that the project was a no-go. As
a representative from Parkwood Pictures put it, the production
company they approached "didn't think it would play on American
network TV."

One American network phenomenon, however, did think my
story would play — I was contacted by *The Jerry Springer Show*
with an invitation to appear. I'd never seen the show, but I knew
enough about it to realize that the issues I was interested in were
unlikely to get a hearing. I was amused by the very idea, though,
and played along for a while, refusing to appear for anything less
than $10,000. To my astonishment, I was told that they never pay
guests and that, if I accepted, I would have to pay for my own flight
to Chicago. (It's hard to believe anyone would accept such terms
for the right to be mocked and abused, but there seems to be no
limit to the number of people willing to debase themselves for a
taste of celebrity.) They kept calling, trying to talk me into it, and
finally took the apparently unusual step of offering to pay for my
hotel in Chicago. I told them to stop calling me. They finally did.

That's how 1995 closed for me. That and my not unexpected
appearance on several media year-end highlights lists. The *Toronto
Sun*'s Christie Blatchford, never quite predictable, included me in
her list of lowlights of the year, describing me as "rumpled, bespectacled, bony-shanked." She got two out of three right. *The Globe
and Mail*'s Liam Lacey alluded to me in the context of a quote from
Salman Rushdie: "One of the things a writer is for is to say the

unsayable, to speak the unspeakable, to ask difficult questions." I ended up on several "I wish they'd just shut up" lists. (I shared more than one with Diana, Princess of Wales. Me and the royals, again!) *Xtra* asked a number of "local creative types" to list their New Year's resolution; mine was, "I resolve to add 'as seen on TV' to my escort ad." (I did, too, much later. It read something like "Do it with a wry prof. As seen on TV!" I couldn't stop being a lippy little bugger. One of my students figured it out and called me on it, for a laugh.) *Frank*, the much-missed Canadian satire magazine, awarded me the number nine spot (of twenty) in its list of The Bores of '95, printing the still from *Symposium* that had started it all, with the cutline: "We'll pay him not to have sex. Gruesome leather boy could scare Sky Gilbert straight. Some alternative. Some lifestyle." An earlier issue of the magazine had used that same photo on the cover, doctored so that writer, broadcaster, and articulate homophobe Michael Coren replaced the young man I was in bed with. The cover draw read, "Bone up for Christmas exams!" My friend Rick Bébout, who was closely monitoring the media reaction, mentioned the following: "In a segment on its New Year's Eve show, CBC's *Royal Canadian Air Farce* cuts to a man in a suit jacket, black panties, red garters, nylons and high-heels — ostensibly at the Department of Justice in Ottawa. The voice-over: 'It looked like the faculty lounge at the Ryerson School of Journalism.'" The Montreal *Gazette* featured an editorial page illustration by Aislin, the country's most famous cartoonist. The text across the top read "Oxymoron of the Year: Journalism professor will also continue to work as a prostitute ..." while a punishingly accurate caricature of me features a thought bubble saying, "Six of one ..."

The most unlikely brush with celebrity came when I took a call from George Stamos, a young Canadian choreographer living in New York. He wanted to create a ballet based on my story. I recall him saying he'd been a hustler himself, though mostly in Amsterdam, I think, and that he had Quentin Crisp involved in the project. It didn't go ahead.

I returned to teaching on Monday, January 8, 1996. I was met with a note from John Miller (copied to my teaching performance file) thanking me for the professional way I had dealt with my students "during a very disruptive time for you and for them," as he wrote. "You were under no obligation to continue evaluating student work while you were suspended, but you very graciously insisted on doing so.... it would have been difficult, if not impossible, to find a replacement who would have been able to fairly evaluate their work. Thanks to your generosity and commitment as a teacher, that was not needed."

I was also met, of course, by the media. The "Ryerson shock prof," as the *Toronto Sun* routinely referred to me, was back at the blackboard. Reporters first clustered just outside the journalism office (Miller shooed them back into the hall), then they followed me out the door and along the street to the building I was to teach in, right up to the classroom door, flashbulbs popping and cameras whirring, my students wondering, I would learn later from one of them, if all this craziness would ever end. The photograph in the *Sun* showed me waving goodbye and closing the door on the press. A story the next day quoted me saying, "The first few minutes were tense because I was nervous. But then they warmed up and I warmed up and class seems to be going just fine." I learned later the students appreciated my professionalism in spending just a few minutes talking about the hysteria and then getting down to teaching journalism. And I could tell, when I got them laughing after the first half hour or so, that classroom life was more or less back to normal. In an unusual move, the administration had adopted a policy of allowing anyone to switch into or out of my class.

Even editorial cartoonist Aislin couldn't resist comment on my Ryerson experience. Cartoon: Aislin

Apparently, only one student switched out, and only because his father insisted.

The student press was also on the story. "Oh boy, Hannon's back" headlined one column. Perhaps the most salient comment came in an editorial in the January 10 issue of *The Eyeopener*. Editor Mathew Shepherd published his list of "Resolutions for the fightin' year," and number one was, "Stop arguing about Gerald Hannon with numbskulls. He doesn't bring it up in class. None of his students have ever complained. What he does on his own time is his business. Thank you and good night."

Ryerson's administration might not have been comfortable being swept up into a media frenzy, but *Forum*, a university newsletter, had to acknowledge in its January 12 issue that coverage had "probably set a record in terms of the amount of Toronto print media attention focussed on Ryerson over a single issue." They'd been keeping track. In the period from November 14 to December 14, "there were at least 122 stories, letters, columns, editorials, cartoons and commentaries in major Toronto print media and in Ryerson's campus press," and that didn't include extensive electronic media coverage "that even encompasses a Gerald Hannon site on the World Wide Web" (a real novelty in early 1996). The article concluded by saying that, "taken together, the coverage fills an inch-and-a-half three-ring binder."

There was more to come. *Spartacist Canada*, the magazine of the Trotskyist League, ran a two-page feature with their usual exhortatory headline: "Stop the Persecution of Gerald Hannon!" The January 13 issue of the *Ottawa Citizen* included a two-page feature, "Gerald Hannon 101." It was largely sympathetic while noting how the controversy had bitterly divided the journalism faculty, with professors shouting at each other during staff meetings.

I was leading multiple lives. On the one hand, I was either a dangerously charismatic poster boy for perversion or a courageous free speech advocate who, in either case, seemed to exist only on radio, on television, or in print media. On the other hand, I lived, or tried to live, something of a normal life. I taught my students. I went to movies. I sang in a choir. I accepted freelance assignments as they came in, including one from *NOW Magazine* to profile John Clarke of the Ontario Coalition Against Poverty.

I was also spending a lot of time with my ailing friend Mike Kibbee. He was thirty-one in 1995, twenty years my junior. Diagnosed with Hodgkin's, he would die less than two years later, on

March 8, 1997. We became good friends, though our tastes and interests didn't much overlap — he was an engineer with little interest in the music or literature that consumed me. We shared a nerdy fascination with the fledgling World Wide Web, even started a little company called Click on This! that designed websites for small companies who weren't quite sure why they should be on the web but felt they had to be. In April 1995, he created the World Wide Cemetery, one of the first internet memorial sites (it still exists at cemetery.org). A few years earlier, he'd become — I hope as a result of my inspiring example — a sex worker, giving us much to giggle over together. That year, though, he was mostly sick; the disease, which he'd thought was in remission, returned with a vengeance in June. We tried the crazy things people try when hope slips through their fingers. I'd heard of an experimental drug called 714-X. We found a sympathetic doctor who ordered it for us, and I injected it while Mike squirmed in agony. It had to be injected into his lymphatic system, the recommended spot being on his abdomen just above his penis. It had to be injected very slowly, my hands trembling, causing him more pain. We abandoned it after only a few injections.

I found him once, late at night, lying out on the grass in front of his building; he told me he was there because he wanted to enjoy the press of the earth against his body and the look of trees against the sky. I sat beside him and held his hand for a while. We didn't say much. We slept together chastely many times, when he was too ill to make it home from my place or didn't want me to leave him alone at his. It felt sometimes as if he were slowly evaporating, the heat rising from his body and carrying him away, leaving less and less of him behind so that I often felt alone in bed by morning, with only a warm tracing on the sheets beside me.

He was an engineer, but he was also a gay man. He said he could not bear the thought of leaving this world in some tacky commercial box, all plush and brass and gewgaws. He coped by making his death a project — he would design and build his own coffin. He insisted on simple pine, and he designed the pattern and angling of the boards, specified a lining of unbleached raw cotton, bridled at his mother's suggestion he be buried in a suit, and asked only to be shrouded in that same raw fabric.

When the coffin was finished, he was pleased with the workmanship, but he had no place to store it. His apartment, a converted garage in Riverdale, was too small. He asked if I would keep it for him until it was needed, and I said I would. I found a place for it in my bedroom at the foot of my bed. We continued to sleep together from time to time, and, though it never seemed to bother him, I was vividly aware that I was sharing my bed with a dying young man and that one day I would, along with other friends, have to prepare the coffin the way he wanted. That day came. He timed it well. He died at home, when most of his friends were with him. I wept, but the opera queen side of me couldn't resist comparing that gathering to the final scene of Puccini's *La Bohème*.

THE RYERSON ADMINISTRATION WROTE to CUPE's Angela Ross to tell her that all three union grievances were denied. I was being closely watched at Ryerson. John Miller sat in on one of my classes. A second teacher observed me as well. Previously, evaluations had been done by my students, and they were mostly positive. Sandra Martin, as part of her research for her *Toronto Life* article about me, came to one of my classes.

Mid-April brought me to the last week of classes at Ryerson. Earlier that month, I had agreed to a proposal from *The Eyeopener* that I participate in their annual parody issue, that year a send-up of the *Toronto Sun*. On April 3, the huge headline on the *Toronto*

Sun blared "Ryerson Prof: I Play Snooker," while the kicker underneath read "Gerald Harmless supplements his teaching income by hustling." The photo inside showed me at a pool table, licking the tip of my cue stick, while the accompanying story was full of sophomoric double entendres about balls and long, hard sticks. It was fun. The photographer was cute. It's interesting that it never occurred to me that keeping a high profile on the issue might not be the best career move, and yet I knew my career as a teacher was heading to a critical juncture. The *Ryersonian*, also on April 3, pointed out that my current contract would end on May 8 and wondered whether I'd be rehired come September. The writer quoted Don Obe as saying he'd recommend me and that he'd do everything he could to keep me on staff. CUPE's Angela Ross mentioned my two National Magazine Awards and the sheaf of excellent student course evaluations, adding that if the university turned to an outside journalist, the union would demand proof that he or she was better qualified. Later in the month, I met with John Miller, who told me that jobs would soon be posted and that he was sure I would qualify. The Rye Report Card in the April 10 issue of *The Eyeopener* gave me an A+. Things seemed hopeful.

My last class happened about a week later, much of it spent talking with my students about ways to change and improve the course. They were free with both praise and criticism, and it pleased me that I'd clearly created an atmosphere where they felt they could speak openly and frankly. There was some tittering in class as they were preparing to leave, and I overheard one of the students say, "Go on, tell him." I asked what was up? It turned out they wanted to let me know they had just watched *After the Bath* in their documentary class, which prompted me to say, "And I do have a great butt, don't I?" That provoked gales of laughter, and then I made a final comment to the effect that the perfectly shameless are the most likely to lead lives of perfect bliss. They would be the last words I would say as a teacher.

That same week, I received a call from Don Obe. He and others had spotted a Ryerson ad in *The Globe and Mail* soliciting applications for part-time instructors in the journalism department, something the school had apparently never done before. It was clear they were looking for someone, for anyone, more qualified than I to teach the course. Angela Ross pointed out that they'd posted publicly before doing so internally, which they weren't supposed to do. Don wasn't sanguine. There would be three people on the committee who would decide whether or not to recommend me.

Then the call came. On June 3, Don Obe telephoned to say that the three-person faculty committee had voted unanimously against rehiring me. "So Miller can smile and smile and be a villain," I wrote in my journal, presumably seeing myself, in a paroxysm of self-importance, as something of a Hamlet figure. Obe had done his best for me. He had tenure, which gave him security, but he was still at risk. (He would tell me later that the first recommendation from a PR firm the university had hired was, "Fire Obe.") He had gone through the contract phrase by phrase with the faculty committee, proving that I was better qualified than the other candidates they were considering, but it made no difference. The critique from the triumvirate was that I had been using the school to advance my own political agenda and boost my notoriety. I was out of a job. The union immediately filed a grievance. And the media mill began again. Andy Barry on *Metro Morning*. Radio-Canada, the French-language CBC. Other stations. Stories in all three newspapers. Heather Bird chimed in, her column headlined "And don't come back no more." Reading through them today, I think it's clear that I was continuing to unravel — my comments were often uncharacteristically sophomoric and cheap: the faculty committee was stocked with dinosaurs, I told *The Globe and Mail*; I told the *Toronto Star*, "It's Jurassic Park down there." (I was quickly admonished for such comments by lawyer Rick Blair and friend Ed Jackson, which somewhat restored me to my senses.) Eventually, I spoke briefly with John Miller, who said he wanted to avoid a public pissing match but also wanted me to know that it had been a wrenching decision for him, painful and done after much soul-searching. But it was the right decision. And then he added, "But I respect you. And I rather like you." Good to know.

Miller received a letter, dated June 7, from five other part-time instructors, protesting the decision not to rehire me. Signed by Lynn Cunningham, Tim Falconer, David Hayes, Paul McLaughlin, and Steve Trumper, it described the vote as "punitive, arbitrary and in contravention of the union's collective agreement." Cunningham wrote Miller a separate letter in which she resigned in protest from the School of Journalism's advisory committee. She was able to point out to Miller the embarrassing fact that the three people to whom the school had offered positions had all refused to accept them once they understood why they were available. She didn't mention names, but within a week the *Globe* leaked two of them — Ron Graham and Heather Robertson — and it was clear the school was aiming for the best and just as clear it wasn't going to get them. (The unsigned *Globe* column was headlined "Wanted: journalism professor with no conscience.") The *Globe* quoted Graham: "When it became clear our jobs involved teaching parts of Gerald's old course, both Heather and I, independently, without having spoken to each other, said we weren't interested." Robertson was well known as a civil libertarian and would go on to lead a successful class action suit against media conglomerates who plundered free-lance work, without compensation, for their websites. Graham had recently become president of PEN Canada, which had supported me. As he put it, "It would have been bizarre if I inadvertently helped Ryerson get rid of Gerald."

There was more to come. Lawyer Rick Blair had attended a grievance hearing and told me the situation between Ryerson and the union was deteriorating rapidly. CUPE had grievances heaped on grievances, prompting the university to grieve the union in retaliation. The administration's Michael Dewson could barely bring himself to look at Angela Ross, and Blair thought the whole thing was about to spill over into a terrible mess. He suggested that, instead of proceeding with our grievances by continuing to examine Dewson, we attempt mediation, engaging the much-respected William Kaplan as mediator, putting our cards on the table, and seeing if we could reach some sort of agreement. I liked that idea. Blair also said he thought the university might offer a financial settlement.

Sensible friends told me I had bought into the Hollywood myth of the revolutionary who never backs down, that I had to get on with my life, that I should face the fact that I'd never teach at Ryerson again. (A story in *NOW* in June reported on "donor revolt" at Ryerson as the reason it was so important to get me out the door. The school was apparently not only deluged by telephone calls and letters, many of those calls came from people withdrawing financial support if I were to continue on staff.) The advice seemed sensible.

In mid-July, I told a friend that I planned to tell Ryerson to stick any money they might offer up their ass. I wouldn't get the chance until mediation hearings started in early September. And then, when I had the chance, I didn't.

I did try one last time to get my job back on the table. During the final mediation meeting, I asked William Kaplan to go to the administration's room — we met in separate rooms, with Kaplan going back and forth with offers and counter-offers — and sound them out on that. We timed how long it took him to return with an answer. He was gone for about ninety seconds. The answer was no, and never, and if we went back to grievance they'd fight me all the way, and if I won they'd take it to judicial review, and it finally became clear to me that I would never work at Ryerson again, at least under that administration.

We moved on to talk money. I have this memory, perhaps not accurate, that we calculated how much I'd have earned if I'd taught until retirement age, rounded it up a bit, and asked for a million dollars. I think Kaplan was gone for less than ninety seconds on that one too. Ryerson lowballed a few offers. We turned them down. On September 9, Kaplan recommended that we make a take-it-or-leave-it proposal. We did, and the administration recessed briefly to leave the building, presumably to meet with President Claude Lajeunesse, though I gather he'd been on conference call during most of this. I hated all that game playing and strategizing and bluffing. But when they came back, we had an agreement.

I received the settlement we'd asked for in the take-it-or-leave-it proposal. The amount was to remain confidential. I agreed not to return to teaching that year and never to apply for a position at Ryerson again. The university agreed to two provisions I'd requested — that there be no repercussions for students or staff who had supported me over the past year and that they hold a competition for the position they were denying me so that those who, for reasons of probity, had refused to accept a job they saw as rightfully mine could reapply. The administration tried to include in the agreement that I be forbidden to guest lecture, but Kaplan made short work of that, and within days I accepted three invitations to do so.

On Friday, at 11:00 a.m., I met the press. Ariane and Angela Ross were there as well, and they spoke first and eloquently. When my turn came, I announced that I would be donating $5,000 of my settlement to create a fund at Ryerson to keep alive the issues raised by this case. Academic freedom, freedom of speech, queerness, deviance, and prostitution had been thrown into high relief over the past year, but those discussions had happened in an all-too-hysterical atmosphere. These important issues deserved the just deliberation of sensible people in an atmosphere the university could provide. I was committed to ensuring that the issues raised by my case did not die with the settlement.

I slammed the institution. Certainly not the students — not even the journalism department. "The administration's handling of this affair," I said, "struck me as cowardly, visionless, moralizing and deeply irresponsible ... The Ryerson community deserves better." I finished with this: "I'd say the Ryerson administration has been screwed — but then that is one of my part-time jobs."

One last chapter to the story of my teaching career. I'd promised to donate at least $5,000 of my settlement to create an award that would recognize and reward students who wrote fiercely and well on controversial topics. I always thought of it as the Shit Disturber Award, though I agreed to the better optics that came with the Gerald Hannon Prize for Dissenting Journalism, "created in order to encourage Ryerson students to investigate controversial subjects, particularly those that test or explore the limits of freedom of expression." The competition would be open to all students enrolled in the university. The prize would be $1,000, and the program would last for five years. (Longer, if there were years in which no prize was awarded.)

I announced the prize in April 1999, the *Ryersonian* reporting that the proposal had already been in the university's advancement office for a month awaiting approval.

At the time, David Hayes reported that President Lajeunesse had been spotted brandishing the *Ryersonian* and fulminating about that "horrible person and his horrible award." Years later, Rick Blair, CUPE's lawyer, would tell me that nothing had infuriated the university's top brass more than my offer for an award. It put them in the awkward position of having to either hold their nose and accept a prize with my name on it or turn down cash that would benefit a student.

True to form, they turned it down. The Gerald Hannon Prize for Dissenting Journalism died a quiet death.

But maybe not.

English writer and humourist Quentin Crisp once wrote, "In an expanding universe, time is on the side of the outcast. Those who once inhabited the suburbs of human contempt find that without changing their address they eventually live in the metropolis." Perhaps he was on to something. In 2019, I resigned after serving many years on the board of directors of Pink Triangle Press. To honour my decades of activism for both sexual freedom and freedom of speech, PTP created the Gerald Hannon Award to support trans and Indigenous students in financial need at Ryerson University. PTP's contribution of $5,000 per year for five years was matched by Ryerson, with apparent full knowledge of our earlier history together. The first awards were made in 2021. The parallels with the earlier proposed prize are striking; sometimes it just takes twenty-two years for change to happen.

Looking back on those few years, from November 1995 until the end of 1999, I sometimes wonder if I wasn't to some degree the author of my own misfortune. The first eighteen months were the most calamitous of my life, outdoing even the turmoil, some twenty years earlier, of the police raid on *The Body Politic* and the subsequent criminal trials. Perhaps, I thought, if I had just refused interviews and kept my opinions to myself, I might be a retired teacher today instead of a famously fired one. Rick Blair thinks not. "It was a witch hunt," he told me, "and you couldn't hide from it. Saying 'no comment' wouldn't have helped." Saying "no comment" was also about as alien to my temperament as it was possible to be. I had come of age in the gay movement at a time when the formerly unspeakable suddenly wouldn't shut up. I still remember how exhilarating it was to talk openly about formerly taboo subjects, and I was certain that everyone would feel the same way, certain that everyone would be thrilled to learn that suburban Italian grandfathers might want to get fucked, that some kids are lustful animals, that some straight guys want their cocks worshipped and don't seem to care if the congregation is largely male. Knowing those things opens the world up, empties one's heart and mind of shadows, and makes everything glisten. I still feel that way. Not everyone does. It was a hard lesson.

I feared also that the notoriety might bring my freelance career to an end. I continued to get assignments from *NOW Magazine* and *Xtra*, but neither paid the $1/word I wanted — for that I needed *Toronto Life*, but I wasn't sure *Toronto Life* needed me. I still had the prostitution income to help me lurch from month to month, but I was becoming paranoid about ever writing for a high-end magazine again. Most writers pitch ideas and stories to editors, but I had rarely done that. I wasn't good at it. What few ideas I'd had were routinely turned down. I don't know if *Toronto Life* decided to take a chance on me again, but in 1999 they assigned me two large pieces — a profile of architect Jack Diamond and a look back at the life of Zena Cherry, who wrote a society column in *The Globe and Mail* for twenty-nine years, from the 1950s until the 1980s. Then *Canadian Art* asked for a profile of artist Tom Dean. It was great to be back at work, and I poured myself into those assignments. I felt I had something to prove — that all the sensationalism and scandal of the previous few years hadn't affected my qualities as a writer.

When the National Magazine Awards announced their nominees for 1999, all three of my articles were on the list. I was in a state of skittery anxiety at the awards gala in May 2000. The National Magazine Awards are the Oscars of the Canadian magazine industry — minus the red carpet, the big names, the glamour, and the money. I almost always went home with a cheque — $1,000 for a Gold Award, $500 for Silver — or a certificate for Honourable Mention. (My first award, a Silver in 1989, came for my profile of John Bentley Mays; the last, a Gold in 2010, for a profile of Toronto mayoral candidate Rob Ford. In between, there were eleven more Golds or Silvers and twenty-four Honourable Mentions.)

The Zena Cherry and Tom Dean pieces didn't win, but "A Monumental Man," my piece on Jack Diamond, took the Gold in the Profiles category. I knew exactly what I wanted to say when I took the stage for my acceptance speech. I thanked John Macfarlane, *Toronto Life*'s editor, for the support shown to me during some very difficult times. Then I held up the award and said, "I guess this proves you *can* lead a horticulture." There was a moment's shocked silence and then a wave of laughter and applause.

I was back in the game.

12

Coda
· · · · · · · ·

I WAS BACK IN the writing game, but I was also briefly back in the news. "Church stifles concert — choir includes sex activist" read the headline in the November 24, 2000, edition of the *National Post*. I'd been singing with community choirs for years by that time, often rehearsing and performing in churches of various denominations. There'd never been a problem, if you don't count the occasional wrong note, until the concert of October 27, 2000, held in St. Basil's, the Roman Catholic church on the grounds of St. Michael's College, where I'd been an altar boy and lost my faith almost forty years earlier. After that October 27 concert, which was to be devoted to new music and to which the choristers had been invited to contribute, I would lose my membership in Kammermusik, the choir to which I then belonged.

Ever since first hearing the "Triumphal March" from *Aida* in Miss Kenzie's grade eight classroom in Marathon, I'd never lost my passion for opera and classical music. I'd joined the U of T chorus shortly after arriving in Toronto, a group accomplished enough to record an album. Years later, I found soulmates in friends Gerry Oxford and Robert Trow, who joined me in a series of choirs, the best being the Royal Conservatory Choir and the most memorable being one with Polish antecedents, which meant a performance, in costume, in the gardens of the Polish Consulate in Toronto.

Eager to improve my singing, I had sought out voice teachers. Some helped, some hindered, but I longed for a fuller understanding of how music worked. I played no instrument and knew nothing of music theory. I decided to fix that, and in the summer of 1990, I registered at the Royal Conservatory of Music for a course in the rudiments of music theory. It was very basic material, so basic that it scarcely justified the exhilaration I felt when my mark represented First Class Honours with Distinction. I continued taking courses until 1998, ending with Grade 5 harmony and analysis. There were no more courses to take. Composition beckoned.

It's impossible to exaggerate my excitement when the Kammermusik director accepted my offer to compose an *a cappella* Kyrie. I would have a world premiere! (I can't resist that pretension.) I'd have a byline for something other than a magazine article. For something that wasn't my profession, for something that seemed a monumental challenge. The fact is, journalistic writing came too easily for me. I was happy about that — it made earning a living a mostly pleasant experience, and my facility made me a writer in demand. But in my fantasy life, I was a musician. I'd already composed a few short satirical birthday odes for friends, and on more than one occasion I'd engaged a small chorus to perform them in my apartment before the birthday boy and a small audience.

My choice of a section of the Latin mass may seem odd, given my atheism and my rocky history with the Church, but I saw the mass as a musical form, rather like a sonata, with no inherent devotional content. I chose the Kyrie, partly because it's short and wouldn't tax my compositional resources, and I chose the key of C minor — a respectable, serious key — but I included some willfully unlikely harmonies. Though I wasn't quite ready for atonality, it was, after all, the year 2000. The concert went well, except for an early entry by one of the choristers, which led the bass section briefly astray. I took a small bow from my place among the men. I was giddy. I foresaw future triumphs (I'd already written a Gloria and had plans for a Credo). I'd forgotten that I was by that time a known name and face.

Someone in the audience recognized me as the notorious Ryerson prof. Presumably horrified that the devil's disciple was not only singing but had composed a piece of church music, he or she complained to the pastor, who alerted Suzanne Scorsone, a spokeswoman for the Roman Catholic Archdiocese of Toronto. She made it clear that my continued presence in Kammermusik would mean the choir would be barred from further use of the space. Either I had to go or the choir did. I went, grudgingly, though not without taking a few supporters with me.

I argued with Scorsone that the church used to welcome sinners. Only if they were penitent, she informed me, and I was not. Broadcaster and author Michael Coren called, not surprisingly given his then commitment to Roman Catholicism's distaste for gay people. He wanted to interview me. I was very polite, and he commended my politesse, in contrast, he said, to the priest at the church, who'd hung up on him. During the Ryerson scandal, I'd learned not to be quite so cavalier about media requests, and I declined to be interviewed on his CFRB show. His column in the *Toronto Sun* on November 11 was headlined "Lord Have Mercy Indeed."

Suddenly, I was a bass without a choir. I wanted very much to find a new musical home and noticed an ad in a music magazine soliciting chorus members for a community opera company called Toronto Opera Repertoire. I phoned and spoke with a man who had a heavy Italian accent; he wondered if I might consider auditioning for a solo role. Later, it became clear that it wasn't because my speaking voice suggested I had talent — it was simply because I was male, and men are rare in community music groups. I said I would sing "Non Piu Andrai" from Mozart's *The Marriage of Figaro.* I did. I got lost in the rapid-fire section at the end and thought, well, that's that. On September 9, 2001, the auditioners were called to meet in the garden of Giuseppe Macina, the artistic director of Toronto Opera Repertoire and the man who had auditioned me. We were told we'd be performing *Tosca* (in Italian) and *Die Fleder-maus* (in English), and then he read the names of the successful candidates. When he reached the Sacristan in *Tosca*, a comically blundering reactionary cleric, he said, "Gerald Hannon." He added that I would also sing the Jailer, a small role in the final act. First audition, two roles! I was ecstatic. I called everyone when I got home. And a few weeks later, I was assigned yet another role — the policeman, Frank, in *Die Fledermaus.* Three roles, but I was that rare thing: a man interested in singing opera.

Toronto Opera Repertoire would be my musical home for the next fifteen years, to the dismay of many friends who felt obliged, or whom I made to feel obliged, to attend performances. Granted, they could be a trial if you expected convincing sets, an orchestra, and trained singers. But the sets gestured toward realism, the piano accompaniment was in the hands of a superb pianist, and lead roles attracted some remarkably talented amateurs. As for me? I was a better performer than a singer; I was very good as a comic character, but I was assigned a major role every year, even when they were wrong for me. The paucity of men sometimes meant that I'd be given significant baritone parts. I'm proud of most of my bass roles, Leporello in *Don Giovanni* in particular. Proud, too, of the ensemble work I had to master — duets, trios, quartets, sextets by the likes of Mozart, Rossini, Donizetti, and Verdi. I

I sang with the Toronto City Opera (TCO) for years. Here I'm playing Baron Zeta in *The Merry Widow* in 2012.
Photo: James Thomson

even had fans! People who recognized me on the street and commended my performance! It doesn't take much to thrill an amateur musician.

The music and my roles meant much more to me than the National Magazine Awards I kept winning.

Although I needed the money that came from writing for the large glossies, tabloid publications like *NOW* and *Xtra* often gave me free rein to write provocatively on subjects more to my tastes. "Metro Sex Academy," in the March 27/97 issue of *NOW*, took me to John School, a city program designed to reduce street prostitution by penalizing its customer base — men arrested for soliciting wouldn't be charged if they took a day-long "class" on the social ills associated with prostitution and weren't apprehended again. On the day I attended, most of the forty-five "students" were men of colour or immigrants with faulty English. Two I spoke with had been entrapped by a female police officer. Many talked about the difficulty of meeting women when you're still coping with a new culture. How every time they turned on the television they saw sex, and yet they couldn't get it. Some were desperately lonely.

My conclusion? John School didn't acknowledge the complexity of desire and the realities of immigrant life, substituting instead an ineffectual "sex is best with love" curriculum.

Another piece I'm proud of is a celebration of park sex, which appeared in the September 11/97 issue of NOW. "If gay people are a minority group," I wrote, "then park sex is our folk dancing. To suppress it is to suppress a venerable part of gay male culture." I had great fun with an August 19/99 article for NOW on what it's like to have sex with whores when you are one yourself. (I'd talked my editor into covering my expenses.) The article featured my favourite opening sentence: "It is a truth universally acknowledged that a young hustler in pursuit of even a modest fortune must not fart in the presence of his john unless, of course, he is specifically asked — and paid — to do so." (The fellow's other social inadequacies led me to imagine creating the Gerald Hannon School of Hustling, Conversation, and Deportment.)

I made a porn movie, and I wrote about the process for NOW. I'd taken part in a Three-Day Workshop for Aspiring Smut-makers organized by Come As You Are, the feminist sex shop. The title? My Cousin Mike. The stars? The young and gorgeous Scott Beveridge, a talented filmmaker himself, as Mike. And I, self-described as "a fifty-four-year-old with severely greying hair, a small-ish cock and moderately porcine features." The story? Cousins have to share a bed at a family reunion. The action? Some groping and masturbation, but no orgasm. The music? The adagio from Leoš Janáček's String Quartet No.2, known as Intimate Pages. The premiere? May 19, 2000, at that year's Inside Out Film Festival. The reaction? From my journal: "People laughed at the funny bits. And the sex looked okay. They laughed at the end, and they were supposed to. And people applauded and hooted. Felt very nice." Mind you, they were primed to be kind — I introduced the film by saying, "After seeing this, people will realize that as a filmmaker, I make a very good journalist."

I had already become something of a go-to guy if local artists needed a performer comfortable appearing in the nude. I'd never been particularly modest, and I rather enjoyed the show-off element. (Voyeurism was my principal perversion — for years, my binoculars and the windows of an adjoining apartment building were inseparable — but I did like to balance it with a little exhibitionism.) It also pleased me that those gigs became a rich source of anecdote, often humorous. "Do it for the anecdote" became my philosophical guide whenever I was asked to participate in projects not everyone would see as appropriate to my age and profession. I kept notes on all of them, and it's clear how obsessed I was and am with seeing penises, any penises, even my own if no others are on display. I usually referred to them as wieners, and yes, I do think my sexuality is a bit puerile. In any case, I'd already appeared in John Greyson's *After the Bath* (several good wieners) and Nik Sheehan's *Symposium* (two wieners, one mine) by the time I agreed to take a role in Scott Beveridge's *Quiver*, which opened at the Toronto International Film Festival in September 1999. It had buzz before the premiere, with the *Toronto Star* describing it as likely the most controversial of the Perspective Canada series. Understandably, perhaps: I play a man who kicks in the door of a small, cell-like room and proceeds to kick, punch, and sodomize the man he finds there. It was an exhausting shoot. The only special effect involved the use of a teapot. I got pee-shy when it came time to urinate on the other actor, so a teapot, out of camera range, filled in with a convincing golden shower.

A year and a half later, in April 2001, I met Peter Kingstone. (Peter Meredith Courtney Kingstone, to give him his full, extravagant name.) An affable bear of a man, six-foot-four, thirty years my

Video artist Peter Kingstone became one of my closest friends. Photo: Lisa Beaudry

junior, a talented artist specializing in video and installation, he became not only a best friend but one impossible to refuse when he needed a performer who'd be naked for the camera. Just a few months after meeting Peter, I was sitting in a chair in my apartment, wearing a mask made out of old socks, my glasses over top, jerking off for his videocam. (I was supposed to come but couldn't.) Peter had been commissioned to create a background video for the indie pop band The Hidden Cameras for their performance at a Bloor Street porno cinema. I wasn't to be the only masturbator; other local luminaries had agreed. The project was cancelled, though, when one of the band members, whose own erect member was to be featured, realized his mother would be in the audience.

I appeared nude on video twice during Nuit Blanche in 2006, once to help Peter create *tableaux vivants* based on paintings by the French artist Delacroix. My other appearance that year was in

John Greyson's *Roy and Silo's Gay Divorce*, on display at the Harrison Baths, where the filming had taken place. (Roy and Silo were famously gay penguins at New York City's Central Park Zoo.) I played the nasty Penguin Books Nude Lawyer, my image projected on the tile walls of the shower room, soaping, showering, and singing (the words coming out backward, though with subtitles reading properly), the water flowing backward, up into the shower head, soap bubbles floating up my body rather than down. There was much, much more. This was all about, to quote the program, "the long march home, away from the tyranny of a wedding industry that reduced them to mere clients. Roy and Silo agreed to divorce — and live together in sin forevermore."

My most challenging appearance for John Greyson was in March 2012 and involved nude lip-syncing, in Arabic, to my own pre-recorded voice. The scene, set in the ruins of Baghdad's National Theatre but shot in a theatre at York University, involved a rehearsal of *Waiting for Godot* with me as Vladimir, a very sexy young actor named Ryan Kotack playing Estragon, and David Phillips, a U of T prof, playing the tree — not a character to be played by an actor in the original Beckett play, but John takes interesting liberties. We performed the scene first in costume and then did it all again in the nude, both times including a passionate kiss between me and Ryan — also not in the Beckett script — and a few quick wiener tugs at the mention of masturbation (most decidedly not part of a conventional staging). David Phillips was worried that his penis and nipple piercings might not seem appropriate for a character playing a tree, but John raised no objections.

IN 2011, THROUGH PETER Kingstone, I met Jonathan Seinen, an actor researching the possibility of a play about the CN Tower. He wanted to speak to people who'd been around during its construction (it was completed in 1976), and I agreed, while admitting that I had very little to say about it, given that my obsession during the 1970s had been gay liberation in general and my work at *The Body Politic* in particular. Very soon, the CN Tower was abandoned as a topic; instead, he wanted to hear more about a publication that had died in 1987. I was willing to talk, and we talked. Jonathan became excited. He'd found his play. Or, rather, Lemon Tree Creations, the ensemble he belonged to, had. They engaged twenty-eight-year-old playwright Nick Green to write a script based on the history of *TBP*. I met the young fellow; he was tall, rather handsome, and had written (but not produced) one play based on the bathhouse raids in Edmonton. This alone seemed to be what qualified him in Jonathan Seinen's eyes, he being the initiator of the whole project. Green had been doing some homework, going to the archives, reading back issues. He wanted to talk, to get a feel for the time, which was impossible. It was — and is — so hard to talk about the past. It's a fabric that doesn't exist anymore; we were in the warp and woof of it, with no sense that it could be any other way. Perhaps I was too pessimistic. History plays can work, though perhaps never quite in the way the subjects imagine.

Body Politic, the play, opened at Buddies in Bad Times on May 21, 2016, and ran for three weeks. It had a cast of five men and one woman. I was often asked what it felt like to see oneself on stage and to have one's history dramatized, but I could truly say I didn't know. Green's characters were composites of the collective in the 1970s, though the sole female character, played brilliantly by Diane Flacks, was clearly modelled on Chris Bearchell. The character Philip, older than the others, would have been thought to have been based on me because in the play he's the author of MLBLM, but I found him somewhat earnest and tiresome. Perhaps I *was* the inspiration. What thrilled me was the fact that a troupe of young people

who hadn't been born in the period covered by the play were grip-
ped enough by the history and politics to do their best to recreate
and reshape it. *Body Politic* was nominated for three Dora Mavor
Moore Awards and won one, for Outstanding New Play.

The night I attended, I took Ali Syed with me. He's fifty-two
years my junior (he was sixteen when we met), was born in Bang-
ladesh, and is straight. I wanted him to have a sense of my past
and the forces that made me. I love him, and he loves me, but,
though I'm also romantically in love with him, he's made it clear
that's not the case for him. I realize how E.M. Forster this sounds:
an aging white colonialist in thrall to a brown boy from South Asia
via Regent Park. Some stereotypes are worth living up to.

We met at the Central YMCA in 2012, thanks to his certainty that
the "l" in "salmon" was pronounced. (I wish I'd said, "Only if the
word following it is Rushdie," but I just took the side of the boy
he was arguing with.) Lust was certainly a factor in my decision
to find a conversational opening, even one as feeble as English
pronunciation. Oddly, he wasn't my type. He's short, and until this
point all my lust objects had been at least as tall as I. He's brown,
and though I've had many a sexual engagement with men of
colour, all my great romances have been with white boys. Unlike
my other great loves, he has a muscular, built body that features
six-pack abs. He also has the loudest speaking voice of anyone
I've ever met, and the day we met he was the charismatic centre of
the small group of teenage boys he'd arrived with. I was delighted
when our exchange led to music, even more so when I discovered
that he not only played the guitar but was studying classical music.
I mentioned composers and asked if he knew Rodrigo. "You mean
Joaquín Rodrigo?" he said.

He was then in his last year of high school at Jarvis Collegiate,
which is across the street from my condo building. Our YMCA

schedules overlapped. He cycled everywhere, as did I. He was so extraordinarily friendly that I figured he might be gay, a young man hoping to meet someone who would at least be a sounding board. (There's no shortage of gay men at the Central YMCA.) Who better qualified than I? I didn't push, but I made it clear I was gay, hoping he might reciprocate and want to talk about the problems being young, brown, Muslim-raised, and gay. There was also the hope that, against all odds, he might find me physically attractive. I invited him to join me for a TSO concert, and he excitedly agreed, but the next time we met at the Y and I mentioned that the date was approaching, he suddenly had to decline, with thanks. Studies had intervened, he said. He looked abashed, and I could tell he was lying. I accepted it as true, though, and asked him to join me some weeks later for a concert at Koerner Hall featuring guitarist Miloš Karadaglić. That proved irresistible. (I discovered only later that his friends and music teacher, on hearing that I was not only gay but old enough to be his grandfather, had strongly urged him to back out. I was sure to hit on him, they said.)

He turned out to be an ideal concert companion. He loved the program, and he was satisfyingly critical; he wasn't about to give unstinting praise just because I'd taken him. He knew most of the pieces and would lean over and say things like, "He really butchered that presto section — doesn't he know the melody is in the bass line?" Or, "Very clumsy scale work." He prefers Bream and Segovia and John Williams and thought this Karadaglić fellow a trendy flash in the pan.

We've been to dozens of concerts over the years, thanks to my media comps, often ending the evenings with talk that goes on until three or four in the morning. He isn't as responsive to vocal music as I am, but he bravely tries it out. He is passionate about chamber and orchestral music.

We kissed, once. Late, late one December night in 2015, the two of us fuelled by single malt scotch. I asked if I could kiss him, and he said I could. He texted me the next day: "I appreciated the long kiss, although it was great you know it's not my favorite but you've proven to be a great kisser! I never doubted you. I don't mind our goodbye peck but I hope we can keep our tongues to ourselves." Goodbye pecks continue to this day.

As I write this, he's a student in mathematics at Ryerson University and has a steady girlfriend who accepts our unusual relationship. She refers to me as "the second wife," and he refers to her as "the mistress."

I'm much gratified by the way he's blossomed through our friendship. My first gift to him, at Christmas, was carefully wrapped, and when he picked it up he said, "I hope it's not a book." It was. Since then, with some prodding by me, he's become not only an inveterate reader but a book lover, one who seeks out particular editions of the books he wants. He relishes challenges, testing Proust for size and *Ulysses* for comprehensibility. Though I pegged him as an indifferent reader when we met, there were signs that there was a devotee buried inside. When school introduced him to a Shakespeare sonnet, he decided to read all of the sonnets. We read *Wuthering Heights* together, the last chapter aloud, taking turns, trying to simulate what we imagined was a North Country accent.

I once asked him what I could get him for his birthday. "How about some of your white privilege?" was his answer. That response, for all his jokey tone, was uncharacteristically acerbic, but he sees white (and class) privilege all the time, and I'm mostly blind to it, rather in the way I'm blind to the fact that the audiences at the concerts and performances we go to are mostly white. And if they're not white, he says, they're probably Asian. I've learned to look at crowds through his eyes, and he reminds me that the situation for him and his girlfriend is much like it was for gays a few decades ago: romance is risky. They're both from Muslim families, neither of which can know they're dating, both of which would disapprove. Both still live at home. Both are lectured regularly. I talk to him a lot about gay history, and the social disapproval gays experienced for so long resonates with him. That's intersectionality of rather a different kind.

I'm not oblivious to the fact that Ali bookends my romantic life. Frank, my college pal, was the first; Ali is surely the last. Both are straight, and though I only fantasized about kissing Frank, Ali's acceptance of a kiss from me fulfilled a longing that echoed back more than fifty years to a shared bed on the floor of a slum house on Charles Street in Toronto.

"BONE WEARY: A FOND Farewell to the Sex Trade," read the poster. "Gerald Hannon celebrates 25 years of working his fingers to your bone," it continued, and then went on to name the date, November 25, 2011, and the venue, Goodhandy's, then a sex-positive bar at 120 Church Street. A donation between five and twenty dollars got you in the door, and all proceeds were to go to Maggie's Toronto Sex Workers Action Project, on whose board I had once sat.

The party wasn't my idea, though retirement was. I had begun to weary of having sex when it suited others and had decided to quietly stop advertising and decline any future calls. Peter Kingstone persuaded me to have a retirement party. I had always treated sex work like a real job, he said, so I ought to exit from it in the traditional manner, though with a twist congruent with my politics: the entertainment would be in-your-face, and the proceeds would go to a charity that supported sex workers in their efforts to have their occupation decriminalized.

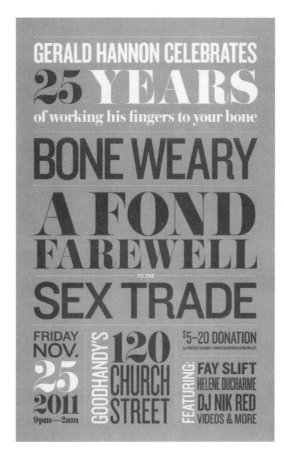

GERALD HANNON CELEBRATES
25 YEARS
of working his fingers to your bone
BONE WEARY
**A FOND
FAREWELL**
···· TO THE ····
SEX TRADE
FRIDAY
NOV.
25
2011
9pm—2am
GOODHANDY'S
**120
CHURCH
STREET**
$5–20 DONATION
ALL PROCEEDS TO MAGGIE'S TORONTO SEX WORKERS ACTION PROJECT
FEATURING:
FAY SLIFT
HELENE DUCHARME
DJ NIK RED
VIDEOS & MORE

Sex work is work. I threw a big party when I retired in 2011. Design: Ryan Crouchman

Retirement wouldn't mean a huge loss of income for me. My records show that I had made just $780 in 2011, almost entirely from regulars, men I kept on because I liked them or they amused me or because it pleased me that it was so easy to make them happy. Mr. Panties, a man my age, would glow when I commended that day's colour choice for the women's panties he'd change into in my bathroom. I'd then pretend to fuck him. Dan-of-the-fistful-of-change was a former Ryerson student who called me "dude" and paid me with whatever coin he had in his pocket. Steve was timid. Jake the Slav was bashful. They kept coming back, and I kept accepting them until one day I decided that their future happiness had to depend on something other than me and my penis. It was an easier decision than I anticipated. And Peter's recommendation that it be marked with a party clinched it.

Peter more or less took over the organizing, once he'd vetoed my wish to have the party end at 9:30 p.m. More in touch with the demimonde than I, he argued for having it begin then. And it did. He had a special rubber stamp made. When guests entered and made donations, their hands were stamped with the word *Whore*. My retirement party was to be a roomful of whores! He secured Fay Slift, politicized drag performer extraordinaire, as one of the entertainers, and Helene Ducharme, whose bare-breasted rendition of the Queen of the Night's aria from Mozart's *The Magic Flute* gave me a whole new insight into that character's demonic powers. The room was packed with friends, political acquaintances, friends of friends, even adult children of friends. An endless loop on video screens showed a compilation Peter had made of hooker-prof headlines and several of my nude appearances in the local art scene. Those may have been a bit of a test for the squeamish in the crowd, but there were very few. Fewer as the night wore on. It was a family affair.

I was presented with gifts: a ballpoint pen engraved with the word "Whore" and a framed condom (I'm assured it was unused) sprayed with gold paint. All the rituals of the traditional retirement party were observed, but tuned to the realities of sex work and a sex-positive crowd.

A few weeks later, I was able to send a cheque for $1,600 as a donation to Maggie's.

SEX WORK DIDN'T END abruptly, of course. It lingered on, rather in the way of an opera diva's final tour. There was always one more engagement to accept, one more regular to make happy, until I finally decided I had to say something to Mr. Panties, who by late 2014 was my only remaining client. It struck him hard. "Why?" he wanted to know. "You enjoy it too!" (Which was something of a testimonial to my acting abilities.) He finally and reluctantly accepted my decision, put the black panties he'd brought with him into the plastic shopping bag he always carried, and left. That was October 6, 2014. After the door closed behind him, I entered his $45 into my receipts ledger — the last of my wages of sin.

Those years of sex for money remain one of the great adventures of my life; like all adventures, it was a mix of peril, tedium, excitement, and drollery. Most importantly, thanks to those risks and joys, I became privy to the ordinary secret lives of men.

Retiring from journalism was slower and nowhere near so dramatic. I declined assignments as they came in, keeping only the classical music listings that I prepared monthly for *Toronto Life*. They were important to me because I could get a pair of media comps to virtually any performance I was interested in, and they were always for seats I could never have afforded on my own. My career in long-form journalism came to an end in October 2015, when I declined a *Toronto Life* assignment that both interested me and was clearly tailored to my interests and strengths. It was very tempting: I'd built a career on juicy *Toronto Life* profiles, and I hated saying no to a magazine that had given me so much work, but I wasn't sure that, at seventy-one, I still had the necessary stamina and resources. Actually, I *was* sure. I didn't.

I don't miss journalism. I don't miss the research and the interviews. I do miss nailing it, the giddy feeling of having written the perfect lede or finding the perfect metaphor or the perfect closing paragraph. When I had an assignment, I wrote nonstop in my head while riding on an exercise bike at the Y, and I often had to stop, get off the bike, find a piece of paper, and write down a phrase I was afraid I'd lose if I didn't record it right away. I miss that urgency.

In early 2019, I resigned from the board of Pink Triangle Press, Canada's leading gay and lesbian media organization. I'd been a member since its formation in 1976 by members of the *Body Politic* collective in response to the corporate structure requirements of a not-for-profit organization. Editorial and political decisions had remained in the hands of the collective.

I resigned for health reasons. Some months earlier, I had been diagnosed with Parkinson's disease, manifesting mostly as chronic fatigue, and pseudobulbar affect, a related neurological disease manifesting as uncontrollable, inappropriate laughter and sudden yelping. Luckily, I have friends whose affection extends to tolerating my new, often noisy self, but my attempts at controlling the PBA behaviours are exhausting. Though I was welcome to stay on the PTP board, I thought it in their best interests and mine to resign.

I've been living as a Parkie (I'm sure that's what the cool kids say) since at least 2018 and have tracked the myriad changes to my social life. I no longer go out without a friend to accompany me. I fell once, when I thought I was up to a solitary stroll, and ended up in hospital for almost a week. I don't participate to the same degree in social badinage. It's very unlikely that I will return to the musical life I so valued. I can't get dressed (or undressed) smoothly or quickly. I haven't attempted a sexual connection, though mas-turbation still sort of works, mostly because my usual hand, the right, is the twitchy one, and it can feel as if someone else is doing the work (which did add to the excitement, at least at first). Though I take medications to control the PBA symptoms, I still often find myself embarrassingly convulsed by laughter when I'm being interviewed by my neurologist. I startle easily. A sudden movement can almost make me leap out of my chair.

I've often wondered what dying is like. Will I sense the transition from living to dead? Perhaps — nothing seems to happen quickly when it comes to Parkinson's. Previously, I imagined a quick death, usually in a bike accident. There were many opportunities. I biked until I was seventy but somehow managed to survive Toronto traffic. Too bad, in a way — I could have written a great article.

My board resignation came at a time that reflected changes in the communities we were serving. The original mission statement of the press, adopted in 1998, began: "We, the members and workers of Pink Triangle Press, are lesbians, gay men, and people of good will. We carry on the work first undertaken by *The Body Politic.*" Though it went on to say, "We bear in mind all those who challenge gender or bend the borders of desire," it sounded like an afterthought to staff members who were trans or gender-fluid. A survey of the staff revealed that though the press ranked very high as a place to work, the mission's emphasis on lesbians and gays rankled. The board undertook to revise the mission statement, keeping in mind staff criticisms.

There's a new mission statement, and those critical sections now read: "We, the members and workers of Pink Triangle Press, are rooted in communities that value diversity and stand for sexual freedom. The outcome that we seek is this — Our passionate communities daring together to set love free." It goes on to define passionate communities: "We have chosen as our public all those who bend the borders of desire or break the bonds of gender. We name here our communities, separately and together, in particular but without exclusion: Lesbian, Gay, Bi, Trans, Queer, Two-Spirit and Allied people."

That was reached with some difficulty. I'm a little ashamed to admit my reluctance to change it. *Who do these kids think they are?* I thought. Don't they know we started everything? Where's the gratitude? Don't they know they're tampering with holy writ? Don't they realize the term LGBTQ+ has become something of a joke, rattled off mechanically? It isn't even a word, and isn't the press all about words? I was clearly thinking as a corporate boss-man in the grip of the past and wasn't taking seriously the importance of naming oneself, even if only by a letter in an acronym. I came around and was the board member responsible for the term "passionate communities." Still learning new tricks.

Nostalgie de la Boue, or My Second Life

HISTORY MAY REPEAT ITSELF, first as tragedy and then as farce, but the indecent are treated first with contumely, then, if they're shameless, as celebrities, and finally as artifacts. I'm at the artifact stage now, in 2022, my seventy-eighth year and the fifty-third anniversary of what is commonly, and mistakenly, called the legalization of homosexuality in Canada. I get trotted out like a rather chipped but colourful piece of pottery from the classic period, asked for my memories of the bathhouse raids and riots, of *The Body Politic*, of a time when life was an exhilarating struggle. I'm asked for my photographs too. I was *TBP*'s principal photographer in the 1970s and 1980s, but I also documented the antics of the communal houses I lived in. Many of those images have become iconic and are much in demand.

In retirement, I seem to have gone from living my life to performing it.

I've tried to live the life I wrote, one that helped, along with thousands of others, to shape the more accepting culture we live in today, in Toronto, in Canada. Shaped it principally for the benefit of white cisgender men and women, but that's who we were, we activists at *TBP* and in the other circles I moved in. There were collateral benefits for the wider community, of course, but it would have been impertinent for us to speak for the gender challengers or the racialized. Or act for them, except as allies. Now they are acting for themselves. I hope they are as selfish as we were.

There is a benign selfishness at the heart of most activism. I am periodically thanked by young people for the roles I played in the early gay movement, almost as if I were doing it for them or for some greater social good. But I wasn't. I and my friends, colleagues, and lovers were doing it for ourselves, sometimes in a rage, sometimes for the sheer joy of stirring things up.

A kiss-in demo at Yonge and Bloor, Toronto, mid-1970s. One of my most requested photos. Photo: Gerald Hannon

Acknowledgements

BOOK PUBLISHING IS RISKY business in Canada at the best of times, but COVID-19 added social, economic, and personal stress to the mix. I want to thank Marc Côté and the staff of Cormorant Books for their unflagging commitment to this project.

Immoral, Indecent & Scurrilous also relied upon the good sense, taste, and historical perspective of Ed Jackson, my close friend of more than fifty years. He acted as my agent, first reader, and first editor. We date back to the earliest days of *The Body Politic*, and it was a pleasure to work with him again.

Freelance editor and friend David Kilgour read an early, unfinished draft of the manuscript, saw promise, and encouraged me to complete it and submit it to a publisher.

Friends played a huge role, partly because Parkinson's disease slowed down my responses and made typing, talking, and meal preparation difficult. I take special note of Hugh Brewster (also a "graduate" of *The Body Politic*), Ian Graham, David Hayes, Peter Kingstone, and Gerry Oxford.

I had the great good fortune to work with the country's most accomplished magazine editors. They stood by me and my writing during several periods of great turmoil and stress. I want to name them: Lynn Cunningham (*Toronto Life*), Sarah Fulford (*Toronto Life*), John Macfarlane (*Toronto Life*), Sarah Murdoch (*The Globe and Mail*).

When I decided to do sex work, I consulted with two friends who had found prostitution a reliable source of extra income. Colin Brownlee and Danny Cockerline helped ease me into the Toronto demimonde.

I am grateful to writers Michael Coren and Stan Persky for taking the time and energy to read and comment on the manuscript. It is much appreciated.

In memory of: Rick Bébout, Yvonne Hannon (my mother), Mike Kibbee, Michael Lynch, Philip McLeod, Don Obe, Herb Spiers, Robert Trow.

Written with the support of the City of Toronto through Toronto Arts Council.

We acknowledge the sacred land on which Cormorant Books operates. It has been a site of human activity for 15,000 years. This land is the territory of the Huron-Wendat and Petun First Nations, the Seneca, and most recently, the Mississaugas of the Credit River. The territory was the subject of the Dish With One Spoon Wampum Belt Covenant, an agreement between the Iroquois Confederacy and Confederacy of the Anishinaabe and allied nations to peaceably share and steward the resources around the Great Lakes. Today, the meeting place of Toronto is still home to many Indigenous people from across Turtle Island. We are grateful to have the opportunity to work in the community, on this territory.

We are also mindful of broken covenants and the need to strive to make right with all our relations.